POPE'S
HORATIAN
POEMS

For his epistles,
say they, are weighty and
powerful; but his bodily presence is
weak, and his speech contemptible.

II COR. 10:10

POPE'S HORATIAN POEMS

By

THOMAS E. MARESCA

OHIO STATE UNIVERSITY PRESS

MAGISTRIBUS
MEIS DEBETUR

Preface

THIS BOOK is an attempt to read some eighteenth-century poems; it is much more a learning experiment on my part than any sort of finished criticism. Such value as it may possess seems to me to rest less in the answers it gives than in the questions it asks, less in the questions than in the poems it asks them of.

I am grateful to the editors of *ELH* for permission to reprint the *Fortescue* essay, which appeared, in slightly different form, in that journal.

I want to thank Don Cameron Allen, Robert C. Elliott, Albert J. Kuhn, and especially Earl R. Wasserman for their comments and criticism: without their help this study could have been neither started nor finished.

T.E.M.

August 22, 1965

[vii]

Table of Contents

POPE'S
HORATIAN
POEMS

Introduction

All translation I suppose may be reduced to these three heads. / First, that of metaphrase, or turning an author word by word, and line by line, from one language into another. Thus, or near this manner, was Horace his "Art of Poetry" translated by Ben Jonson. The second way is that of paraphrase, or translation with latitude, where the author is kept in view by the translator, so as never to be lost, but his words are not so strictly followed as his sense; and that too is admitted to be amplified, but not altered. The third way is that of imitation, where the translator (if he now has not lost that name) assumes the liberty, not only to vary from the words and sense, but to forsake them both as he sees occasion; taking only some general hints from the original, to run division on the groundwork, as he pleases.[1]

Despite the fact that Dryden's distinctions are familiar enough to amount almost to cliché, they have only infrequently been applied seriously in any criticism of Pope's *Imitations of Horace,* where they would seem to be particularly useful.[2] This is not, I suggest, because of any limitation inherent in the distinctions themselves, but more directly in this case because readers have been unsure of the precise nature of the "words and sense" that Dryden frees the poet to vary and forsake, and all too often because they have been almost completely unaware of what is involved in the "groundwork" on which he is to build.[3] Our one thing needful has been, and is, an investigation of the Horace the eighteenth century and Pope saw or thought they saw—it amounts to the same thing—in the satires and epistles. Only in this light can Dryden's remarks start making sense when applied to Pope's poems.

Recent critical studies of Pope have sought to define his poetic accomplishment in terms of a broadened awareness of what the eighteenth century called wit and what we more pretentiously label mythopoeia. We have moved beyond ideas of decorum and form as final explanations of what happens in a Pope poem, beyond an understanding of Pope's artistry as an exercise in laughter and style. That his achievement can be located in wit, we are still agreed; but it now seems clear that the fullest significance of Pope's poetry must be found in that more serious meaning the Augustans attached to wit: the ability to discern and articulate—to "invent" in the classical sense—the fundamental order of the world, of society, of man, and to express that order fittingly in poetry.

The following study concerns itself with the serious ethical and aesthetic content of the *Imitations of Horace*, with what they say about Pope's view of his world and his art. It tries to discover how Pope used the Horace his culture gave him and to understand the nature of the wit of these poems. It is, quite simply, an investigation of what the *Imitations of Horace* are about.

---

1. *Preface to the Translation of Ovid's Epistles*, in *Essays of John Dryden*, ed. W. P. Ker (Oxford, 1900), I, 237; *The Poems of John Dryden*, ed. James Kinsley (Oxford, 1958), I, 182. All quotations from Dryden's prose will be taken from Ker; all quotations from his poetry will be taken from Kinsley.

2. In fact, criticism of these poems has tended to be directly antithetical to the spirit of Dryden's remarks; most often the *Imitations* have been considered from the standpoint of their validity as translations, and praised or condemned, according to the reader's bias, for slavishly following or cavalierly abandoning Horace. Samuel Johnson's was the first major criticism of these poems as a group, and his comments established the tone and basis of most subsequent appraisals: "The *Imitations of Horace* seem to have been written as relaxations of his genius. This employment became his favorite by its facility; the plan was ready to his hand, and nothing was required but to accommodate as he could the sentiments of an old author to recent facts or familiar images; but what is easy is seldom excellent: such imitations cannot give pleasure to common readers. The man of learning may be sometimes surprised and delighted by an unexpected parallel; but the comparison requires knowledge of the original, which will

likewise often detect strained applications. Between Roman images and English manners there will be an irreconcileable dissimilitude, and the work will be generally uncouth and party-coloured; neither original nor translated, neither ancient nor modern" (*Lives of the English Poets,* ed. George Birkbeck Hill [3 vols.; Oxford, 1905], III, 278).

3. This has been largely due to critical failure to consider the differences between the twentieth-century and the eighteenth-century view of Horace. Our contemporary critics have tended to see Horace as a fellow spirit, as a "cultivated man of the world," urbane, sophisticated, sensitive, unmarked by a sense of sin—all of which, as I hope the next chapter will show, is far from the eighteenth century's conception of him. An important exception to this attitude is Aubrey Williams' perceptive essay, "Pope and Horace: *The Second Epistle of the Second Book,*" in *Restoration and Eighteenth-Century Literature,* ed. Carroll Camden (Chicago, 1963), pp. 309–22.

[5]

Chapter I

Horace

TO UNDERSTAND the Horace of the *Imitations* properly, it is essential to approach him through the texts and editions available to Pope, to place him in the general framework of thought provided by neoclassical critical documents. This Horace is not the playful Epicurean twentieth-century critics have posited, but a poet who took life and literature seriously. "Aut prodesse volunt, aut delectare Poetae," he had said; and the eighteenth century believed him. Critic after critic echoes the Horatian dictum; critic after critic traces the origin of poetry to Holy Writ and explains that Moses was the first poet, that from the beginning of time poetry conveyed morality, philosophy, science, and God's law to the minds and hearts of men.[1] They claimed for it a present function as impressive as its pedigree: Tasso, for instance, toyed with the speculation of Maximus Tyrius, "that philosophy and poetry were one thing, double in name but single in essence,"[2] and then went on to prefer poetry, as teacher, to scholastic philosophy—"to move readers in this way with images, as do the mystic theologian and the poet, is a much more noble work than to teach by means of demonstrations, which is the function of the scholastic theologian."[3] Ben Jonson asserts no less: for him, poetry combines the learning of philosophy, divinity, and statesmanship, and teaches all of them well.

> I could never thinke the study of Wisdome confin'd only to the *Philosopher,* or of *Piety* to the *Divine,* or of *State* to the *Politicke*: But that he which can faine a *Common-wealth* (which is the *Poet*), can gowne it with *Counsels,* strengthen it with *Lawes,* correct it with *Iudgements,* informe it with

[7]

Religion and *Morals,* is all of these. Wee do not require in
him meere *Elocution,* or an excellent faculty in verse, but the
exact knowledge, of all vertues and their Contraries, with
ability to render the one lov'd, the other hated, by his proper
embattaling them.[4]

In the Preface to *Gondibert,* Sir William Davenant spins
out the implications of such remarks, down to their most
specific and tedious details. He starts with the praises of
poets and poetry, and then proceeds to the sacred poets—
Moses, David, and Solomon—and the favor their verse
won with God. He then harangues the divines because they
failed to use poetry to smooth the unruliness of the people;
this negligence has earned its proper return in the disobedience and sectarianism with which the masses, for lack
of poetry's soothing didactic influence, oppose the clergy.[5]
Davenant recommends poetry to generals to rouse the
courage of their troops and to statesmen to inculcate the
principles of morality and order in their subjects.

> But Poets, who with wise diligence study the People, and
> have in all ages by an insensible influence governd their
> manners, may justly smile when they perceive that *Divines,
> Leaders of Armies, Statesmen,* and *Judges* think *Religion,*
> the *Sword,* or (which is unwritten *Law* and a secret Con-
> federacy of Chiefs) *Policy,* or *Law* (which is written, but
> seldom rightly read) can give without the help of the *Muses*
> a long and quiet satisfaction in government.[6]

Poetry, Davenant asserts, is indispensible to the proper
functioning of all branches of civil life. Poets excel as
promulgators of religion and teachers of nature and divinity;
they are the most pre-eminently useful of all moralists.

> For Poesy, which like contracted *Essences* seems the utmost
> strength & activity of Nature, is as all good Arts subservient
> to Religion, all marching under the same banner though of
> less discipline and esteem. And as Poesy is the best Expositor
> of Nature, Nature being misterious to such as use not to
> consider, so Nature is the best Interpreter of God, and more
> cannot be said of Religion. And when the Judges of Religion,

which are the Chiefs of the Church, neglect the help of the Moralists in reforming the People (and Poets are of all Moralists the most useful), they give a sentence against the Law of Nature: For Nature performs all things by correspondent aids and harmony. And 'tis injurious not to think Poets the most useful Moralists, for as Poesy is adorn'd and sublim'd by Musick, which makes it more pleasant and acceptable, so Morality is sweetned and made more amiable by Poesy.[7]

Such commonplace opinions represent the shared critical stance of the English Augustans; their attitude toward satire in particular grows naturally out of these ideas. In addition to the prestigious historical background it shares with poetry in general, the genre was regarded as peculiarly didactic, and was recognized, at least in theory, as a most effective means of accomplishing moral reformation. The comments of Pope's fellow satirist Edward Young offer a fair idea of its pedigree and prestige:

But it is possible, that Satire may not do much good: men may rise in their affections to their follies, as they do to their friends, when they are abused by others: It is much *to be feared,* that misconduct will never be chased out of the world by Satire; all therefore that is to be said for it, is that misconduct will *certainly* be never chased out of the world by Satire, if no Satires are written: nor is that term unapplicable to graver compositions. Ethics, Heathen and Christian, and the Scriptures themselves, are, in a great measure, a Satire on the weakness and iniquity of men; and some part of that Satire is in verse too: nay, in the first Ages, Philosophy and Poetry were the same thing; wisdom wore no other dress: so that, I hope, these satires will be the more easily pardoned that misfortune by the severe. If they like not the fashion, let them take them by the weight; for some weight they have, or the author has failed in his aim. Nay, Historians themselves should be considered as Satirists, and Satirists most severe; since such are most human actions, that to relate is to expose them.[8]

Dryden agrees: he quotes with approval Heinsius' definition, that "Satire is a kind of poetry, without a series of actions,

[9]

invented for the purging of our minds; in which human vices, ignorance, and errors, and all things besides, which are produced from them in every man, are severely reprehended. . . . " [9] Such ideas reverberated through the poetical and critical tracts of the late seventeenth and early eighteenth centuries. Buckingham's *Essay on Satire* informs us that

> Poets alone found the delightful Way,
> Mysterious Morals gently to convey
> In charming Numbers, that when once Men grew
> Pleas'd with their Poems, they grew wiser too.
> *Satire* has always shin'd among the rest,
> And is the boldest Way, perhaps the best,
> To shew Men freely all their foulest Faults;
> To laugh at their vain Deeds and vainer Thoughts.[10]

Some theorists pushed their respect for satire's strength far beyond the limits of Buckingham's encomium. It was even common to regard satire in quasi-legal light as a supplement to the laws of the nation, as an effective weapon to terrorize sinners who have no fear of the laws of the land or of religion.[11]

In many ways, Joseph Trapp's *Praelectiones Poeticae* constitutes the definitive statement of this body of Augustan theory. He conglomerates elements from every aspect of the critical tradition to draw out its fullest implications and articulate what well may be the most elaborate presentation of neoclassical criticism:

> The word *Satire* was anciently taken in a less restrain'd sense than it is at present, not only as denoting a severe Poem against Vice, but consisting of Precepts of Virtue, and the Praises of it: And even in the Satires, as they are call'd, of *Horace, Juvenal,* and *Persius,* &c, which are principally levell'd against the Weaknesses, the Follies, or Vices of Mankind; we find many Directions, as well as Incitements to virtue. Such strokes of Morality, *Horace,* particularly, is full of; and in *Juvenal* they occur very frequently. . . . All

of them sometimes correct Vice, like Moralists, I may say, like Divines, rather than Satirists: what less can we say of this of Persius?

> O curvae in terras animae, & caelestium inanes!
> O souls, in whom no heav'nly Fire is found.
>
> *Dryden.*

Sentiments, these, one would think, were fetch'd from true Religion, not from unassisted Reason; and which we might expect from the Christian, more than the Stoic.[12]

Trapp's statement draws upon a traditional body of literary criticism that runs far back into the Renaissance and makes explicit the inherent tendency of that tradition to approximate pagan philosophy to Christian faith. It allocates the name satire entirely, or at least primarily, to the three Roman greats, Horace, Persius, and Juvenal. Satire for the Augustans seems often not so much a literary genre as a living creature, a three-headed beast named Horace-Persius-Juvenal. Mention of satire inevitably conjures them up; mention of any one of them inescapably calls forth the other two.[13] For the neoclassicists, classical verse satire was one solid body of work, tending toward one end: moral instruction. In Dryden's *Discourse concerning the Original and Progress of Satire* the three Latin poets are considered alike in purpose, in their attempt to correct and instruct a foolish and wicked world. The only differences among them are those of technique and success, as his comparison of the merits of Juvenal and Horace evidences:

That Horace is somewhat the better instructor of the two, is proved from hence, that his instructions are more general, Juvenal's more limited. So that, granting the counsels they give are equally good for moral use, Horace, who gives the most various advice, and most applicable to all occasions which can occur to us in the course of our lives,—as including in his discourses, not only all the rules of morality, but also of civil conversation,—is undoubtedly to be preferred to him who is more circumscribed in his instructions, makes them to fewer people, and on fewer occasions, than

[11]

the other. I may be pardoned for using an old saying, since 'tis true, and to the purpose: *Bonum quo communius, eo melius.* . . . Horace is teaching us in every line, and is perpetually moral. . . . [14]

Dryden's concession of Horace's superiority as a teacher, despite his personal preference for Juvenal, is also a well-established prop of the traditional view: by the beginning of the eighteenth century, few readers dispute the pre-eminence of Horace as a moral instructor. Dunster, in the preface of his translation, tells us that Horace's satires and epistles "were written, as he himself assures us, for the Instruction of Mankind; they abound with many excellent Rules and Precepts, the Knowledge of which contributes very much to be Improvement of Life, by imprinting in our Minds just and true and lively Sentiments of Moral Honesty and Vertue." [15] Edward Young is equally confident, and somewhat more sophisticated:

> Moreover, Laughing Satire bids the fairest for success: the world is too proud to be fond of a serious tutor; and when an Author is in a passion, the laugh, generally, as in conversation, turns against him. This kind of Satire only has any delicacy in it. Of this delicacy Horace is the best master: he appears in good humour while he censures; and therefore his censure has the more weight, as supposed to proceed from judgment, not from passion.[16]

Thus the Augustan poets and critics formulated their vision of Horace. The seriousness with which they regarded poetry generally and satire specifically molded their conception of the first great satirist: Horace was inevitably for them earnest, serious, "perpetually moral," and ever instructive, a source of guidance in matters of ethics and civility both.

I

Alongside Renaissance and Augustan critical and poetic pronouncements about literature, there flourished a complementary tradition of scholarly commentary. From the earliest Renaissance printing of Horace through the eighteenth century (well into the nineteenth for that matter; the Delphine edition was still being reprinted during the Romantic period), editions flowed off the presses in numbers increasing to match Horace's ever-growing popularity.[17] It is no doubt superfluous to say that these editions were totally unlike the prim classics texts we have become accustomed to, but the point needs to be emphasized. A representative Renaissance edition of Horace—say, that of Cruquius or of Christoforo Landino—tosses the reader adrift in a sea of commentary, with only a spar or two of text to cling to. The commentary itself is a hodgepodge of heterogeneous materials—philology, interpretation, verbal criticism, philosophy, variant readings, allegorizations, comparisons with other classical satirists or with similar *loci* in other Horatian poems, or with Scripture. But perhaps the most impressive aspect of the commentaries is their general unanimity: in almost all important cases, and certainly in the larger areas of interpretation, they are usually at one. The same annotations recur in commentator after commentator, generally without mutual acknowledgment; plagiarism is never a consideration. This can be easily demonstrated by tracing the annotations on any given line of Horace chronologically through editions.[18] The scholars evidently felt that their task was to document what was common knowledge, to write down and restore to the public what was originally its own, to publish the conclusions any right-thinking man would come to. This accounts for their silence about their predecessors, broken only when a faulty derivation or a particularly ingenious reading and interpretation disturbs the tranquillity of some scholarly soul, and calls—in the interests of truth—for a crushing refutation, ending more often than not in vituperation. Such unity within confusion is the basic condition of the scholarly Horatian tradition.

Out of this welter of elements grows a consistent and coherent image of Horace, and a conception of him and his poetry that is perfectly at one with—in fact, is an amalgam of—the critical and scholarly traditions. This view has been shaped in many cases by the very same minds, but always by the same kind of minds, that had formed those attitudes; and it is, of course, inescapable that the same opinions should reappear. Horace's moral pronouncements are related to similar dicta in the poems of the other satirists on the same or like themes, or they are reinforced by comparison to like statements in the Old and New Testaments. Horace, the chorus of annotators tells us, has written seriously and importantly, imparting rules for the wise governance of human life. Torrentius puts it briefly:

> At studiose & sedulo singula Horatii poemata lege & perpende: inuenies non disputationes quidem subtiles, aut ratiocinationum acumina: sed pleraque omnia quae ad recte, sancte, tranquille, beateque viuendum a profano homine proficisci possunt, argute ac graviter praecepta, exemplisque poetarum historiarumque & vitae communis de copia depromtis explicata, confirmata, ac quasi condita. Hic enim mos, haec ratio philosophandi, vnice Horatio placuit.[19]

That is, in essence, the traditional Horace, the Horace whom Pope and the Augustans knew. André Dacier, whose scholarship and sensitivity Pope admired, explains the implications of such statements more fully: like the figures of the Sileni, whose homely exteriors hid images of all the gods, Horace's playful surface matter conceals the doctrine of all the virtues, which should be the constant pursuit of everyone who wishes to correct his vices.[20] The satires and epistles constitute an almost complete course in morality:

> Ce n'étoit pas là la difference qu'on devoit établir entre les Satires et les Epitres; il y en a une plus essentielle, et plus digne de nôtre curiosité. Il falloit faire voir qu'Horace s'étant aperçû que le défaut de ceux qui, avant lui, avoient entrepris de combatre les vices, et de donner des preceptes pour la vertu, venoit de ce qu'ils n'avoient gardé aucun ordre ni aucune methode, il a voulu rendre son Ouvrage plus complet, et mieux suivi; et pour cet effet il a divisé et rangé

sa matiere avec beaucoup de jugement. Il a mis d'abord ses
deux premiers Livres de Satires, parce que dans le premier
il travaille à déraciner les vices ; et que dans le second il
s'efforce d'arracher les erreurs et les fausses opinions. Après
ces deux Livres, viennent les Epitres, qui peuvent fort bien
être appellées la suite de ses Satires ; et il les a mises après
les Satires, parce qu'ils s' attache à y donner des preceptes
pour la vertu, et à allumer dans nos coeurs l'amour qu'elle
merite. Ainsi ces quatre Livres font un cours de Morale
entier et parfait.[21]

This is the Horace of the Renaissance and of those who
were bred, as Pope was, in the final days of the Renaissance
tradition; he was for them, as he could never be again after
their reverential attitude toward Augustan Rome passed
away, a nearly unimpeachable moral arbiter and guide, on
the level of authority almost with the Scriptures to which
his sentiments were so often compared.

The ultimate tests of the grasp that any idea has on the
minds of men are the instances of its practical application;
and everywhere, the men of the eighteenth century proved
by their deeds that they quite firmly believed in their
conception of Horace. Essay after essay calls upon the
authority of Horace to reinforce its didactic point; writer
follows writer in his turn to bow at the shrine of ever moral,
ever instructive Horace.[22] Men as diverse as Henry Fielding
and Lord Chesterfield in effect agree: one looked to Horace
as the great master of the equanimity he tried to practice;
the other drew from him a conception of personal integrity
and innocence as the source of human happiness.[23] Horace
was their sure guide, as he was the firm and unquestioned
authority for many of the laws Addison dictated to his little
senate and to an England proud (and occasionally embar-
rassed) to call itself Augustan.[24]

Pope in no way stands apart from his time, except in the
brilliance of his talent. These assumptions about the nature
of satire, about the matter of Horace, were his by birthright.
His poetic statements do not imply that he disagreed with
the Renaissance critical tradition he inherited; his poetic

[15]

practice in translating Homer forcefully suggests the opposite.[25] His careful attention to the translation and notes of
Mme Dacier and the commentary of Eustathius (translated
for him by Broome and Fenton), which frequently guided
his translation of the Greek text, indicates, not the feeble-
ness of his knowledge of Greek as his contemporary enemies
claimed, but a sturdy respect for the matter and authority
of the learned tradition, a position quite in line with his
conservative stance in many other areas of thought.

In employing such aids in his poetic task, Pope in no way
enslaved himself to the mind of another, or sacrificed his
own "artistic freedom." He did what any sensible poet
would, what there was much honorable precedent for. His
English master Dryden had done as much in his translation
of Virgil, apparently regarding it as a duty incumbent upon
him; he accepted the responsibility of knowledge laid upon
him by the commentary tradition as a natural and essential
part of his poetic task:

> I return to our Italian translator of the *Æneis*. He is a foot-
> poet, he lacqueys by the side of Virgil at the best, but never
> mounts behind him. Doctor Morelli, who is no mean critic
> in our poetry, and therefore may be presumed to be a better
> in his own language, has confirmed me in this opinion by
> his judgment, and thinks, withall, that he has often mis-
> taken his master's sense. I would say so, if I durst, but am
> afraid I have committed the same fault more often, and more
> grossly; for I have forsaken Ruaeus (whom generally I
> follow) in many places, and made expositions of my own in
> some, quite contrary to him. . . . [26]

This and his other frequent apologies for deviation from the
commentators' interpretations[27] make it more than clear
that Dryden recognized the authority of this scholarly tradition as a factor not lightly to be set aside; and it hardly
needs to be said that Dryden's example in so crucial a
matter would carry great weight with Pope.

Dryden's practice, of course, is not unique, nor is Pope
in following him merely obeying the peculiar whim of an
esoteric poet. Both exploit a knowledge and a tradition that,

until the early eighteenth century at least, lay squarely in
the public domain. In one of the few Augustan public statements of policy on the business of poetic translation, the
Earl of Roscommon strongly urges poets to turn the commentators to advantage if they would translate aright:

> Take pains the genuine meaning to explore,
> There sweat, there strain, tug the laborious oar;
> Search every comment that your care can find,
> Some here, some there, may hit the poet's mind.[28]

In the light of such pronouncements and such examples, it
is impossible not to conclude that Pope employed the lore
of the annotators in his *Imitations of Horace*, and that his
achievement was guided and influenced by it and by the
traditional conceptions of Horace that his age inherited
and cherished.

But even more specific evidence (if it be needed) indicates
that Pope utilized the labors of the scholars and expected
his readers to recognize their influence in his poems. Lilian
Bloom has long ago brought to our attention the fact that
Pope possessed at least four different editions of Horace,[29]
and there is every likelihood that he was familiar with the
contents of even more. The four that he certainly owned
were those of Bentley, Cunningham, Heinsius, and Desprez.
Of these, Pope was probably aided least by Bentley's edition,
however much he may have been guided by him in establishing a text. Bentley, of course, stood in the vanguard of
the new classical scholarship that was busily engaged in
undermining the prestige of the older editors and obliter-
ating their accumulated learning from the pages of Latin
and Greek authors. Pope, conservative here as in politics,
remained true to his humanist heritage and heaped scorn
and literary damnation on the narrow specialization of the
exponents of the new *Wissenschaft*.

> Pains, reading, study, are their just pretence,
> And all they want is spirit, taste, and sense.

Comma's and points they set exactly right,
And 'twere a sin to rob them of their Mite.
Yet ne'er one sprig of Laurel grac'd these ribalds,
From slashing Bentley down to pidling Tibalds.

(*Epistle to Arbuthnot,* 159–64)[30]

Cunningham's edition is only lightly annotated and, although anti-Bentleian in tone, continues the kind of verbal scholarship that Bentley had for all practical purposes begun. Heinsius had prepared his edition for the Elzevir press, which had set itself the task (continuing the work of the Aldine press) of issuing uniform, sound texts of the classics, relatively unencumbered by commentary. Still, this edition managed to cram the entire Horatian corpus into its first half, leaving the remainder for Heinsius' bulky annotations that were, in addition, frequently reinforced by his lengthy and highly influential essay *De Satyra Horatiana Libri duo.* This latter filled as many pages as did the text of the Roman poet. Pope's fourth edition, that of the French Jesuit Desprez, was one of the series of classical texts published *in usum Delphini* (the Delphine editions). This is a volume in the grand Renaissance tradition, in which a postage stamp of Horace is often surrounded by an outsized envelope of commentary. The annotations themselves form a confluence or digest of the main streams of the Horatian tradition, which by this time had settled down into rather marked channels of thought. This particular edition appears to have been highly instrumental in shaping Pope's Horatian poems.

In addition to these, a letter of Pope's to the Duke of Buckingham gives ample evidence that Pope was familiar with yet another important edition, Dacier's.

I cannot think quite so highly of the Lady's [Mme Dacier's] learning, tho' I respect it very much. It is great complaisance in that polite nation, to allow her to be a Critic of equal rank with her husband. To instance no further, his remarks on Horace shew more good Sense, Penetration, and a better

[18]

Taste of his author, and those upon Aristotle's art of poetry more Skill and Science, than any of hers on any author whatever.[31]

Pope's interest and the point of his praise turn on Dacier's ability, not as an emendator of texts in the manner of Bentley, but on his perspicuity as a commentator on Horace. Dacier's edition, published in ten volumes from 1681 to 1689 and reprinted many times thereafter, constitutes, like Desprez', an *omnium gatherum* of the main elements of the established commentary tradition—with this difference: while the space and format requirements of a uniform edition restrained the exegetical tendencies of the French cleric, the French classicist was free to spin out to their finest the threads of meaning and implication with which the previous commentaries were woven. As a result, his volumes are fat with annotation and explanation, all of it building on the work of the savants who preceded him. In Dacier, the neoclassical image of Horace appears drawn most clearly; in him, Horace attains most overtly the semi-divine status the Augustans were so willing to confer upon him. Dacier's Horace is a man both serious and moral, dedicated to the philosophical pursuit of the true and the good. His poetry is a compendium of theoretic and useful knowledge about conduct and character and the duties a man must discharge in life. As Dacier often points out, it pleasantly leads young people into the necessary rigors of philosophy; and it contains, for both young and mature, an almost complete course of moral philosophy, according to the best of classical knowledge.

That Pope employed, and wished his readers to recognize, Dacier's commentary is also fortunately quite clear. A note of Warburton's demonstrates this:

Dacier laughs at an able Critic, who was scandalized, that the antient Scholiasts had not explained what Horace meant by *a wall of brass;* for, says Dacier, "Chacun se fait des difficultez à sa mode, et demande des remarques proportionées à son goût:" he then sets himself in good earnest about this important inquiry; and, by a passage in Vegetius, luckily discovers, that it signified an *old veteran* armed cap-a-pie in *brass,* and placed to cover his Fellow. Our Poet has happily served himself of this impertinence to convey a very fine stroke of satire.[32]

This remark presents certain problems that will be taken up in discussion of Epistle I.i., but its meaning and its intent are plain. Pope has employed Dacier's commentary, and he or his editor (if it makes any real difference) is here calling attention to it. In effect, Warburton warns the reader that if he doesn't remember his Dacier, he will miss this satiric thrust. The whole statement and the detail with which Dacier's explanation is reported strongly imply much beyond this: they suggest that familiarity with Dacier may well convey many a "very fine stroke of satire."

It is evidently essential, then, to consult Pope's Horaces in order to understand Pope's Horace. Neither Dacier nor any other critic can be considered alone; if he were idiosyncratic, he could not possess the authority he does for Pope and for the eighteenth century.[33] It is as another voice in a long tradition, a compiler of knowledge that has almost the hallowed seal of the *concensus gentium,* that Dacier is valued; and it is in company with his cultural brothers in that tradition that he must be employed to illuminate the poetic achievement of Alexander Pope.

II

In addition to understanding the neoclassical Horace, it is important also to examine the component parts of satire as the eighteenth century understood them. Fortunately, our contemporary critical equipment here stands us in better stead than in evaluating Horace; there is a stability about literary kinds that literary ideas frequently and distressingly lack. The basic pattern of satire, at least in its most rigorous manifestation as formal verse satire, has changed little since Horace solidified the genre. Verse satire, for the eighteenth century as for him, demanded that the poet empty his whole bag of rhetorical tricks in denunciation of a single vice or group of related vices, often choosing as the foil for his artistic fury a straw-man *adversarius,* who can also serve to counterpoint the heroic virtue of the satirist.[34] Equally essential is the active presence in the satire of positive norms, either explicitly or implicitly stated.[35] If there is any real difference between our contemporary theory of satire and that of the Augustans, it centers on the degree of importance attached to this factor. For the Renaissance and the eighteenth century, the presence of such norms is crucial, as Trapp's statement, quoted above,[36] should indicate. It is, of course, the presence of such moral norms that won the palm for Horace against his two rivals; his "many excellent Rules and Precepts" constituted the superiority of his satires.

For the eighteenth-century reader, one of these norms was presented ready-made in Horace himself. The Augustan reverence for the golden age of Roman civilization and language endowed Horace with an authority that, as we have seen, was little short of canonical. With this as his pre-text, Pope's moral dicta in the *Imitations* were already half-sanctified by the mere fact of their existence in the Horatian original; thus his criticisms of eighteenth-century England had behind them the massive weight of Horace's denunciations of first-century Rome; or, inversely, Pope's scorn is all the more withering if he condemns where Horace could praise—as when George Augustus is weighed in the balance with Augustus Caesar, and found wanting. Horace and the noble Roman civilization of which he is the moral and poetic spokesman reinforce every barb and every taunt Pope points at his England: it is noble to be worthy of Horace's praise, damnable to merit his scorn; the good life, the life worthy of rational man, is described in his poems, and poetic damnation awaits the eighteenth-century sinner who falls short of it. By classical standards the neoclassicists are judged.

More important than this, however, is the norm by which the classics themselves are judged: the ethical standards of Christian religion. The relations of Christianity and classical culture had, of course, always been tangled in a hopeless ambiguity. Church fathers who denounced the errors of the pagans and the seductions of classical letters also quoted from them to bolster their own arguments. However much the evil influence of classical literature may have been deplored, it was most certainly never ignored; and the practice of assimilating pagan authors by showing their likenesses to Scripture may truthfully be said to have begun even before the patristic aversion to them had entirely waned. By the late seventeenth and early eighteenth centuries, this practice had become almost commonplace, and was applied to the greater part of classical literature.

Inevitably, an even more curious ambivalence rose out of this process of assimilation: as respect for the ethical thought of the ancients grew, that thought more and more resembled, in contemporary interpretations, Christian morality. The dividing line between pagan and Christian narrowed from the great gulf the fathers had fixed to an almost invisible seam in the cloak of Renaissance culture: in many Renaissance texts, it is difficult to distinguish the pagan from the Christian, the light of reason from the illumination of faith. The scholars of the Renaissance labored mightily to explain these similarities. In some cases they were attributed to the clarity of classical reasoning; in others, they were held to stem from the preservation of traditional truths first known to Adam. Alexander Ross, eccentric in other matters, is typical here: he explains, for instance, that the pagans of India believed in the immortality of the soul by the light of natural reason, and that this doctrine was professed also by the "learned Gentiles"—and to prove this he cites Zoroaster, Trismegistus, Phocillides, the Pythagoreans, Socrates, Plato, Aristotle, "the Poets," Cicero, and Seneca.

"Many such passages may be seen in his [Seneca's] writings: and that generally the Gentiles believed this truth, is plain by their opinion they had of torments in Hell, and the joyes in their *Elysian* fields." [37] Nor was this the only orthodox doctrine known and believed by the ancients: they—or at least those of them that the Renaissance was concerned with, the poets and philosophers—were also practicing monotheists. Ross remarks, in the course of a discussion of classical polytheism, that "we must observe, that although the ignorant multitude among the Gentiles did worship many Gods, yet the wiser sort acknowledged but one true God. . . . " He then goes on for two pages naming poets and philosophers to substantiate that statement.[38] But the orthodoxy of the pagans does not end here. The same exclusive group was aware of even more esoteric Christian doctrines:

> . . . It was held an act of justice and mercy both to bury the dead; of justice, that earth should be restored to earth, and dust to dust; for what could be more just than to restore to mother earth her children, that as she furnished them at first with a material being, with food, rayment, sustentation, and all things needful, so she might at last receive them again into her lap, and offer them lodging til the Resurrection, whereof some of the wiser Gentiles were not ignorant. . . . [39]

Ross's statements may fairly be taken as representative of his time on these matters. For educated men of the Renaissance, the "wiser sort" of the ancients had, whether by reason or traditional revelation, attained a moral state and a body of beliefs similar to, and all but identical with, Christianity.

Theophilus Gale's *The Court of the Gentiles* stands as the summation and culmination of this attitude toward the religion and knowledge of the ancients. His research both advances the prestige of the classical thinkers and provides a pedigree that would make that prestige acceptable to the most scrupulous of Christians. The full title of his work is its own best explanation: *The Court of the Gentiles: or a Discourse Touching the Original of Human Literature, both Philologie and Philosophie, from the Scriptures, and Jewish Church.* Although no previous writer had handled these materials with the thoroughness and devotion Gale brings to them, the prefatory advertisements to his study give some idea of the intellectual history, repute, and popularity of his central thesis. He began this study because he found hints "in *Grotius* and others, touching the *Traduction of Human Arts* and *Sciences* from the *Scriptures,* and *Jewish Church.* . . . " By further research, he "found a general *concurrence* of the Learned, both *Philologists* and *Divines,* of this and the former Age, endeavoring to *promote* this *Hypothesis.*" There follows a list of the major authorities that make the muster of Gale's troops: Steuchus Eugubinus, Ludovicus Vives, "with other learned Papists of the former Age," Julius Scaliger, Joseph Scaliger, Serranus, Vossius, Sandford, Heinsius, Bochart, Selden, Jackson, Hammond, Usher, Preston, Owen, Stillingfleet, "with others among the Protestants," Josephus, Origen, Clement of Alexandria, Eusebius, Tertullian, Augustine, Johannes Grammaticus, "with others, as is shown in the Bodie of this Discourse." The first of his two lengthy, learned volumes concerns itself with proving that pagan poetry in its entirety—form and matter and purpose—is derived from the sacred poetry of the Hebrews and from their stock of divine knowledge; the second accomplishes the same feat for pagan philosophy. His purpose is the strictly edifying one, welcome to all Renaissance Christians, of showing the incapacity of mere unaided reason to attain the highest truth and of demonstrating the necessity of a divine revelation.

A farther *Designe* the Author has in promoting this *Hypothesis* is, to beat down that *fond persuasion,* which has of late crept in among, and been openly avowed by many, too great *Admirers* of *Pagan Philosophie,* (especially that of *Plato*) as if it were all but the *Product of Natures Light.* Whereas, I take it, the author has, or will in what follows, evidently

[24]

evince, that the choicest *Contemplations of Gentile Philoso-phie,* were but some corrupt *Derivations,* or at best but broken *Traditions,* originally traduced from the *Sacred Scriptures,* and *Jewish Church.*

He accomplishes this lofty aim by tracing the dispersal of Judaic tradition through Egyptians, Syrians, Phoenicians— "*Sanchoniathon* and *Mochus,* those great *Phenician Soph-ists,* who, as 'tis very likely, had *immediate* and *frequent* Conversation with the *Jews;* [and] the *Egyptian Priests,* who seem to have been instructed first by *Joseph* who founded and endowed a college for them. . . . " Gale then goes on to argue what almost everyone in the Renaissance conceded, "that several of the first *Poets, Sophists,* and *Philosophers* of *Greece,* travelled into *Egypt* and *Phenicia;* and made considerable abode there, at those very times when the *Jews,* in great multitudes, frequented those parts." The main body of his argument concerns itself with proving that in this way Orpheus, Linus, Homer, Hesiod, Solon, Thales, Pherecydes, Pythagoras, and Plato acquired their highest and truest ideas.[40] By this mode of argumentation, Gale both explains the basis of the similarities between pagan and Christian thought and makes that thought ac-ceptable and useful to the most tender-conscienced Chris-tians. Rather than being demonically inspired, as some of the early fathers had charged, the "wiser sort" of the ancients were in much the same situation as the Jews: they were pre-Christians, waiting for the fulness of God's revelation.

This attitude did not satisfy everybody, of course. There were those who maintained that what the pagans knew, they knew by the light of reason, and that this natural knowledge was sufficient for salvation. These deists would not disagree with Gale's conclusions about the content of ancient belief, but they did quarrel with him over its mode of acquisition and over the necessity of a special revelation.[41] Lord Herbert of Cherbury is the most important early spokesman for this view. In his tract *De Religione Gen-*

tilium, he concludes that the pagans held these five essentials of true religion:

> I. That there is one Supreme God. II. That he ought to be worshipped. III. That Vertue and Piety are the chief Parts of Divine Worship. IV. That we ought to be sorry for our Sins, and repent of them. V. That Divine Goodness doth dispense Rewards and Punishments both in this Life, and after it.[42]

In his *De Veritate,* these conclusions are applied even more broadly: he argues that every past religion has acknowledged, and every future religion will acknowledge, one sovereign deity. No race, however savage, has ever been found without this belief, as well as the concomitant doctrines of providence and grace. Priestcraft and superstition supply in themselves the sole causes of the corruption or distortion of this sound belief, which was nevertheless preserved in its purity by the "wiser sort" of the ancients.[43]

Lord Herbert's statements are the basis of the deist position: later deists elaborated upon them, but did not alter them in their essentials. Wollaston, for instance, in *The Religion of Nature Delineated,* documents many of Herbert's "Common Notions" by reference to, and quotation from, innumerable classical authors. To support the thesis of a universal belief in a single supreme being, for example, he quotes Horace's "Nec veget quid quam simile aut secundum," which he translates, "Nor is there any being in the world like or anything near to him." [44] And the two most important English deists of the eighteenth century, John Toland and Matthew Tindal, are equally explicit and outspoken on the subject of the pagans' knowledge of true religion. Toland seems to be mingling Alexander Ross and Herbert of Cherbury when he remarks, in the course of explaining away pagan polytheism, that "the more learned and virtuous had many times better Notions of Things," yet were prevented from promulgating them by the persecutions of the priests and the superstitious rabble.[45] Toland

makes a clear distinction between these preservers of the
true light of reason and the debased and priest-ridden mob,
and refuses to even consider such a person as Cicero, for
instance, a heathen.[46] Tindal seems to extend the franchise
of salvation even further by arguing that the truths of
religion are at all times equally apparent to all men (he
quotes Horace to prove this) and that God's justice demands that this be so. He cites the "wisest Heathens" and
the Stoics to prove that the path to salvation was at all
times open and easy to know.[47]

The orthodox response to all this was necessarily awkward: the divines found themselves committed to granting
as much to pagan knowledge as did the deists, and, at the
same time, showing the absolute necessity of a special
revelation. Tindal in particular mercilessly exposed the contradictions of their position, quoting their own pronouncements to the effect that whatever was necessary to be known
of God was clear in all ages.[48] This did not deter other
ecclesiastics from falling into the same trap: in essence,
orthodoxy had committed itself to Theophilus Gale's thesis.
It had, therefore, no choice but to repeat his conclusions
and content itself with the paradoxes of pagans as proto-
Christians and an indispensable divine revelation that
seemed completely unnecessary.[49]

That, at any rate, fairly accurately summarizes the common opinion of the ancients and their religion at the time
Pope was writing. Everyone agrees, in effect, that the
ancients were monotheists who knew at least the essentials
of the requirements for salvation, and in many cases much
more. However much the theologians and polemicists argued
about the sources of pagan knowledge, almost no one found
it incompatible with the major doctrines of Christianity,
and certainly not in conflict with Christian ethics.

Naturally, Horace shared fully in the effects of this general
tendency to find correspondences between pagan and Christian ideas. Renaissance *Polyanthea,* for instance, clearly
revealed the results of this sort of conflation or assimilation:

[27]

there the apothegms of the Bible and the fathers are printed side by side with those of Horace and other classical writers as representing the body of received and authoritative opinion on any given subject.[50] Equally striking are the overtly Christianized Horaces produced throughout the Renaissance. The Polish Jesuit Sarbiewski—"the divine Casimir"—wrote his Latin and heavily moralized odes in direct imitation of Horace: he was, in fact, known as the "Christian Horace."[51] Their popularity carried them through many editions and many translations (including one in English in 1646), and the poems themselves left their marks in the works of several English poets, especially Vaughan. Thomas Sagittarius brought out a *Horatius Christianus, sive Parodiae sacrae ad Horatii ductum noviter accomodatae*, which consisted of adaptations of Horatian poems to Christian themes. This often meant as little as changing the dedication, as when he converts Ode I.i. to orthodoxy by transforming Maecaenas to the Messiah, and expunging all reference to the pagan gods.[52] There is even a specifically Horatian emblem book—also quite popular and frequently reprinted—the *Horatius Emblematus*, which draws its denunciations of vice and praise of virtue indiscriminately from odes, satires, and epistles, and never fails to parallel them with like remarks from the Bible or the fathers.[53]

Such ideas and attitudes toward Horace would also naturally belong to his Renaissance editors, and influence their commentaries. Here, for example, is an annotation of Dacier's on line 79 of Satire II.ii.:

> Divine Particulam Aurae) Une particule du souffle de la Divinité. C'est-à-dire une partie de la Divinité même, qui n'est qu'un esprit, & que Platon appelle l'ame du monde. Cette idée du souffle de la Divinité, est venuë sans doute aux Anciens de l'Histoire de la Création, qui leur étoit connuë. Dieu après avoir formé l'homme de la poussiere, lui inspira un souffle de vie: *inspiravit in faciem ejus spiraculum vitae.* Et c'est souffle de vie qu'ils ont appellé *particulam divinae aurae.*[54]

This brief paragraph contains all the elements of the traditions we have discussed. It directly confronts classical poetry with biblical narrative; it overtly states that the ancients knew and believed and utilized a piece of Judeo-Christian truth that came to them through their acquaintance with the Mosaic account of creation. It implies that Platonic philosophy is based—at least in part—on that account; and it clearly demands an understanding of Horace that is markedly not twentieth-century and hedonist, but Renaissance and Christian.

All these same attributes stand out in Pope's rendering of the passage:

> How pale, each Worshipful and rev'rend Guest
> Rise from a Clergy, or a City, feast!
> What life in all that ample Body, say,
> What heav'nly Particle inspires the clay?
> The Soul subsides; and wickedly inclines
> To seem but mortal, ev'n in sound Divines.
>
> (*Imitation of Sat. II. ii.*, 75–80)

It is obvious that Pope's poem makes use of the allusion that the commentators (Desprez also notes it) have provided. Horace's "divinae particulam aurae" has been transmuted into a "heavenly Particle" that scripturally "inspires the clay" of which man is made. Seen in the context of the poem, Pope's gluttons here reveal the extent of their alienation from God: their depravity is the undoing of his creation and the restoration of primal chaos. Their souls do quite literally subside and stoop to become gross matter. Pope's moral point is quite clear and quite Christian: for him, the same point appears to have been already clear in Horace, in very much the same terms as those he uses.

This vision of Horace—a serious moral poet whose best and highest ideas were only slightly distorted versions of Hebraic truth—is clearly ideal for a Christian satirist who, however great his reverence for the ancients, believes that the ultimate court of appeal for human conduct must be

[29]

found in the full revealed truth of Christianity. Given this propensity in the tradition, combined with Pope's own preoccupation with ethics and morality, it is to be expected that he will follow the commentators' lead and buttress his satire with the authority of Scripture and Christian tradition. He probably did not even need Dacier's specific advice to urge him to do this:

> Homere ajoute ces derniers mots pour faire entendre que ces tromperies surprennent bien plutôt les esprits fins & délicats, que les esprits lourds & grossiers; & la Poésie en est d'autant plus dangereuse. C'est pourquoi il faut bien examiner la doctrine qu'elle présente, & éplucher ces opinions, pour rejetter les fausses, & pour confirmer les véritables, par les lumieres sûres que nous donne la verité.
>
> . . . Je m'en étonne, car Plutarque en avoit ouvert le chemin dans son excellent Traité sur *la maniere dont il faut lire les Poëtes,* où il donne des avis très-utiles pour mettre les jeunes gens en état de discerner dans les Poëtes ce qu'ils ont de bon, d'avec ce qu'ils ont de mauvais, & pour leur donner dans cette lecture comme un avant-goût de la Philosophie. Au lieu de le suivre, on s'est contenté d'expliquer litteralement leurs maximes sans les approfondir, & sans en montrer la fausseté ou la verité, en les appliquant à la véritable regle.
>
> C'est pourtant ce que nous pouvons faire aujourd'hui beaucoup mieux, & plus sûrement que Plutarque ne l'a fait. Car, outre que la verité de la Philosophie ne lui étoit pas entierement connue, la superstition lui a fait souvent prendre pour contraires à la Religion & aux moeurs des choses qu'il auroit trouvé très-veritables, s'il avoit mieux connu la nature de Dieu, & s'il avoit pu remonter jusqu'aux véritables sources.[55]

All the weight of Renaissance learning works to this same end, to enable Pope to understand and employ Horace as a moral instructor illuminated by the best of classical knowledge, and to be further brightened by the light of Christian revelation. The Horace his culture presented to him was a poet serious, moral, didactic, and—to use a congenial twentieth-century term—committed. His poetry, as seen through the prism of commentators and scholars, formed a thorough study of ethics and practical morality, and reflected a life passionately spent in the pursuit of reason, truth, and virtue. It is this Horace that Pope knew and utilized; and it is precisely the harmony of pagan knowledge and Christian faith that the Renaissance strove after, and which it thought it found implicit in Horace, that Pope has worked into great satire.

1. For such ideas about literature, see, for instance, André Dacier's *Preface to Aristotle's Art of Poetry* (English trans. 1705; Augustan Reprint Society, no. 76, Los Angeles, 1959), pagination A3–A4recto; Joseph Trapp, *Lectures on Poetry* (London, 1742; originally published in Latin in 1711 as *Praelectiones Poeticae)*, pp. 1–12; and Sir Thomas Pope Blount's *De Re Poetica: or, Remarks upon Poetry* (London, 1694), pp. 1–9. J. E. Spingarn's three volumes of *Critical Essays of the Seventeenth Century* (Oxford, 1957) are, of course, a storehouse of like opinions. George Chapman, for example, prefaces his translation of Homer with a long encomium of poetry, in the course of which he informs us that poetry is of all human activities most closely bound to truth, "as hauing perpetual commerce with the diuine majesty, and embracing and illustrating al his most holy precepts, and enioying continual discourse with his thrice perfect and most comfortable spirit" (Spingarn, I, 67–68). See also Henry Peacham, *The Complete Gentleman* (Spingarn, I, 116–18); Henry Reynolds, *Mythomystes* (Spingarn, I, 151–75); and Sir William Temple, *Of Poetry* (Spingarn, III, 86–88). Ernst Robert Curtius describes an identical attitude toward poetry in Renaissance Spain: see *European Literature and the Latin Middle Ages,* trans. Willard R. Trask, (New York, 1953), pp. 547–48.

2. Torquato Tasso, *Discourses on the Heroic Poem,* in *Literary Criticism: Plato to Dryden,* ed. Alan H. Gilbert (New York, 1940), p. 469.

3. *Ibid.,* p. 476.

4. Ben Jonson, *Timber, or Discoveries* (Spingarn), I, 28. See also pp. 51–52.

5. Sir William Davenant, Preface to *Gondibert* (Spingarn), II, 32–35.

6. *Ibid.,* p. 38.

7. *Ibid.,* pp. 48–49.

8. Edward Young, Preface to *Love of Fame; or, The Universal Passion,* in Johnson's *English Poets,* LX (London, 1790), 71–72.

9. John Dryden, *A Discourse Concerning the Original and Progress of Satire* (Ker), II, 100; (Kinsley), II, 660.

10. *The Works of John Sheffield, Earl of Mulgrave, Marquis of Normanby, and Duke of Buckingham* (London, 1729), I, 112, lines 7–14.

11. See the Earl of Rochester's "In Defense of Satyr," in *Poems on Several Occasions,* ed. James Thorpe (Princeton, 1950), p. 45; Walter

Harte's "An Essay on Satire," in Anderson's *British Poets* (London, 1795; Harte's poem was first published in 1730), IX, 825; William Melmoth, *The Letters of Sir Thomas Fitzosborne on Several Subjects* (London, 1795; first ed., 1742), letter 48, pp. 234–35.

12. Pp. 223–24.

13. See, for example, Heinsius' *De Satyra Horatiana Libri duo,* in his edition of Horace (Leyden, 1629) ; or Casaubon's *Persiana Horatii Imitatio,* in his edition of Persius (Leipzig, 1839; first ed. 1605), pp. 344–67.

14. Dryden, *Discourse* (Ker), II, 82–83; (Kinsley), II, 648. See also pp. 81–82, 84, 97–98 in Ker, II, all of which are concerned with Horace's excellence as a moral instructor. It is important for an understanding of the traditional nature and authority of these ideas to realize that Dryden's essay is greatly indebted to Dacier's Preface to his own edition of Horace, and, in fact, frequently translates whole pages of it. Dacier's essay in turn draws heavily upon Casaubon.

15. *Horace's Satires, Epistles, and Art of Poetry done into English with Notes by S. Dunster* (London, 1739), pp. A4–A5.

16. Preface to *The Love of Fame* in Johnson's *English Poets,* LX, 73.

17. The following are the editions that I have principally used in tracing the vagaries of the Renaissance Horace and in examining Pope's Horatian poems:

Opera cum quatuor Commentariis et Figuris nuper additis (Pomponius Porphyrio, Pseudo-Acron, Cristoforo Landino, and Antonio Mancinelli) (Venice, 1509; first ed., 1492).

Horatii Ode, Carmen, Epodon et seculare, cum exactissima A. Mancinelli; Sermones et Epistole cum . . . Explanatione B. Ascensii (Paris, 1503).

Quinti Horatii Flacci Poemata, novis Scholiis et Argumentis ab Henr. Stephano illustrate (np., 1588; first ed., 1549).

Q. Horatii Flacci Sermonum Libri quattuor . . . a Dionysio Lambino Monstroliensi . . . (Venice, 1566; first ed., 1561).

Q. Horatius Flaccus . . . cum Commentariis antiquis expurgatus & editus, opera Iacobi Crvqvii Messenii . . . (Antwerp, 1599; first ed., 1578).

Q. Horatius Flaccus, cum Commentariis selectissimis variorum: & Scholiis integris Johannis Bond . . . (Leyden, 1658; first ed., 1606).

Q. Horatius Flaccus, cum erudito Laevini Torrentii Commentario . . . item Petri Alcmariani in Artem Poeticem (Antwerp, 1608).

Quintus Horatius Flaccus accedunt nunc Danielis Heinsii (Leyden 1629; first ed., 1612).

Oeuvres d'Horace, en Latin, traduit en François par M. Dacier, et le P. Sanadon. Avec les remarques critiques, historiques, et géographiques de l'un et de l'autre (Amsterdam, 1735; first ed., 1681–89).

Quinti Horatii Flacci Opera. Interpretatione et Notis illustravit Ludovicus Desprez . . . (London, nd; first ed, 1691).

I have also employed, to a lesser extent, the following:

Opera, (Venice, 1483).

[32]

Poemata omnia. Annotationes Aldi Manutii (Venice, 1527; first ed., 1501).

Carmina atque Epodos. Bernardini Partheni Spilimbergii (Venice 1584).

Quinti Horatii Flacci . . . Poemata omnia (Frankfurt, 1600).

Quinti Horatii Flacci Opera . . . (Cambridge, 1699).

Q. Horatii Flacci Eclogae, cum selectis Scholiastarum veterum, et Guilielmi Baxteri, Io. Matthiae Gesneri et Io. Car. Zeunii Annotationibus (Leipzig, 1822; Baxter's edition appeared in 1701).

Q. Horatius Flaccus, ex Recensione et cum Notis atque emendationibus Richardi Bentleii (Berlin, 1869; first ed., 1711).

Poemata, ed. Alexander Cuningamius (The Hague, 1721).

Quinti Horatii Flacci Opera (London, 1733).

The Odes, Satyrs, and Epistles of Horace. Done into English by Thomas Creech (London, 1684).

Horace's Satires, Epistles and Art of Poetry done into English with Notes by S. Dunster (London, 1739; first ed., 1709).

Œuvres d'Horace traduites en François par le P. Tarteron . . . avec des remarques critiques sur la traduction par Pierre Coste (Amsterdam, 1710).

18. For example, in explaining line 20 of Horace's Satire II.i., almost identical opinions (opinions not readily apparent to twentieth-century readers) are offered by Porphyrion, by Cruquius and his Vetus Commentator, by Desprez, by Torrentius, and by Dacier; in addition, in order to explain the grammatical usage of "undique tutus" in the same line, many of these commentators refer with the same conformity to Virgil's phrase, "tuta lacu nigro."

19. Pagination ***2verso, in his essay *De Q. Horatii Vita ac Scriptis,* prefaced to his edition of Horace. "Carefully read and consider each poem of Horace: you will not find subtle disputations or cunning syllogisms, but almost all the rules that enable profane man to progress towards living in a right, holy, peaceful, and blessed manner disclosed and arranged and, as it were, ornamented with models chosen from the riches of poets and history and human life. This usage, this mode of philosophizing especially pleased Horace."

20. Dacier, V, xv. Dryden translates this section in his *Discourse* (Ker), II, 97; (Kinsley), II, 657–58.

21. Dacier, VI, 325.

22. Caroline Goad's exhaustive compilation of Horatian motifs has long ago demonstrated this point. See especially her appendix of references to Horace in the works of the authors she deals with, *Horace in the English Literature of the Eighteenth Century* (New Haven, 1916), pp. 293–620.

23. See Fielding, "Proposal for Making an Effectual Provision for the Poor," in *The Complete Works of Henry Fielding,* ed. W. E. Henley (London, 1903), III, 193; and Philip Dormer Stanhope, Fourth Earl of Chesterfield, *Letters,* ed. Bonamy Dobrée (London, 1932), VI, letter 2453, pp. 2762–63. See also in the same volume letter 2555, p. 2879, and III, letter 1560, p. 1148.

24. This can be demonstrated most conveniently by reference to Goad's appendix on Addison, pp. 297–334. The other appendixes offer similar evidence for the authority of Horace in the writings of Rowe, Steele, Prior, Gay, Pope, and Swift.

25. Pope's letter to Parnell of May 25 or June 1, 1714, will give some idea of the extent to which he employed the commentators while translating Homer: "The minute I lost you Eustathius with nine hundred pages, and nine thousand Contractions of the Greek Character Arose to my View— Spondanus with all his Auxiliaries in Number a thousand pages (Value three shillings) & Dacier's three Volumes, Barnes's two, Valterie's three, Cuperus half in Greek, Leo Allatius three parts in Greek, Scaliger, Macrobius, & (worse than 'em all) Aulus Gellius: All these Rushd upon my Soul at once & whelm'd me under a Fitt of Head Ach, I curs'd them all Religiously, Damn'd my best friends among the rest, & even blasphem'd Homer himself. Dear Sir not only as you are a friend & as you are a Goodnatur'd Man, but as you are a Christian & a Divine come back Speedily & prevent the Encrease of my Sins: For at the Rate I have begun to Rave, I shall not only Damn all the Poets & Commentators who have gone before me, but be damned my Self by all who come after me . . ." *(The Correspondence of Alexander Pope,* ed. George Sherburn [Oxford, 1956], I, 225).

26. Dryden, *The Dedication of the Æneis;* (Ker), II, 221; (Kinsley), III, 1050.

27. See, for example, *Dedication,* (Ker), II, 173, 174, and 176; (Kinsley), III, 1016 and 1018; and *Preface to Sylvae,* (Ker), I, 252 and 258; (Kinsley), I, 390 and 394.

28. Wentworth Dillon, Earl of Roscommon, "An Essay of Translated Verse," in Johnson's *English Poets,* XV, 85. This was first published in 1684.

29. "Pope as Textual Critic: A Bibliographical Study of his Horatian Text," *JEGP,* XLVII (1948), 150–55.

30. All quotations from Pope and from the Latin text of his Horatian poems will be taken from the Twickenham Edition of the *Poems of Alexander Pope* (gen. ed. John Butt; [London, 1939–61]), hereafter referred to as TE.

31. *Correspondence,* I, 492.

32. Note to line 95, Ep.I.i., *To Bolingbroke, The Works of Alexander Pope,* ed. William Warburton (London, 1753), IV, 112; TE, IV, 285.

33. For Dacier's prestige and reputation, see S. H. Monk's introduction to *The Preface to Aristotle's Art of Poetry,* pp. i–iv.

34. For a full discussion of the nature of formal verse satire, see Mary Claire Randolph's "The Structural Design of Formal Verse Satire," *PQ,* XXI (1942), 368–84, and her unpublished dissertation, "The Neo-Classic Theory of the Formal Verse Satire in England, 1700–1750," (University of North Carolina, 1939). Also pertinent are Maynard Mack's "The Muse of Satire," *Yale Review,* XLI (1951), 80–92; Northrop Frye's "The Nature of Satire," *UTQ,* XIV (1944–45), 75–89; and Alvin Kernan's *The Cankered Muse* (New Haven, 1959), pp. 2–31.

35. Miss Randolph's article makes this clear, as does her dissertation, pp. 79–182 *passim*. See also Northrop Frye, *The Anatomy of Criticism* (Princeton, 1957), pp. 224–25.

36. On pages 10–11.

37. Alexander Ross, *Pansebeia: or, A View of All Religions in the World* (4th ed.; London, 1672), pp. 86–87.

38. *Ibid.*, pp. 126–28.

39. *Ibid.*, pp. 131–32.

40. All these citations are drawn from the "Advertisements to the Reader" in *The Court of the Gentiles* (Oxford, 1669), I, pagination *2recto–*4verso; they form a concise summation of the main lines of Gale's massive and detailed argument. For specific arguments on the relation of pagan theology and poetry to the Hebrew traditions, see I, 8–17, 99–129, and especially 275–97; in this last, he demonstrates in particular that pagan poetry is derived from Scriptural poetry and like it in its purpose, instruction and edification.

41. For a concise review of the deist position and its dependence upon the works of previous orthodox theoreticians, see Frank Manuel, *The Eighteenth Century Confronts the Gods* (Cambridge, Mass., 1959), pp. 57–65. Manuel makes quite clear the prevalence of a belief in pagan monotheism, at least on the part of an intellectual elite.

42. Edward, Lord Herbert of Cherbury, *De Religione Gentilium*, trans. William Lewis (London, 1705), p. 304. See also pp. 158–67, 168–84, 184–218.

43. Herbert of Cherbury, *De Veritate* (trans. Mayrick H. Carré; [Bristol, 1937]), pp. 291–94. See also pp. 298–99, 301–2, 312.

44. William Wollaston, *The Religion of Nature Delineated* (8th ed.; London, 1759), p. 124. His citations of Horace are frequent: see pp. 60, 112, 201, 247, 253, 296, 323, 337, and 338.

45. John Toland, *Letters to Serena* (London, 1704), p. 114.

46. *Ibid.*, pp. 115, 116–17.

47. Matthew Tindal, *Christianity as Old as the Creation: or, The Gospel, A Republication of the Religion of Nature* (London, 1731), pp. 268–70. Toland's volume, *Christianity not Mysterious: or, A Treatise Shewing That there is nothing in the Gospel Contrary to Reason, Nor Above it.* (London, 1702), argues at length the very same point.

48. *Christianity as Old as the Creation*, pp. 247–48.

49. John Conybeare, *A Defence of Reveal'd Religion against the Exceptions of a late Writer, in his book, intituled, Christianity as Old as the Creation* (3rd ed.; Dublin, 1739), pp. 285–86. John Leland, *An Answer to a Late Book Intituled, Christianity as Old as the Creation* (Dublin, 1733), II, 555–57.

50. For examples of the citation of Horace in such circumstances, see the articles on *divitiae* in Laurentius Beyerlinck's *Magnum Theatrum Vitae Humanae* (Leyden, 1678), II, 995, col. 2; and Domenico Nani Mirabelli's *Polyanthea* (Geneva, 1600), p. 253.

[35]

51. His poems cover such topics as "That the shortnesse of mans life is to bee lengthened by good deeds," "A Departure from things humane," and outright biblical paraphrases: see *The Odes of Casimire, Translated by G. Hils* (1646; Augustan Reprint Society, no. 44, Los Angeles, 1953), pp. 14–25 and pp. 30–45.

52. Thomas Sagittarius, *Horatius Christianus* (Jena, 1615), pp. A–A3.

53. Octavio van Veen, *Quinti Horatii Flacci emblemata* (Brussels, 1684). An entry in Horace Walpole's Commonplace book (Huntington MS 1271), which is supposedly from Spence, attributes to Pope a rather detailed familiarity with the work.

54. Dacier, V, 517.

55. Dacier, I, 39; also, in the same volume, pp. 47–48: "Mais comme la Philosophie des Payens n'étoit pas exempte d'erreurs dans les Philosophes même, on ne doit pas s'attendre à la trouver plus sane et plus pure dans les Poëtes. On y trouve souvent des maximes qui pourroient être dangereuses, et qu'il faut ou corriger ou expliquer, afin, comme dit Plutarque, *que les jeunes gens soient instruits par cette lecture, et que la poésie les rends amis de la Philosophie, et leur serve auprès d'elle d'introducteur.* Car c'est une grande erreur de croire que la lecture des poëtes n'est qu'un délassement et qu'un amusement où l'on ne cherche qu'à réjouir l'esprit par de nobles expressions, de belles peintures, de fines allusions, et par toutes les finesses et les tours les plus ingeneux d'une langue riche et feconde. C'est une étude agréable à la verité, mais qui doit préparer à une étude plus solide."

Chapter II

The Theory and Practice of Satire
The First Satire of the Second Book of Horace, Imitated

CHRONOLOGICALLY the first of the *Imitations*, Pope's dialogue with Fortescue embodies most of those elements of neoclassical satiric theory that have so far concerned us. It portrays, far more accurately than any of my descriptions can, the features of Horace as Pope's age saw them. The twin facts that it stands near the beginning of Pope's most intensive satiric activity and that it is his first finished poem in the imitative mode only hint of its significance in the canon of his works. It constitutes not only a major literary accomplishment in its own right, but also an important—perhaps the most important we possess—articulation of Pope's satiric position and methods, with consequent implications for a broad area of his poetry. It is a mistake to regard it only as a shield, an excuse, for the supposedly more ambitious *Epistle to Bathurst*: rather, this carefully wrought defense of satire boldly proclaims Pope's literary and moral and political orthodoxy, and forms the firm base upon which the *Bathurst* and Pope's other satires can be built.

I

The *Fortescue* was written within the framework of a well-defined and easily recognizable subgenre of literature, the satirist's apologia. The primary concern of the poem is, of course, satire, and the central effort of the poem is to distinguish what Pope's satire is and does from what it is

[37]

not or should not be. The precise question is whether Pope's verses constitute satire or libel, as his *Advertisement* makes clear:

> And indeed there is not in the world a greater Error, than that which Fools are so apt to fall into, and Knaves with good reason to incourage, the mistaking a *Satyrist* for a *Libeller;* whereas to a *true Satyrist* nothing is so odious as a *Libeller,* for the same reason as to a man *truly Virtuous* nothing is so hateful as a *Hypocrite.*

The problem that confronted Pope was not by any means a new one. Horace, Persius, and Juvenal had established precedents and provided an elaborate ethical and literary background for Pope's poem by answering just such charges in their own apologias. Pope's solution to the problem, however, appears to be unique. In the *Epistle to Augustus*, he characteristically clears satire of all such slurs by defining it as the virtuous mean between the vicious extremes of flattery and libel:

> At length, by wholesom dread of statutes bound,
> The Poets learn'd to please, and not to wound:
> Most warp'd to Flatt'ry's side; but some, more nice,
> Preserv'd the freedom, and forebore the vice.
> Hence Satire rose, that just the medium hit,
> And heals with Morals what it hurts with Wit.
>
> (256–62)

Satire attacks vice only to redeem the vicious; it virtuously preserves the golden mean between hypocritical flattery and pernicious libel. These ideas are not in themselves complex or abstruse, but they provide the essential keys to the intricate dialectic of Pope's defense of his calling, his verse, and himself.

From the very outset, the *Fortescue* makes clear the antitheses that are to absorb most of its energy, and whose resolution is to be its focal point. His verse is too harsh, his verse is too weak; it is libelous, it is utterly innocuous.

There are (I scarce can think it, but am told)
There are to whom my Satire seems too bold,
Scarce to wise *Peter* complaisant enough,
And something said of *Chartres* much too rough.
The Lines are weak, another's pleas'd to say,
Lord *Fanny* spins a thousand such a Day.

(1–6)

This is a significant example of Pope's satiric and rhetorical technique: he undermines the charge of libel in the very act of presenting it by referring to his attacks, in the *Epistle to Bathurst*, upon Peter Walters and Chartres, two notorious reprobates, of whose public guilt there could be absolutely no doubt.[1] But beyond this, the passage presents what amounts to the "situation" of the Imitation—in rhetorical terms, its *narratio* and *partitio*, the statement of the case and its divisions.[2] Some claim Pope has libeled Walter and Chartres; others claim that his poems are the very same as those of Lord Fanny—the *beatus Fannius* of Horace's Sat.I.iv. (another defense of satire), whose popular and empty verse contrasts significantly with the fear Horace's satires rouse in the guilty crowd. The words are never used, but the ideas are plain enough: Pope's poetry has been accused simultaneously of both opprobrious extremes, flattery and libel; and it is particularly for this last reason that he must seek "Council learned in the Law" (8).

What his lawyer, Fortescue, tells him is quite practical advice. He urges Pope to flatter rather than satirize:

Better be *Cibber*, I'll maintain it still,
Than ridicule all *Taste*, blaspheme *Quadrille*,
Abuse the City's best good Men in Metre,
And laugh at Peers that put their Trust in *Peter*,
Ev'n those you touch not, hate you . . .
A hundred smart in *Timon* and in *Balaam*:
The fewer still you name, you wound the more;
Bond is but one, but *Harpax* is a Score.

(37–44)

But his attempt to dissuade Pope from satire merely serves as the stimulus for a long justification of that very thing. In point of fact, Fortescue's remarks have already been undercut by being themselves incorporated into the satiric process. It is always important to remember the physical and moral presence of Horace's poem on the facing page of Pope's editions and the possibilities of cross-reference offered by such an arrangement. In the Horatian original, Trebatius says,

> Quanto rectius hoc, quam tristi laedere versu
> Pantolabum Scurram, Nomentanumve nepotem?
> Cum sibi quisque timet, quanquam est intactus, & odit.
>
> (21–23)

The English version slyly makes Fortescue equate "the City's best good Men" (39), whom he is ostensibly defending, with Horace's despicable "Pantolabum Scurram, Nomentanumve nepotem." The remainder of his remarks constitute in themselves a succinct satire on the age: general satire is even more cutting than particular, because more of the apparently innumerable guilty are hit.[3] Thus Pope's defense of satire has been strengthened in advance by the interplay of the Latin and English texts, which have betrayed Fortscue, the voice of practicality and law in the poem, into committing (and simultaneously demonstrating the inevitability of) the same sort of offense that Pope is charged with.

Pope's apology proceeds from this point in a manner parallel to Horace's. He claims that satire is his pleasure, as various vices are the pleasures of Scarsdale and Ridotta, and that

> I love to pour out all myself, as plain
> As downright *Shippen,* or as old *Montagne.*
> In them, as certain to be lov'd as seen,
> The Soul stood forth, nor kept a Thought within;
> In me what Spots (for Spots I have) appear,

Will prove at least the Medium must be clear.
In this impartial Glass, my Muse intends
Fair to expose myself, my Foes, my Friends;
Publish the present Age, but where my Text
Is Vice too high, reserve it for the next:
My Foes shall wish my Life a longer date,
And ev'ry Friend the less lament my Fate.

(51–62)

Horace has compared himself to Lucilius, who wrote

quo fit ut omnis
Votiva pateat veluti descripta tabella
Vita senis.

(31–33)

The idea that Pope seizes upon and develops is contained
in *votiva tabella*, the comparison of satire to a religious
object or act. This is made abundantly clear by Pope's insistence upon his satire as a reflection of his "spotted" soul
and upon its value as a mirror of his spiritual state. The
use of these images here, far more complex than in the
Horatian original, is not the result of a departure from
Horace, but is an expansion of his text, the product of the
insistent christianization of pagan ideas.

On its most readily apparent level, the passage employs
the rather commonplace conception of satire as the glass
that exposes to the reader the truth about himself and his
times. But the prominent mention of soul, spots, and
medium does not accord with this usage, and the reasons
for their presence must be sought in another and equally
common occurrence of the mirror image. Such a conjunction
of ideas is found in a cluster of biblical passages, all making
use of the metaphor of the glass. The most famous of these
is probably the "For now we see through a glass darkly"
of St. Paul, but the most pertinent for Pope's context occurs
in Wisdom of Solomon 7:26:

[41]

For she [Wisdom] is the brightness of eternal light, and the unspotted mirror of God's majesty, and the image of his goodness.[4]

Biblical exegetes were unanimous in deciding that Wisdom was to be identified with Christ, who was truly the immaculate mirror of God's perfection. They further agreed in distinguishing two other kinds of less perfect mirrors: one, the human mind, made to the image of God but nevertheless not without spots, and the other, creatures, in whom are reflected traces of the Trinity.[5]

The glass to which Pope's context has immediate reference is the human mind, and particularly poetry as a creative work of the mind that mirrors God's own act of creation. The relevance of such an idea to Pope's view of satire can be readily grasped; like Horace, he places satire in the perspective of a religious act, an almost sacramental self-revelation and confession. He goes far beyond the pagan poet, however, by suggesting that in so doing he discharges fully his duty as man, by thus faithfully reflecting the image of God within him and reproducing, in little, God's creation of the universe through the agency of the Word. The classical *votiva tabella* to which Horace refers depicted episodes in the suppliant's life that showed the active intervention of the gods in his affairs. Its presence on the facing page of Pope's editions and in the minds of his readers would have provided sufficient clue to the religious nature of his own "impartial Glass": satire becomes for him very literally a sacred tablet, the medium through which he reveals the continuing presence of God in his soul. The only thing that the satiric glass will not reflect is "Vice too high" (60); and the reservation of that for later judgment is, like the total satiric theory of which it is a small part, a successful mingling of classical and Christian ideas—in this case, of Cicero's rhetorical advice and the admonitions of Scripture.[6] In this manner, Pope's particular pleasure (the excuse he had given for his penchant for satire) dis-

[42]

covers itself as an almost sacred act, in distinct contrast to the vicious pleasures of the foils with whom he opened his defense.

Having in this way established the basically religious character of his craft, Pope goes on to explain precisely what his satire expresses:

> My Head and Heart thus flowing thro' my Quill,
> Verse-man or Prose-man, term me which you will,
> Papist or Protestant, or both between,
> Like good *Erasmus* in an honest Mean,
> In Moderation placing all my Glory,
> While Tories call me Whig, and Whigs a Tory.
>
> (63–68)

This passage elaborates the character of the man who writes such sacramental satire as Pope has described, and he is strikingly presented as a living exemplar of that ideal of moderation that achieved its most succinct expression in St. Paul.[7] But the doctrine of the mean is here depicted not so much as the median between two extremes as it is the reconciliation of them; the basic unspoken unitive element of the passage is the traditional conception of *concordia discors rerum*.[8] This harmonization of discordant opposites is accomplished not only in, but by, Pope's writings: head and heart meet in his quill; it is in his compositions that he appears to be, simultaneously, verse-man and prose-man, Papist and Protestant, Whig and Tory. The satiric glass reflects faithfully the state of the author's soul and of his poetic world, and, as a consequence, shares in his concordant nature (itself a reflection of the image of God, in whom all opposites are reconciled). Pope has now shown his satire, which he had already displayed in a clearly religious light, to be in itself an exemplification of apostolic moderation and divine harmony.[9]

This has been implicit in Pope's satiric theory from the very beginning. By the terms of his definition of satire, it partakes of some of the characteristics of both flattery and libel—that is, as a mean between the two, it reconciles in itself elements of both. It takes from flattery honest praise and its constructive elements; from libel it borrows its cutting edge and destructive tendency. Fused and reconciled, these disparate factors produce satire, which "heals with Morals what it hurts with Wit." Since satire itself is a concord, a harmonization of opposites, it is with complete consistency that Pope describes it as the vehicle for the concordant sentiments of the golden mean.

So also the targets of his satire become the "sad Burthen of some merry Song" (80). Vice and the vicious are the inevitable refrain of satire, and, in Pope's verse in particular, they are worked into the greater harmony that constitutes the whole satiric song. The line that states this is itself a *concordia discors,* balancing and linking the opposites "sad" and "merry" in a miniature of the larger universal harmony of which Pope's poetic creation is an echo. Because of this, Pope can claim that the butts of his satire are "Sacred to Ridicule" (79). They have been incorporated (as vicious extremes, but incorporated nevertheless) into a poetic universe that achieves its own harmony by a careful internal balancing of opposite concepts and themes, and so is an accurate model of the divine creation. All this is done within the general context of Horace's poem,[10] which constantly supports Pope's points with the sanctions of classical culture.

After making clear in this manner exactly what his satire is, Pope demonstrates equally clearly what it is not by presenting a gallery of libelers:

> Slander or Poyson, dread from *Delia's* Rage,
> Hard Words or Hanging, if your Judge be *Page*
> From furious *Sappho* scarce a milder Fate,
> P-x'd by her Love, or libell'd by her Hate:
> Its proper Pow'r to hurt, each Creature feels,
> Bulls aim their horns, and Asses lift their heels,
> 'Tis a Bear's Talent not to kick, but hug,

And no man wonders he's not stung by Pug:
So drink with *Waters,* or with *Chartres* eat,
They'll never poison you, they'll only cheat.

(81–90)

Besides changing the Latin names to more contemporary
type-names, Pope has insinuated into his rendering a consideration, not present in the original, of the misuse of
language. In Horace, this passage is the final statement of
the poet's resolution to follow his natural bent and write
satire. Pope, however, has shifted the emphasis and con-
verted it into a passage uncovering the antithesis of his
satire. Its primary concern is announced with its first word,
"Slander," and continues on through "Hard Words"[11] to
libel, to culminate in a complete transformation of Horace's
poisoner into a contemporary confidence man. All these
things, as Pope's equation of them with poison, hanging,
and the pox demonstrates, are the vile extremes that his
satire avoids. They are as well serious abuses of the faculty
of language, in glaring contrast to his careful use of it.

These lines are complicated, and their meaning further
adumbrated, by a highly significant deviation from the
Horatian original, to which Pope calls attention by inserting
index guides from the English to the Latin text at the
pertinent places.[12] His line 85, "Its proper Pow'r to hurt,
each Creature feels," corresponds only roughly to Horace's
"Ut, quo quisque valet, suspectus terreat, utque/ Imperet
hoc natura potens" (50–51); but it translates almost exactly
a line of Lucretius that the editor of the Delphine text
(which Pope owned) cites in his commentary.[13]

At varios linguae Sonitus Natura subegit
Mittere, & Utilitas expressit nomina rerum:
Non alia longe ratione, atque ipsa videtur
Protrahere ad gestum Pueros infantia linguae,
Cum facit, ut digito, quae sint praesentia, monstrent.
Sentit enim vim quisque suam, quam possit abuti,

[45]

Cornua nata prius vitulo quam frontibus extent,
Illis iratus petit, atque insensus inurget.[14]

The similarity of Pope's English line to Lucretius' "Sentit enim vim quisque suam, quam possit abuti" will be readily apparent, and the significance of its occurrence in Pope's poem will not be farther off. In Lucretius, the line occurs in the context of his explanation of the growth of civilization and the beginnings of concord and justice among men, and is part of his argument that language arose naturally out of the need of human beings to communicate ideas to each other. Speech is for Lucretius the means by which the bond of society was forged, the indispensable element by which men articulated their desire for peace and justice. Viewed in this light, Pope's Delia, Sappho, and Waters cannot easily be dismissed. Their abuse of language is not simply a breach of decorum, but an irresponsible act that strikes at the foundation of civilized society and threatens to undo the ties that hold it together. It is scarcely accidental that of the characters Pope chooses to present at this point, one makes a mockery of the judicial system, one grotesquely parodies the normal love relationship, and two effectively destroy the basis of contractual business dealings. All four represent a total perversion of the purpose and nature of language, and, consequently, an inversion of its effects. Lucretius' use of *concordia* (V.1024) is crucial here, for what the malevolence of Delia, Page, Sappho, Waters, and Chartres amounts to is an attempt to destroy that harmony that Pope as true poet labors to perpetuate, and to reduce mankind to its original savagery and discord. This is the true nature of libel, and, as Pope is at pains to make clear, it is the exact opposite of real satire.

The values that Pope here and in the mirror passage attaches to language, and especially to poetry, help establish the interchangeability of artistic achievement and morality. By his theory of language and literature, right usage becomes a symbol, a metaphor, for right morals and social

[46]

standards, for personal and political rectitude. In such a world, the dunces, for instance, will inevitably sin against God, man, and art simultaneously; and the poetasters of the *Epistle to Arbuthnot* are inescapably hacks, Hanoverians, and Low-Churchmen. The good poet *is* the good man and the good citizen, the scribbler, a blasphemer and Whig. Offense in any one area signifies guilt in all others: concord once violated can yield only greater and greater discord. Consequently, it can be no surprise to find Pope concluding his defense of himself as satirist by announcing his intention to continue to "Rhyme and Print" (100). "Rhyme" is metaphor for the poet's vocation, to properly employ language to produce harmony on all levels; "print" is metaphor for the moralist's, to "publish the present Age." Given the character Pope has so far established for his satire and himself, he could do nothing else.

II

Character has been a concern of almost paramount importance in the poem from that point, at least, at which Pope began defending satire as his pleasure and his natural talent. The Imitation has preserved an undercurrent of interest in this problem almost from its beginning, when it was sounded in somewhat muted form in the first Pope-Fortescue interchange:

> *F.* I'd write no more.
> > *P.* Not write? but then I *think,*
> And for my Soul I cannot sleep a wink.
> I nod in Company, I wake at Night,
> Fools rush into my Head, and so I write.
> *F.* You could not do a worse thing for your Life.
> Why, if the Nights seem tedious—take a Wife;
> Or rather truly, if your Point be Rest,
> Lettuce and Cowslip Wine; *Probatum est.*
>
> > > > > (11–18)

[47]

This section provides a subdivision of the topics of the poem, and introduces the grounds of its third area of discussion, the satirist's character. Pope has already detailed the antithetical charges leveled against his poetry, and now, in response to Fortescue's suggestion that he abandon satire altogether, he replies, in effect, that he *must* write because of an inner compulsion—"And *for my Soul* I cannot sleep a wink." Fortescue sets up by his rejoinder a clear dichotomy of values in terms of which Pope will have to vindicate his character and moral stance. "You could not," he tells Pope, "do a worse thing *for your Life.*" As satirist, Pope's conduct is subject to judgment both according to private, moral norms and according to public, social ones. This dilemma has remained secondary as long as the poet was engaged in the act of defending satire itself: as soon as that is accomplished, the question of his character re-emerges and demands consideration.

Fortescue once again introduces it, in his lament over Pope's resolution to continue writing satire, by reverting to terms similar to those of his first warning:

> Alas young Man! your Days can ne'r be long,
> In Flow'r of Age you perish for a Song!
> Plums, and Directors, *Shylock* and his Wife,
> Will club their Testers, now, to take your Life!
>
> (101–4)

The already explained virtuous nature of the song for which Pope risks his life draws a good deal of the sting from Fortescue's objection, but there still remains, at the very least, a residual level of social disapproval of the satirist and his vocation. Pope's retort, in lines 105–42, attempts to reverse this opprobrious judgment by demonstrating both his personal integrity and his public possession of the esteem of worthy judges—that is, to show himself as a moral man and an aid to society rather than a threat.

Pope immediately responds to Fortescue's warning by elaborately defending his virtue in a passage that approaches the oratorical sublime:

> What? arm'd for *Virtue* when I point the Pen,
> Brand the bold Front of shameless, guilty Men,
> Dash the proud Gamester in his gilded Car,
> Bare the mean Heart that lurks beneath a Star;
> Can there be wanting to defend Her Cause,
> Lights of the Church, or Guardians of the Laws?
> Could pension'd *Boileau* lash in honest Strain
> Flatt'rers and Bigots ev'n in *Louis'* Reign?
> Could Laureate *Dryden* Pimp and Fry'r engage,
> Yet neither *Charles* nor *James* be in a Rage?
> And I not strip the Gilding off a Knave,
> Un-plac'd, un-pension'd, no Man's Heir, or Slave?
> I will, or perish in the gen'rous Cause.
> Hear this, and tremble! you, who 'scape the Laws.
> Yes, while I live, no rich or noble knave
> Shall walk the World, in credit, to his grave.
> TO VIRTUE ONLY AND HER FRIENDS, A FRIEND,
> The World beside my murmur, or commend.
>
> (105–22)

Horace, of course, has sheltered himself under the authority and example of Lucilius, and Pope parallels this by introducing Dryden and Boileau, who not only wrote satire unmolested but were actually rewarded by their respective kings. They, like Pope, reprimanded the vicious extremes of behavior, flattery and bigotry—two targets obviously quite significant for a poem concerned with flattery and libel.[15] That Pope is now criticized for the very same thing is shown really to reflect on his age rather than on himself; under a previous (and Stuart) king, satire was honored, but the reign of George II obviously cannot endure such looking into. The precedent of Dryden's satire under a legitimate monarch betrays the inversion of values and the growth of corruption under what Pope regarded as a German usurper.

The authority of Dryden and Boileau is reinforced by classical examples. There is, first of all, the active presence of Horace and the exemplar he cites, Lucilius. In addition, Pope has managed to bring to bear upon his poem materials from the apologias of both Juvenal and Persius, thus anchoring it firmly in the classical tradition and simultaneously presenting an overwhelming weight of authority to vindicate the integrity and public utility of the satirist. His lines about Dryden and Boileau (111-14) are based upon Persius' decription of the satire of Horace and Lucilius, as is also the form and content of the lines following them (115-16). Here is the most relevant portion of Persius' statement in Dryden's translation:

> Yet old *Lucilius* never fear'd the times;
> But lash'd the City, and dissected Crimes.
> *Mutius* and *Lupus* both by name he brought;
> He mouth'd 'em, and betwixt his Grinders caught.
>
> .   .   .   .
>
> Cou'd he do this, and is my Muse controll'd
> By Servile Awe? Born free, and not be bold?[16]

And shortly before this, in lines 105-6, Pope has echoed Dryden's translation of Juvenal's appeal to the precedent of Lucilius:

> But when *Lucilius* brandishes his Pen,
> And flashes in the face of Guilty Men,
> A cold Sweat stands in drops on ev'ry part;
> And Rage succeeds to Tears, Revenge to Smart.[17]

The multiplication of authorities that has taken place in this passage is staggering. Horace cites the example of Lucilius; Pope in imitating him has the advantage of his and Lucilius' precedent, but names Boileau and Dryden, echoing the latter's translations of Juvenal's and Persius' defenses, and particularly drawing upon the contexts in which they refer to their predecessors, Lucilius and Horace. This brings the argument full circle, and silences absolutely those who objected to Pope's satire on moral grounds, since he, in naming "shameless, guilty Men," has done exactly what they did, and accomplished a deed that was formerly recognized as praiseworthy. By so adapting the posture and language of the Roman poets, Pope has manipulated the entire bulk of classical tradition and demonstrated his right to its protection in the very act of claiming it.

Pope's interpolation of these lines from Juvenal and Persius should not be mistaken for merely personal associations based on his own private insights and preoccupations. Besides the obvious fact that the passages deal with the same subject for the same reasons in poems that are all designed to justify their creators' satire, both Juvenal's and Persius' lines had been repeatedly linked with Horace's by the editors and annotators of all three authors.[18] Pope's use of them here then is not to be construed as the esoteric whim of a scholarly poet, but rather as his exploitation of materials that lay well within the bounds of the common knowledge of educated men. They are drawn from the public domain, and Pope could in all probability rely on at least the most alert portion of his audience to recognize their provenance and relevance.

Pope had announced in his prefatory *Advertisement* both his reasons for writing this defense and his reasons for imitating Horace:

> The Occasion of publishing these *Imitations* was the Clamour raised on some of my *Epistles.* An answer from *Horace* was both more full, and of more Dignity, than any I cou'd have made in my own person; and the Example of much greater Freedom in so eminent a Divine as Dr. *Donne,* seem'd a proof with what Indignation and Contempt a Christian may treat Vice or Folly, in ever so low, or ever so high, a Station.

[51]

The very fact that Horace's poem so nearly "hit his case" was in itself a vindication of Pope's legitimate standing as a satirist, and this parallelism he has been cleverly exploiting through the Imitation. Besides this support, his *Advertisement* (which functions as a sort of topical outline for the poem) points to another exemplar, John Donne, not as an authority of the stature of Horace, but specifically as a precedent for *Christian* satire. Pope has already established the religious nature of his verse: it is only logical, then, that his enumeration of classical sanctions for his activities should also embrace and be bolstered by a Christian justification for the writing of satire.

Appropriately enough, this justification has been presented at the very beginning of Pope's argument. The index guides correlate the first line of the "arm'd for *Virtue*" passage with Horace's

> Quid? cum est Lucilius ausus
> Primus in hunc operis componere carmina morem,
>
> (62–63)

which it could not possibly translate. What Pope has actually done is to call into play at this point Horace's earlier pun on *stylus*,[19] which enables him to equivocate between pen and sword and to at least symbolically combine both in one weapon. The significance of this implied metaphor is to be found in the addition of the words "arm'd for *Virtue*" (105) to the opening of the passage. If the Christian life is a constant warfare against evil, as Renaissance and eighteenth-century divines assured their cures it was, the life of a Christian satirist is even more so. It is entirely consistent with the tenor and content of Pope's poem to recognize here a reference to the apostolic injunction that had for centuries armed the Christian warrior and supplied his arsenal; Paul's exhortation to "put on the whole armor of God" (Ephesians 6:10-17). The final weapon Paul catalogues, "the sword of the Spirit, which is the word of God," is the one that matches Pope's and fits coherently into his view of satire as a religious act. Horace's *stylus*, like Horace's conception of satire, has become a valid weapon in the Christian's spiritual struggles. Its occurrence at the beginning of this section of Pope's defense casts his entire elaboration of the satirist's mission into the broader context of the Christian's righteous warfare against the father of lies and his earthly minions, who are the legitimate targets of both preachers and a poet concerned to clear himself from false charges of libel. Such standards provide the final stamp of approval necessary to vindicate his personal morality.

Pope's social worth can best be demonstrated by describing his relationships with worthy noblemen who are themselves possessed of notable public virtues. To this end, he carefully selects two names, prominent respectively in peace and war, Bolingbroke and Peterborough. Returning once again to his previous use of the *concordia discors* pattern, he links these two in a passage that presents himself as a thoroughly concordant individual, reconciling extremes in himself and those about him and living in perfect harmony with the great men whose esteem far outweighs the petty cavils of the mob.

> Know, all the distant Din that World can keep
> Rolls o'er my *Grotto,* and but sooths my Sleep.
> There, my Retreat the best Companions grace,
> Chiefs, out of War, and Statesmen, out of Place.
> There *St. John* mingles with my friendly Bowl,
> The Feast of Reason and the Flow of Soul:
> And He, whose Lightning pierc'd th' *Iberian* Lines,
> Now, forms my Quincunx, and now ranks my Vines,
> Or tames the Genius of the stubborn Plain,
> Almost as quickly, as he conquer'd *Spain.*

(123–32)

[53]

Once more, the concept of *concordia discors* is the main unitive element. The harmonius linking of soldier and statesman is further extended by the higher harmony of the mixture of active and contemplative lives presented in the picture of the two former officials meeting in a contemplative rural retreat.[20] This is elaborated even into the details of their avocations by the two couplets on Peterborough, which liken and, in effect, merge his peacetime gardening with his wartime soldiering.[21] The vocabulary of the lines devoted to gardening shows clearly by its application of military terms to horticulture the extent of the interpenetration and harmonization. Peterborough "forms" the quincunx, "ranks" the vines, and "tames" the plain. Bolingbroke's part is to "mingle" mind and spirit with conviviality in "the Feast of Reason and the Flow of Soul." This latter should also recall Pope's earlier aspirations to pour himself out in his writings so that his soul might stand forth: we are being subtly reminded that even in relaxation Pope and his companions employ language properly, with intelligence and morality. By locating the scene of this concord in his own grotto and garden, Pope has made it clear that this harmony flows from him, that he is responsible for the good order of this miniature society of statesmen and soldiers. In social matters as in literary, Pope has pictured himself as a source of harmony—appropriately enough, if we consider seriously his earlier allusion to Lucretius. Language was invented to establish concord among men, and Pope displays his own proper use of it in the vignette of his relations with Bolingbroke and Peterborough. By thus emphasizing the constructive, edifying role played by himself and his poetry, he answers the objections brought against the satirist as a disrupter of society.

A larger pattern of harmonized opposites can be traced through these various vindications of the satirist's calling. In order to defend his private morality in writing satire,

Pope has had recourse to citing classical and scriptural authority for his public actions; and in order to absolve himself from charges of threatening the social order, he has found it expedient to expose his private life to view. In addition, his defense of his personal morality has been accomplished by proving the social utility of his writings, while his demonstration of his social worth could be brought about only by dismissing the extreme opinions of the mob in favor of the more moderate and competent judgment of a few personal friends. He has inextricably intermingled public and private in yet another harmonious fusion, all of it spreading outward in concentric circles from the focal point of satire as itself a reconciliation of opposites and, simultaneously, the glass of Pope's soul reflecting the divine creation. He has made his defense of satire fully embody his own theory of satire. Form and meaning are completely united.

After all this, the final verse paragraph of Pope's defense (133-42) has something of the character of a legal summation. He reminds Fortescue that, despite contrary charges, he has received impressive marks of social approval (133-34); that he is *not* a malicious libeler (135-36), but rather one who uses language charitably "To help who want, to forward who excel" (137); and, finally, he reminds his lawyer once again of his personal indifference to the real libels of the "Mob" (139-40). His final appeal to his "Council learned in the Laws" (142) has, after the high moral line he has taken, an unmistakable quality of gently mocking irony;[22] "Learned in the Laws" no longer indicates Fortescue's abilities, but his limitations. The phrase has, as it were, fallen back into the Latin word of which it is a literal translation, *Iurisconsultus,* which all the commentators use to describe Horace's Trebatius, and which signifies no more than "lawyer."

Fortescue's very lawyer-like reply (143-49) returns the poem to the problem from which it set out, the legal charge

of libel. Pope has incorporated Fortescue into the pattern
of his satiric thrusts without violating the decorum of the
lawyer's persona; his precise, legalistic comment contains
in itself an acknowledgement of Pope's innocence (143) and
a gibe at a tyrannical king (144-46; that Pope meant
George is, of course, beyond doubt). Despite the satire inherent in his remarks, Fortescue still insists that Pope's own
"very honest Rhymes" (146) are covered by the laws concerning libel. It is Pope's retort (150-53), the poem's
refutatio, that reduces this to a mere legal quibble. Putting
aside Horace's pun on *mala carmina,*[23] which side-steps
rather than answers the question, he makes a distinction in
kind between his writings and "*Libels* and *Satires!* lawless
Things indeed" (150). Lest there be any doubt about what
he is actually doing, Pope's use of the adjective "lawless"
recalls the opening of Horace's poem, where one of the
charges brought against him is that "ultra legem tendere
opus" (1-2); and it is precisely this sort of verse that Pope
denies writing. Instead, he composes "grave *Epistles,* bringing Vice to Light" (151); that is, his verses are not malicious
lampoons, but didactic poems whose constructive value
compensates for any injury their wit causes.[24] Despite his
disavowal of the name, it is clear that Pope is here claiming,
as he has all through the poem, that he writes true satire.
Fortescue's final words bear this out:

> The Case is alter'd—you may then proceed.
> In such a Cause the Plaintiff will be hiss'd,
> My Lords the Judges laugh, and you're dismiss'd.
>
> (154–56)

This is the ideal result of true satire: the plaintiff, the satiric
butt, will be hissed from the court amid the curative
laughter that satire is supposed to rouse. The legal charge
of libel has no relevance because there is a real and
demonstrable (and, by this point, fully demonstrated)
difference in nature and effect between libel and satire.

[56]

III

In accordance with his conception of satire as the virtuous mean between vicious extremes, Pope's repudiation of the charge of libel is paralleled by his disavowal of flattery. Fortescue had brought this problem to the fore early in the poem. In the same passage wherein he first raised the dichotomy in values expressed by the poles of "Life" and "Soul," he concluded by advising Pope to "Write *Caesar's* Praise:/ You'll gain at least a *Knighthood*, or the *Bays*" (21-22). That is, he asks him to compose such verses as Lord Fanny or Colley Cibber write, and points out that such flattery is the sure road to royal favor. Pope's reply and the dialogue that ensues are masterpieces of satiric *double entendre*.

> *P.* What? like *Sir Richard,* rumbling, rough and fierce.
> With Arms, and George, and Brunswick crowd the Verse?
> Rend with tremendous Sound your ears asunder,
> With Gun, Drum, Trumpet, Blunderbuss & Thunder?
> Or nobly wild, with *Budgell*'s Fire and Force,
> Paint Angels trembling round his *falling Horse?*
> *F.* Then all your Muse's softer Art display,
> Let *Carolina* smooth the tuneful Lay,
> Lull with *Amelia*'s liquid Name the Nine,
> And sweetly flow through all the Royal Line.
> *P.* Alas! few Verses touch their nicer Ear;
> They scarce can bear their *Laureate* twice a year:
> And justly Caesar scorns the Poet's Lays,
> It is to *History* he trusts for Praise.
>
> (23–36)

Blackmore and Budgell are the Georgian versions of Virgil and Pindar, and, as Pope's index guide makes clear,[25] Horace's excuse for not writing heroic poetry is literally true of them: their talents are insufficient. The best that the "tremendous Sound" of their verse can do is depict the melodramatic scene of George's sole military adventure, Oudenarde, during which his horse was killed.

At this point, the ever-present tensions between Pope's English and Horace's Latin poem mesh finely to produce a telling satiric thrust that indicates exactly how great the difference is between George Augustus and Augustus Caesar. In the original, the episode pictured involves a wounded Parthian falling from his horse, and the commentators identify this incident as the slaying of Pacorius, king of the Parthians.[26] Pope's English rendering, by dwelling lovingly on the circumstances of George's mishap, has slyly transformed him into the barbarian king rather than his ideal prototype, Augustus. In point of fact, if we follow the lead provided by Warburton's Scriblerus-like note, we will be forced to see the Stuart Pretender playing the role of the unharmed Caesar to George's stricken barbarian:

> The horse on which his Majesty charged at the Battle of Oudenarde; when the Pretender, and the Princes of the blood of France fled before him.

That this episode was in reality seriously celebrated in one of Budgell's panegyrics on George is an indication of far more than Pope's personal dislike of his king. Played off thus against Horace's legitimate praise of *Caesaris invicti* (11), it reveals that George has totally perverted the king's role: praise of him can only be satire in disguise, as Pope will later say and demonstrate in the *Epistle to Augustus*.

Even Fortescue's next suggestion, that Pope turn from heroic panegyric to lyric and praise the royal family, shares this same condition: from seeming encomium it degenerates to actual insult. The muse's questionable "softer Art" falls into the opposite extreme from the "rumbling, rough, and fierce" verse of George's flatterers, but the difference is only verbal: they reflect exactly the same inanity and vacuity. The "tuneful Lay" promptly acquires the characteristics of a lesser Dulness and lulls even the muses themselves to sleep with Amelia's "liquid" name, before flowing diarrhetically on through the rest of the royal family. What is lacking from these lines is as important as what is present: there are no domestic virtues to celebrate, no filial love, and, in the face of Horace's praise of Augustus' civil achievements, no wise government, none of the arts of peace. To balance the dubious glory of George's exploit at Oudenarde, there is only the absolute emptiness of sweetly flowing verse. Pope's explicit reference to the laureate makes quite clear that this soporific nonsense is the only poetry Cibber can write, the only poetry the royal family can inspire.

Such satire is not a manifestation of Pope's personal animosity for the Hanoverians, but an integral part of the developing argument of the poem. As the first and briefest section of the poem's *confirmatio,* it constitutes a complete repudiation of the first and flimsiest of the charges brought against Pope. It is proof by demonstration that flattery under such a king is impossible and can only result in the very lowest form of satire—in fact, in libel itself. Heroic panegyric ends in a ridiculous farce, in which George is denigrated by simple juxtaposition to Augustus. Lyric panegyric of his private life cannot even be attempted, since he notoriously lacked the private virtues to an even greater extent than the public. An awkward attempt to substitute the praises of his family produces a stream of trivia worthy, Pope intimates, of Cibber. In such an inverted world, what Juvenal says of his Rome is perfectly applicable: *difficile est non saturam scribere.*

Throughout the poem, there is a constant recurrence to the theme of the total corruption of society under George. Fortescue raises the issue again when he says,

> The fewer still you name, you wound the more;
> *Bond* is but one, but *Harpax* is a Score,

(43–44)

which indicates a degree and extent of guilt that spreads far beyond the limits of the court. Pope's response covertly develops this suggestion, while its surface statement accomplishes a correlative task:

> Each Mortal has his Pleasure: None deny
> *Scarsdale* his Bottle, *Darty* his Ham-Pye;
> *Ridotta* sips and dances, till she see
> The doubling Lustres dance as fast as she;
> *F*—loves the *Senate, Hockley-Hole* his Brother
> Like in all else, as one Egg to another.
>
> (45–50)

The ostensible argument, in reply to Fortescue's objection, is that if Scarsdale's drunkenness, Dartineuf's gluttony, and Ridotta's profligacy are tolerated, the same courtesy should be extended to Pope's more innocent pleasure, writing satire. Once again, however, Pope's index guides—and the Horatian commentators—indicate a great deal beyond this.

The guides attach Pope's phrase "Each Mortal has his Pleasure" to Horace's two lines "Quid faciam? Saltat Milonius, ut semel icto/Accessit fervor capiti numerusque lucernis" (24–25), which it clearly does not even approximate. It is closer to Horace's "quot capitum vivunt, totidem studiorum/Millia," which occurs two lines later and which is bound by its own index guide to another dissimilar English phrase. The reason for this apparent confusion is that Pope is following up a lead provided by the commentators and is, I believe, using this displacement of the index guides to draw attention to it. In conformity with their habit of explaining Horatian passages by comparison to similar ones in other authors, many Renaissance editors noted at this point of the text Persius' "Mille hominum species et rerum discolor usus;/ Velle suum cuique est nec voto vivitur uno." [27] This begins a passage that describes the ways in which most people waste their lives, as opposed to the philosopher's devotion to truth and virtue. Persius then goes on to list several more or less vicious pursuits, including gluttony, sloth, politics, and profligacy.[28] That

Pope's "Each Mortal has his Pleasure" resembles Persius' lines more closely than it does Horace's phrase is evident, and Pope's use of Persius' succeeding catalogue of vices rather than Horace's briefer and more innocent list of avocations makes the presence of the allusion certain. The relevance of this to Pope's context as a complement to Fortescue's remark is also apparent: many are offended by satire, because many are guilty of the offenses that satire lashes—idleness, gluttony, lechery, and so on. The passage simultaneously explains the widespread animus against satire and shows the absolute necessity of writing it. Needless to say, Pope's description a few lines later of the virtuous nature of his poems will stand out in bold contrast to this general corruption.

Still missing from this argument, however, is the link that ties this degeneracy to the court and locates there the cause of this universal immorality. This too is supplied by the ministrations of the commentators, who point out the similarity between Horace's description of Milonius and a passage from Juvenal's famous satire on women.

> Quid enim Venus ebria curat?
> Inguinis, & capitis quae sint discrimina, nescit;
> Grandia quae mediis jam noctibus ostrea mordet,
> Cum perfusa mero spumant unguenta Falerno,
> Cum bibitur concha, cum jam vertigine tectum
> Ambulat, & geminis exsurgit mensa lucernis.[29]

Juvenal supplies Pope's passage with a type-named dissolute woman, with the instance of objects apparently moving with the drunken dancer, and with specifically doubled lights in place of Horace's more general *numerus*. The significance of the English poet's use of this locus goes far beyond the graphic picture of female depravity it presents, and includes the whole Juvenalian context of which this is a small part. The larger concern of Juvenal's poem is the total corruption of the women of his age, who had in former

[61]

times been the repository and symbol of the old, solid, Roman virtues. The lines that Pope here makes use of occur, fortunately enough for his purposes, in a section of the poem wherein Juvenal explains the cause of this universal vice. Roman women, he claims, were chaste when Italy was poor and threatened by Hannibal; now, "We suffer all th'invet'rate ills of Peace . . . / Since Poverty, our Guardian-God, is gone" (Dryden's translation). Juvenal is equally specific about the source of this sin:

> Pride, Laziness, and all Luxurious Arts,
> Pour like a Deluge in, from Foreign Parts:
> Since Gold Obscene, and Silver found the way,
> Strange Fashions with strange Bullion to convey,
> And our plain simple Manners to betray.[30]

The origin of corruption is laid squarely at the door of a protracted peace—an attribution that could not fail to suggest to English readers of the 1730's the similar and much lamented effects of Walpole's peace policies. Juvenal's further tracing of this vice to foreign manners and foreign wealth would unequivocally pinpoint the Hanoverian king and court as the fountainhead of the depravity that Pope sees overwhelming England.

The same theme re-emerges when Pope explains the circumstances that force him to satire.

> Satire's my Weapon, but I'm too discreet
> To run a Muck, and tilt at all I meet;
> I only wear it in a Land of Hectors,
> Thieves, Supercargoes, Sharpers, and Directors.
> Save but our *Army!* and let *Jove* incrust
> Swords, Pikes, and Guns, with everlasting Rust!
> Peace is my dear Delight—not *Fleury*'s more:
> But touch me, and no Minister so sore.

(69–76)

The "Land of Hectors,/ Thieves, Supercargoes, Sharpers, and Directors" is clearly the corrupt and vice-ridden England that has obliged Pope to defend himself with this present satire. He cleverly adapts Horace's prayer for personal tranquillity to an ironic thrust at the controversy over the standing army and, once again, at Walpole's peace policy. His mention of Fleury's ardent desire for peace implies that such a policy benefits foreigners far more than Englishmen, and hammers home in the political realm the point that his allusion to Juvenal has established in the moral. The simple presence of the word "Minister" in line 76 fastens the satire directly upon Walpole, and emphasizes the fact that the court is principally responsible for the disorder of England and so indirectly responsible for Pope's compulsion to write satire.

All these political considerations are focused most clearly in Pope's final defense of his calling and character in lines 105–42. Herein Pope explains the virtuous intent of his satire, and points out that under other kings, satirists, not flatterers, had been rewarded with royal favor. Louis had pensioned Boileau; Charles and James made Dryden laureate. George has chosen Cibber for his laureate, and that is proof enough of where the corruption—in taste at least—originated. The morality of satire can have no honor at George's court, but there are rewards enough for the immorality of lying flattery. In such a world, Pope implies, it is inevitable that satiric honesty be miscalled libel. Fortescue directly substantiates this point when he warns the poet that, although his case is good, "Laws are explain'd by Men" (144). He hardly needs to add the instance of the tyrant king, Richard III (who was also, appropriately enough, a usurper), to make clear the target of the stroke (145). For these same reasons, when Pope seeks to demonstrate his social acceptability, he cannot show to any effect that he is esteemed by any of the court: he has already totally devaluated their opinion. Instead, he has recourse to displaying his friendship with statesmen and soldiers of

the reign of Anne, which he has "mythologized" into a
golden age of virtue, justice, and order, in complete contrast
to the reign of George II. Indeed, the very fact that such
paragons as Bolingbroke and Peterborough are "Chiefs,
out of War, and Statesmen, out of Place" (126) is in itself
a commentary on those who have filled their posts under
George, and points once again to the degeneracy and corruption spreading outward from the king.

These political and social references serve as a carefully
channeled undercurrent in the flow of Pope's argument. As
he has demonstrated earlier in the poem, honest praise of
the Hanoverians is impossible: the panegyrics of the various
court poetasters are only disguised satires, or libels not
understood. The confrontation of the deeds of George and
Augustus proves that merely to tell the truth is satire
enough. In this way, Pope makes all his political asides
provide in themselves further justifications of his satire,
and paradoxically convicts the hireling court flatterers of
the libels with which he is charged.

IV

The interaction throughout the poem of the persona Pope
has assumed with the character he has assigned Fortescue
is also carefully manipulated to the end of exonerating Pope
entirely from the charges brought against him. He has cast
himself as a *naïf*, an innocent whose exaggerated shock
indicates that he cannot comprehend the outcry against
his poems:

> There are (I scarce can think it, but am told)
> There are to whom my Satire seems too bold.
>
> (1–2)

He carefully describes himself as the exact opposite of the
aggressive, malicious libeler he has been called—"Tim'rous

[64]

by Nature, of the Rich in awe" (7)—and his approach to his friend for help is at once humble and ingratiating. Fortescue, on the other hand, is the voice of experience and authority in the poem, a legal expert who knows thoroughly the practical, day-to-day world. He represents that body of opinion that Pope must sway if he is to win his case, since, paradoxically, the *ingenu* Pope is also forced to become a lawyer delivering a set oration in his own defense, and the lawyer Fortescue simultaneously becomes a judge. It is in his capacity as the embodiment of the opinion of society that Fortescue raises the dichotomy of values between Pope's implicit claim that he writes *for his soul,* and his own opinion that the poet could not do a worse thing *for his life.* It is as a practical man of the world that he advises Pope to praise George and tries to dissuade him from satire. These pragmatic judgments Pope has no difficulty in setting aside, by simply modulating his own voice from its ingenuous opening comments to the sterner and more idealistic tones of the *vir bonus,* whose devotion to virtue necessitates his writing satire.[31]

Still, his skeptical *adversarius* reverts to the practical aspects of the case and warns him once again of the public disapproval of his attacks. This forces the poet to display yet another side of his persona, his innocent friendship with the great. This concludes his presentation of the case, but his counsel, still not entirely convinced, warns him yet again. This time Pope answers on legal rather than moral grounds by showing that the charge of libel is not applicable. Fortescue capitulates completely, and endorses Pope's future satiric activities. What this really means is that Pope has manipulated the voice of public opinion so that by the end of the poem it is in complete agreement with him, and opposed to those who have carped at his poetry—a total reversal of Fortescue's initial position. This is shown most clearly in Fortescue's final statement, the closing lines of the poem, which indicate a shift in his viewpoint from the

[65]

practical world for which he has been spokesman to the theoretical, ideal world out of which Pope has acted.

> P. *Libels* and *Satires!* lawless Things indeed!
> But grave *Epistles,* bringing Vice to Light,
> Such as a *King* might read, a *Bishop* write,
> Such as Sir *Robert* would approve—
> >>>>>>>>>> *F.* Indeed?
> The Case is alter'd—you may then proceed.
> In such a Cause the Plaintiff will be hiss'd.
> My Lords the Judges laugh, and you're dismiss'd.
>
> >>>>>>>>>> (150–56)

Pope's claim that he writes such poems as "a *King* might read, a *Bishop* write,/ Such as Sir *Robert* would approve" is clearly not based upon the reality of Georgian England— indeed, in that context the statement is heavily ironic and bitterly comic—but upon a conception of an ideally ordered world where kings and ministers do read satire and do not think it any reflection on themselves. Fortescue's acceptance of this argument involves his simultaneous acceptance of the larger world order that Pope has defended throughout the poem, the world wherein theoretic distinctions between genres and the theoretic roles of language and literature are meaningful and accurate indexes of the ultimate realities. Thus his final lines are also the conclusion of Pope's theory of satire: in the ideal world, the satiric butt *is* hissed off the stage, and satire *does* successfully wage war on vice with morally therapeutic laughter. In this manner, Pope's critics are vanquished, and *adversarius* is metamorphosed into coadjutor.

The ideally harmonic worlds of God's creation and man's rational state have been the underlying supports of Pope's poem. The poem itself, incorporating all those concords already noted, has attempted to reproduce this world by carefully balancing, in its dialectic, the extremes of flattery and libel against each other and picking a concordant

[66]

median path between them, by harmoniously mingling classical and Christian in a consistent and coherent literary and moral program. Thus the plan of the poem, as well as its subject matter, mirrors the ideal world upon which it depends, at once claiming its support and demonstrating its presence. So it is that the dialogue ends with Fortescue's sudden corroboration of that world: the poem breaks through the petty quibbles of the phenomenal into the higher reality of the ideal; it closes with the burst of curative laughter that it is the end of true satire to produce. Thus, since it has been the whole purpose of the poem to prove that Pope does write true satire, the poem validates itself and proves its own argument. In the ideal world where God's creation and man's actions are equally rational and concordant, real satire is greeted, not with scorn or fear, but with appreciative laughter. It is the reality and validity of this world that Fortescue—and Pope's poem—affirms.

1. *Bathurst,* 20, 86, and 123. This is a trick Pope learned from Horace, who does the same thing in line 22 of this satire, where he quotes a line from his earlier (Sat.I.viii) attack on Pantalobus and Nomentanus.

2. This Imitation is built around a carefully worked out rhetorical framework, and employs the divisions of a formal oration except the two that would violate the decorum of its dialogue form, the *exordium* and the *peroratio.* The first fifteen lines of the poem present simultaneously a *narratio* and a *partitio,* a statement of the situation and its divisions. Pope lists the antithetical charges that will be the two main concerns of the poem, and Fortescue's advice, coupled with Pope's response, introduces the third problem, that of the satirist's character. The *confirmatio* falls into three parts corresponding to these topics: lines 21–36 repudiate the charge of flattery; lines 37–100 deal with the question of libel; lines 101–42 are devoted to the defense of Pope's character. The final rhetorical division of the poem is the *refutatio,* which extends from line 143 to the end. Here, Pope shows the legal charge of libel to be completely inapplicable, and accomplishes that final suasion of his audience that is the end of all rhetoric.

3. This expansion of Horace's text is traceable to the commentators, who pointed out that consciousness of his own crime causes each guilty man to fear the satirist. See the commentaries of Acron and Christoforo Landino in *Opera cum quatuor Commentariis et Figuris nuper additis* (Venice, 1509), pp. 212verso–213recto. It is worth noting that these lines also provide Pope's answer to the controversy over the propriety of particular satire, in which he had been directly involved through widespread misapplication of the Timon passage in the *Epistle to Burlington.*

[67]

4. Pope appears to have used at various times all three major versions of the Bible. For the sake of uniformity, I quote regularly from the King James, except for those books that, although apocryphal for Protestants, are canonical for Roman Catholics; for these, I quote from the Douai version.

5. See, for instance, Hugo de Sancto Charo, *Opera omnia in universum vetus, & novum Testamentum* (Venice, 1703), III, 152verso, col. 1: "Et nota quod Filius dicitur speculum & imago Patris, cum tamen in rebus inferioribus imago sit in speculo, ad notandum quod idem est speculum & imago. Et sicut in rebus inferioribus in speculo videtur imago rei, & per imaginem res, sic in Filio, & per Filium videtur Pater. In Filio videtur, quia est speculum; per Filium, quia est imago. Item Filius non speculum simpliciter, sed speculum sine macula dicitur ad differentiam faciendam inter hoc speculum & alia specula. Tria siquidem sunt specula Dei. Unum est mens humana, facta ad similitudinem Dei, sed non est sine macula. Aliud est quaelibet creatura, in qua relucet vestigium Trinitatis totius, ut dicit *Aug.* . . . De isto speculo dicitur I *Cor.* 13.d. Videmus nunc per speculum aenigmate, etc. Sed nec illud speculum verum est. Speculum est Christus, & illud est sine macula omnino."

6. See Cicero on the limits of the use of ridicule, *De Oratore*, II.lviii.237. For typical biblical pronouncements about the reservation of the wicked for judgment, see II Peter 2:4 and 2:9. The omission of "Vice too high" from the scope of satire is quite standard literary theory: see Mary Claire Randolph, "The Neo-Classic Theory of the Formal Verse Satire in England, 1700–1750," p. 76 and pp. 260–61. The purpose of this concentration of diverse elements in Pope's lines appears to be to show at once his rhetorical, satiric, and moral orthodoxy, and to place yet another prop beneath both his ethical and his literary program.

7. Phil. 4:5: "Let your moderation be known to all men." This counsel was interpreted in such a manner that Pope could easily fit it into the context of the golden mean and *concordia discors*. "Now hence it follows, *1st,* That Moderation can have only Place in Things which are not always evil in themselves, but become so, by exceeding that Rule, and Measure, which is praescrib'd for the due Management of them. . . . *2ndly,* Hence it is demonstratively evident, that Moderation is always a Virtue, it being always virtuous to restrain the Excesses of our Passions, and Appetites, and the Exorbitances of our angry Passions, and to regulate our Words, and Actions, according to the Rule, and Measure, by which we ought to act." Daniel Whitby, *A Paraphrase and Commentary on The New Testament* (London, 1727), II, 402, col. 2.

8. For basic information about the *concordia discors* theory, see Leo Spitzer, "Classical and Christian Ideas of World Harmony," *Traditio,* II (1944), 409–64, and III (1945), 307–64. For its importance to Pope, see Maynard Mack's introduction to TE, III, pt. i, xxxiv–xxxv, and E. R. Wasserman, *The Subtler Language* (Baltimore, 1959), pp. 101–68 *passim.* Edgar Wind concisely states the connection between *concordia discors* and the golden mean: " 'There is,' as we may remember from Pico, 'this diversity between God and man, that God contains in him all things because he is their source, whereas man contains in him all things because he is their centre.' In the centre the opposites are held in balance, but in the source they coincide. In so far as man therefore approaches his own perfection, he distantly imitates the deity. Balance is but an echo of divine

transcendence" (*Pagan Mysteries in the Renaissance* [New Haven, 1958], p. 88).

9. This sort of poetic theory had an independent existence of its own in European literature, and can be traced as a minor current through the Middle Ages—notably in Hugh of St. Victor's *Didascalicon*—until it received fresh impetus from the neoplatonism of the Florentine Academy. The essential premise of this view is the Christian one that man is made in the image of God. Since God is the resolution of all contradictions and the allaying of all paradoxes, man's highest spiritual faculty resembles, in its humbler way, that divine harmony. Wisdom too mirrors the nature of the deity, and she manifests her presence in the human soul through and in the various arts. Finally, language is also a mirror, reflecting man's innermost nature: thus poetry itself becomes yet another reflection of the deity, revealing the divinely ordained pattern of creation. Cowley's ode "Of Wit" exemplifies and explains the concept:

> What is it then, which like the *Power Divine*
> We only can by Negatives define?
> In a true piece of *Wit* all things must be,
>   Yet all things then *agree*.
> As in the *Ark,* joyn'd without force or strife,
> All *Creatures* dwelt; all *Creatures* that had *Life.*
>   Or as the *Primitive Forms* of all
>   (If we compare great things with small)
> Which without *Discord* or *Confusion* lie,
> In that strange *Mirror* of the *Deitie.*

10. The hint for all this is taken from Horace's lines 35–39, wherein he states that he is unsure whether he is an Apulian or a Lucanian, because his native Venusia borders on both. Needless to say, Pope's witty exploitation of this hint makes of it something very different from whatever Horace may have intended.

11. "Hard Words" mean not only vituperation, but also difficult words, thus adding another item to Pope's list of misuses of language. See DeWitt T. Starnes and Gertrude E. Noyes, *The English Dictionary from Cawdrey to Johnson* (Chapel Hill, N.C., 1946), pp. 190–92.

12. The index guides consist of a pair of matching numbers or letters, connecting ideological fragments of Horace's poem with their usually equivalent English versions. It occasionally happens, however, that a significant deviation of Pope's poem from its Horatian original is signaled by a displacement of these guides, or by their being attached to passages that only remotely, and sometimes not at all, translate or paraphrase each other. The guides were present in all editions during Pope's and Warburton's lifetimes. See the table of index guides in Appendix A.

13. *Opera interpretatione et notis illustravit Ludovicus Desprez,* p. 432, note to line 52. Desprez quotes in full the relevant portions of the Lucretian passage.

14. *De Rerum Natura* V, 1027–34. The text of Lucretius is that of Thomas Creech, 2nd ed. (London, 1717). Here is Rouse's translation (from the Loeb Classical Library edition) of this passage and its immediately preceding context: "Then also neighbours began eagerly to join friendship amongst themselves to do no hurt and suffer no violence, and asked protection for their children and women-kind, signifying by voice and gesture

with stammering tongue that it was right for all to pity the weak. Nevertheless concord could not altogether be produced, but a good part, nay the most kept the covenant unblemished, or else the race of mankind would have been even then wholly destroyed, nor would birth and begetting have been able to prolong their posterity.

"But the various sounds of the tongue nature drove them to utter, and convenience pressed out of them names for things, not far otherwise than very speechlessness is seen to drive children to the use of gesture, when it makes them point with the finger at things that are before them. For each feels to what purpose he is able to use his own powers. Before the budding horns stand out on the calf's forehead, these are what he uses in anger to butt with and pushes viciously."

15. The designation of "you who 'scape the Laws" as the targets of satire is once again quite orthodox literary theory: see Randolph, pp. 260–61, and such contemporary sources as Walter Harte's *Essay on Satire;* William Melmoth's *The Letters of Sir Thomas Fitzosborne* (pp. 234–35); and Joseph Trapp's *Lectures on Poetry,* wherein the opinion of Vossius and others is considered (p. 228).

16. This passage is from "The First Satyr of Aulus Persius Flaccus," lines 227–30, 239–40 (Kinsley) II, pp. 748–49; it corresponds to lines 114–19 of Persius' poem.

17. "The First Satyr of Juvenal," 251–54, (Kinsley) II, p. 677; Juvenal I.165–67.

18. The relevance of the passage from Persius was noted by Landino, p. 213verso; Cruquius, p. 413, col. 1; Torrentius, pp. 518–19; and Dacier, V, p. 466. Casaubon's edition of Persius (*Satirarum Liber, cum . . . Isaaci Casauboni notis* [Leipzig, 1839]) cites the Horatian locus in his commentary, p. 111. Giovanni Britannico, in his edition of Juvenal *(Opus, interprete Joanne Britannico* [Venice, 1523]), refers to the same passage in Persius, and Badius Ascensius' notes in the same volume refer to that in Horace, p. 18verso, cols. 1 and 2.

19. Lines 39–41: "Sed hic stylus haud petit ultro/ Quenquam animantem; & me veluti custodiet ensis/ Vagina tectus . . ."

20. For the importance of the rural retreat as a scene of ethical and religious activity, see Maren Sophie Röstvig, *The Happy Man* (Oxford, 1954–58), II, 117–22, which have special reference to Pope. In this connection, see also Atterbury's sermon "Of Religious Retirement," *Sermons and Discourses on Several Subjects and Occasions* (London, 1740), I, 349–75.

21. Landino, in his commentary on line 66 of Horace's poem, quotes Virgil's famous description of the Scipios as *duo fulmina belli (Aeneid* VI.842), "two thunderbolts of war." This connection provides the rationale for the presence of Peterborough's "Lightning" in line 129, and at the same time furnishes him with an extremely handsome compliment through the implied comparison to Scipio.

22. This irony has been seen in the original by at least one Horatian commentator, Cruquius, p. 413, col. 2.

23. Lines 82–84; "'Si mala condiderit in quem quis carmina jus est/ Judiciumque.' Esto, siquis mala; sed bona siquis/ Judice condiderit laudatur

Caesare . . ." Horace's pun turns on the two possible meanings of *mala*, "evil and unlawful," or "of poor quality."

24. Pope says in effect the same thing in a letter to Swift, April 2, 1733, *Correspondence*, III, 365–66: "That I am an Author whose characters are thought of some weight, appears from the great noise and bustle that the Court and Town make about any I give; and I will not render them less important or interesting, by sparing Vice and Folly, or by betraying the cause of Truth and Virtue. I will take care they shall be such as no man can be angry at but the persons I would have angry. . . . I have not the courage to be such a Satyrist as you, but I would be as much, or more, a Philosopher. You call your satires, libels; I would rather call my satires, Epistles: they will consist more of morality than wit, and grow graver, which you will call duller." The purpose of this equivocation seems to be to provide for all his satires the same sort of firm rhetorical structure he has employed in this poem, since the epistle was conceived of in the Renaissance as a miniature oration, governed by all the rules of formal rhetoric. See Jay Arnold Levine, "The Status of the Verse Epistle before Pope," *SP*, LIX (1962), 658–84, for the connection of rhetoric and the epistolary form. Pp. 667–68 are especially pertinent.

25. It links Sir Richard's name with Horace's "vires/ Deficiunt" (12–13).

26. See Dacier, V, 451, note to line 15.

27. *Sat.* V.52–53. The following Horatian commentators cite the Persius passage: Landino, p. 213recto; Cruquius, p. 411, col. 1; and Desprez, p. 431. Schrevelius' edition of Persius (Leyden, 1648) reciprocates by quoting the Horatian passage to explain Persius (see page 610), attributing the comment to unnamed *veteres scholastiae*.

28. Here is the passage in Dryden's translation, "The Fifth Satyr of Aulus Persius Flaccus," 67–82, (Kinsley) II, 774:

> Nature is ever various in her Frame:
> Each has a different Will; and few the same:
> The greedy Merchants, led by lucre, run
> To the parch'd Indies, and the rising Sun:
> From thence hot Pepper, and rich Drugs they bear,
> Bart'ring for Spices, their *Italian* Ware.
> The lazy Glutton safe at home will keep;
> Indulge his Sloth, and batten with his Sleep:
> One bribes for high Preferments in the State,
> A second shakes the Box, and sits up late:
> Another shakes the Bed; dissolving there.
> Till Knots upon his Gouty Joints appear,
> And Chalk is in his crippled Fingers found;
> Rots like a Doddard Oke, and piecemeal falls to ground.
> Then, his lewd Follies he wou'd late repent:
> And his past years, that in a Mist were spent.

29. The text quoted is *D. Junii Juvenalis Aquinatis Satyrae*, ed. Henricus Christianus Henninius (Utrecht, 1685), Sat. VI. 300–305. Grangaeus' notes, printed in this volume, cite the pertinent Horatian line (p. 156), as do Giovanni Britannico's in his edition, p. 73verso, col. 1. The following Horatian commentators note the correspondence with Juvenal's passage:

Landino, p. 213recto; *Vetus Commentator* in Cruquius, p. 408, col. 1; Desprez, p. 431; and Torrentius, p. 516.

30. For the entire passage in Dryden's translation, see "The Sixth Satyr of Juvenal," 397–423, (Kinsley) II, 706–7.

31. Maynard Mack has already made some of these same points about the use of the poet's persona. See "The Muse of Satire," *Yale Review,* XLI (1941), 80–92.

Chapter III

Apologia pro vita sua: *An Epistle to Dr. Arbuthnot*

A N EPISTLE TO DR. ARBUTHNOT belongs to
the same literary tradition as Pope's Imitation of
Sat. II.i., and shares with it many interests and
themes. Pope appears to have worked at both poems
simultaneously, and the manuscripts of the Epistle contain
many passages that were eventually fitted into the Imitation. Structurally, the two poems are strikingly alike: the
Epistle borrows its dialogue format and general plan from
the Horatian satire, and the *adversarius* Arbuthnot is himself manipulated in much the same way as his predecessor
Fortescue, and frequently echoes his lines.[1] Both poems
are concerned with defending Pope and his writings from
false and vicious allegations. The Epistle is a more elaborate
defense of the satirist's calling than Pope's Imitation, but
is nevertheless a defense articulated by similar means and
in the same mode.

The major difference between the two poems is that of
scope. Where the Imitation focused clearly on a satire and
Pope's use of it, the field of vision of the *Arbuthnot* encompasses almost the whole of Pope's literary life. This
difference in range causes, naturally enough, a shift in
emphasis: for the *Fortescue*'s predominant concern with
ethical *literature*, the *Arbuthnot* substitutes an overriding
interest in literary *ethics*. Faced with the problem of justifying not simply his conduct in one literary genre but the
conduct of his whole life, Pope grounds his defense on
morality rather than on esthetics, and triumphs through his
virtue rather than his artistry—or so, at least, his artistry
would have it seem.

[73]

I

An Epistle to Dr. Arbuthnot announces its intentions and its methods at the outset. Pope endures not simply the assaults of hacks and would-be poets but of scribblers who derive lineally from the pests who plagued Horace and Juvenal: "The Dog-star rages" (3), and with it the rhymers who were its concomitant in Juvenal's complaint.[2] Pope's use of classical reminiscences establishes nicely his cultural and poetic respectability while it renders his opponent more certainly contemptible. The presence of a classical name, such as Pitholeon (49) or Codrus (85), calls to mind the similarities existing between his enemies and the versifiers who plagued the Roman poets, and simultaneously, by virtue of the parallel, vindicates Pope's position while it more fully damns the dunce in question. A good many of Pope's targets share this classical pedigree:

> Is there, who lock'd from Ink and Paper, scrawls
> With desp'rate Charcoal round his darken'd walls?
>
> (19–20)

This particular unfortunate was condemned for literary eternity in an epigram of Martial's that Pope's couplet echoes.[3] He and his fellows "rave, recite, and madden round the land" (6); the line recalls the end of the *Ars Poetica,* wherein Horace satirizes a representative of the inept poets who plagued him and his city;[4] it partially establishes the nature of the world in which Pope and his poem must live. Imperial Rome provides the background for the *Arbuthnot,* and Juvenal, Persius, and Horace, the elements of the character Pope has chosen for himself. He is the true poet, cast solidly in their mold, suffering the same fate they endured: the constant assault of favor-seekers and libelers.

These opening lines accomplish more than this, however; if half the poetic landscape of the *Arbuthnot* derives from

classical literature, the other half proceeds from the corpus
of Christian polemical writings. Pope very carefully convicts
the poetasters of impiety:

> No place is sacred, not the Church is free,
> Ev'n *Sunday* shines no *Sabbath-day* to me:
> Then from the *Mint* walks forth the Man of Ryme,
> Happy! to catch me, just at Dinner-time.
>
> (11–14)

And they are guilty of sacrilege too.

> Is there a Parson, much be-mus'd in Beer,
> A maudlin Poetess, a ryming Peer,
> A Clerk, foredoom'd his Father's soul to cross,
> Who pens a Stanza when he should *engross?*
> Is there, who lock'd from Ink and Paper, scrawls
> With desp'rate Charcoal round his darken'd walls?
> All fly to *Twit'nam,* and in humble strain
> Apply to me, to keep them mad or vain.
> *Arthur,* whose giddy Son neglects the Laws,
> Imputes to me and my damn'd works the cause:
> Poor *Cornus* sees his frantic Wife elope,
> And curses Wit, and Poetry, and *Pope.*
>
> (15–26)

The poet who seeks his muse in beer sins just as enormously
as the parson who searches for inspiration in drunkenness,
and Pope has joined the two in one figure (15) to establish
the symbolic identity of literary and theological offense in
the cosmos of his poem.

But the real keys to the poem's dialectic are initially
provided by the hapless clerk and by Arthur's "giddy Son."
The lines devoted to them sound themes that would have
inescapably recalled to eighteenth-century readers contemporary religious issues: "foredoom'd his Father's soul to
cross," "neglects the Laws," "imputes," "damn'd works"—

[75]

all these touch on ideas intricately involved in the predestinarian controversy and in the argument about the efficacy of good works as opposed to faith. All echo phrases from St. Paul's Epistle to the Romans, which provided the canonical fuel for that sectarian fire.[5]

Pope's allusions to St. Paul's epistle at the beginning of his own indicate the context into which his argument is going to fit. Arthur's false imputation and his reference to Pope's "damn'd works" align him with the Calvinist dissenters (at the time the *Arbuthnot* was written, perhaps specifically with the "enthusiastic" Methodists), in which group it also appears logical to place the predestined hack of line 17. At the same time, Arthur's concern for "the Laws" also associates him and Pope's other enemies with St. Paul's opponents, and involves them in the orthodox condemnation consequent upon that fact. Pope has conglomerated eighteenth-century dissenters with the proto-heretics of apostolic times: further, he has linked the poetically inept with the religiously heterodox and symbolically equated poetasters with dissenters, so that they have become the concrete images of anarchy in both culture and religion. Pope becomes by this same means both symbol and champion of orthodoxy, and his "damn'd works" should be understood as a metaphorically apostolic act, the same sort of preaching of the truth for which St. Paul was attacked by first-century lovers of "the Laws."

Pope has cast himself as true Christian and true poet: the task of the *Epistle to Arbuthnot* is to validate both claims. The poem accomplishes this through a dialectic of works, distinguishing Pope's meritorious poetic works from the chaotic deeds of the dunces. The materials Pope has drawn from the Epistle to the Romans must therefore be kept in a careful and exact perspective. The sin of the poetasters is at once poetic and theological: "the Laws" that Arthur's son neglects are as much those of poetry as they are those of the Mosaic code to which St. Paul refers; the abuse of poetry by the parson, Arthur's son, and the rhyming peer constitutes the degradation of a way of life and a potential means of salvation. The clerk's case is identical: he is sinful because he has no real calling to poetry; his proper task is to engross. Against this background, the main arguments of the *Arbuthnot* attempt to disentangle Pope's works from the charges of the dunces, to free them and Pope from a false imputation of damnation and win for them the imputation of righteousness they have merited. The real goal of the poem is to explain the full meaning of the "virtue's better end" that Pope has served throughout his literary career: this conception of virtue is most fully presented in the portrait of Pope's father that climaxes the poem. The *Arbuthnot* completes its own work when its audience agrees that "Thus far was right, the rest belongs to Heav'n."

II

Perhaps it is easiest to determine precisely what Pope is defending by first analyzing what he attacks. Of all his targets, none is more famous than Sporus, and, equally, none is more liable to misconstruction than this satiric vision of the lie made flesh. The characteristics Pope enumerates form the composite picture of Satan, the father of lies, in human shape, engaged in his eternal work of deceit and corruption. Pope's sketch does not describe Hervey or any other specific person, though it is also a condemnation of Hervey in so far as he corresponds to the description. Nevertheless, the picture remains irreducibly that of Sporus, and Sporus is depravity in human form.

> Whether in florid Impotence he speaks,
> And, as the Prompter breathes, the Puppet squeaks;
> Or at the Ear of *Eve,* familiar Toad,
> Half Froth, half Venom, spits himself abroad,
> In Puns, or Politicks, or Tales, or Lyes,

[77]

Or Spite, or Smut, or Rymes, or Blasphemies.
His Wit all see-saw between *that* and *this,*
Now high, now low, now Master up, now Miss,
And he himself one vile Antithesis.
Amphibious Thing! that acting either Part,
The trifling Head, or the corrupted Heart!
Fop at the Toilet, Flatt'rer at the Board,
Now trips a Lady, and now struts a Lord.
Eve's Tempter thus the Rabbins have exprest,
A Cherub's face, a Reptile all the rest;
Beauty that shocks you, Parts that none will trust,
Wit that can creep, and Pride that licks the dust.

(317–33)

Sporus is the embodiment of total disharmony, a jangling heap of discordant elements that reveal him as a complete perversion of God's harmonic being. His every action contradicts its predecessor. The phrases that describe this chaos most succinctly spill over out of the balanced couplet form into the only triplet of the poem, portraying in themselves the imbalance and disorder of the creature they describe— "himself one vile Antithesis," the very reverse of the divine reconciliation of opposites. Sporus, like Milton's Satan, becomes a grotesque parody of the God he rebels against.

Sporus-Satan most threatens the man of letters in his capacity as father of lies, for the act of lying corrupts the channels of communication and subverts the very function of language. Thus Pope identifies Sporus' speech as venom, and defines that venom as a heterogeneous and chaotic mixture of truth and untruth, seeming poetry and irreligion, "Puns, or Politicks, or Tales, or Lyes,/ Or Spite, or Smut, or Rymes, or Blasphemies." Sporus' aim is Satan's, to corrupt the imaginative faculty (both the well-spring and the receptor of poetry) and to reproduce in his victim his own sin of pride—in Milton's words,

Assaying by his Devilish art to reach
The Organs of her Fancy, and with them forge

[78]

Illusions as he list, Phantasms and Dreams,
Or if, inspiring venom, he might taint
Th' animal spirits that from pure blood arise
Like gentle breaths from Rivers pure, thence raise
At least distemper'd, discontented thoughts,
Vain hopes, vain aims, inordinate desires,
Blown up with high conceits ingend'ring pride.

(*PL*. IV. 801–9)

As the *Epistle to Arbuthnot* evidences, Sporus succeeds in every way: Eve does fall, and with her, her fatuous husband (in Pope's poem, George II); the world order is shattered, and all other mortals share in the pride that generated this original sin and the discordant effects consequent upon it. The fallen world is the cosmos of the *Epistle to Arbuthnot*.

In Milton's poem, of course, Satan's success is a hollow one, made void by Christ's redemptive act. The rebellious demon's attempt to disrupt creation is nullified by God's providential order. Pope shared this conception: in his *Epistle to Bathurst*, for instance, the extremes of evil are reconciled by God's ordered government of the world into a harmonious pattern of balanced opposites.[6] In this poem, Sporus is characterized by "florid Impotence," in distinct contrast to God's omnipotence. This idea also explains Pope's choice of the name Sporus: Nero's castrated favorite is the fitting symbol of the master-miss's complete discord and sterility. Not accidentally, the Sporus passage concludes with the biblical and Miltonic curse pronounced upon Satan and the punishment visited upon him in the shape in which he sinned.[7] Like Satan, Sporus is condemned for all eternity, and his punishment embodies in itself the discord of which he is the source: his high-aspiring pride is forced into the lowly shape of the serpent—"Pride that licks the dust" (333). In the *Epistle to Arbuthnot*, Pope wreaks this divine vengeance upon Sporus and reveals the satanic toad in his true form. Imagistically, his satire has become the divine weapon, the Ithuriel's spear, which exposes and punishes this literary manifestation of the Christian's eternal enemy.

The simple fact that his verse reproduces the punishment exacted by divine justice is a guarantee of his essential righteousness, and the best possible defense of his satire. Its justice is confirmed by its correspondence with the divine decree.[8]

Sporus, then, is the poem's emblem of the basic sin of pride, and its representation of the forces of total disorder. He climaxes a long series of similar and lesser offenders whose trespasses have all involved these same elements. From the early, light strokes at Bentley and the poetasters, through Atticus and Bufo, pride has been designated as the besetting sin of these dunces, both great and small. It is, in Christian tradition, the original offense from which all others flow; in Pope's world system and critical plan, it is the sin that destroys the world order and the order of art.[9] Thus it is finally embodied in a vision of the great prototype of pride incarnate, and Pope's verbal laceration of it in that form places him squarely in the ranks of the proponents of virtue and orthodoxy.

That Bufo and Sporus share the same basic sin explains why they also share similar traits: they embody different aspects of the same offense, and are ideologically identical. Bufo is, as his name proclaims, the toad whose form Sporus-Satan adopts; he too swells with sinful pride.

> Proud, as *Apollo* on his forked hill,
> Sate full-blown *Bufo,* puff'd by ev'ry quill;
> Fed with soft Dedication all day long,
> *Horace* and he went hand in hand in song.
> His Library, (where Busts of Poets dead
> And a true *Pindar* stood without a head)
> Receiv'd of Wits an undistinguish'd race,
> Who first his Judgment ask'd, and then a Place:
> Much they extoll'd his Pictures, much his Seat,
> And flatter'd ev'ry day, and some days eat:
> Till grown more frugal in his riper days,

He pay'd some Bards with Port, and some with Praise,
To some a dry Rehearsal was assign'd,
And others (harder still) he pay'd in kind.
Dryden alone (what wonder?) came not nigh,
Dryden alone escap'd this judging eye:
But still the Great have kindness in reserve,
He help'd to bury whom he help'd to starve.

(231–48)

Like Sporus, Bufo attempts to undo God's work by diabolically usurping his place: he becomes a satanic false god. The comparison of him to Apollo, for instance, involves many layers of analogous perversion. Apollo is both sun god and god of poetry, and, in the opinion of most mythographers, a symbol of Christ. Bufo, of course, falls as far short of Apollo as he does of Christ. He is Satan in the guise of an angel of light, Lucifer impersonating the sun of righteousness, the false god of poetry who usurps the place and role of a rightful patron and set himself up instead as a protector of poetasters.[10] For this reason, Dryden alone, synecdoche for all true poets, escaped "this judging eye." Iconographical tradition commonly attributes the all-seeing eye of judgment to God, whose prerogative Bufo has seized: he is attempting to substitute his own order (or disorder) for God's providence and his own taste (or lack of it) for God's wisdom.[11]

Bufo, Sporus, and Satan are further linked by the common purpose of their various pursuits. The effects of Bufo's patronage, in particular, parallel the aims of Milton's toad. In a grim parody of Satan's explosion to his true height at the touch of Ithuriel's spear, Bufo is "puff'd by ev'ry quill" of his train of flatterers. Because they misuse the craft of writing, they become by a curious perversion parodies of Ithuriel, fallen angels who are themselves simultaneously victims and tempters, their own pens inflating the false god's pride yet higher. Bufo too is his own victim: like

Satan, he is self-tempted. At the opening of Pope's passage, he is presented as already fallen, already "blown up with high conceits ingend'ring pride," and actively engaged in corrupting the "Organs of Fancy" in others. Bufo and his hacks, Sporus, and Satan are all caught up in a single concerted attempt to undo the established order of the world—both literary and moral—by perversion and usurpation.[12]

In the context of literature, the combination of Bufo and Sporus effects a total corruption of the "whole *Castalian* State" (230). Sporus destroys the meaning and efficacy of true poetry: he has tainted the imaginative faculty and debased it. Bufo eliminates the possibility of true poets surviving or even existing: he patronizes flatterers and starves Dryden. This is the significance of Pope's abandoning to him the "whole *Castalian* state": the proper and equitable relationship between poet and patron constitutes an ordered state in little, a hierarchic and harmonious kingdom of letters; and it is this good order and concord that the false patron, Bufo, has effectively subverted. Bufo and Sporus, like the satanic toad whose nature they share between them, have with their "froth and venom" thoroughly polluted the symbol and source of poetic inspiration, the Castalian stream that flows from Mt. Parnassus—the "forked hill" that Bufo has usurped. Between them, they have destroyed both the poetic life and the poetic act.

Bufo and Sporus stand at the apex of a ladder of pride and disharmony that reaches far back into the poem. Just as the chaotic materials of Sporus' talk and writings signify his interior disharmony and depravity, so, too, in a lesser degree, the works of minor offenders function as the external symbol of their degradation. The sketch of Atticus is a case in point. He does not fully partake of the total evil that is Sporus, but is described rather as a man of true genius who has, through pride, abused his gift. Consequently, because he does not exercise his abilities rightly, his actions reflect some of the disorder that is the essence of Sporus:

Peace to all such! but were there One whose fires
True Genius kindles, and fair Fame inspires,
Blest with each Talent and each Art to please,
And born to write, converse, and live with ease:
Shou'd such a man, too fond to rule alone,
Bear, like the *Turk,* no brother near the throne,
View him with scornful, yet with jealous eyes,
And hate for Arts that caus'd himself to rise;
Damn with faint praise, assent with civil leer,
And without sneering, teach the rest to sneer;
Willing to wound, and yet afraid to strike,
Just hint a fault, and hesitate dislike;
Alike reserv'd to blame, or to commend,
A tim'rous foe, and a suspicious friend,
Dreading ev'n fools, by Flatterers besieg'd,
And so obliging that he ne'er oblig'd;
Like *Cato,* give his little Senate laws,
And sit attentive to his own applause;
While Wits and Templers ev'ry sentence raise,
And wonder with a foolish face of praise.
Who but must laugh, if such a man there be?
Who would not weep, if *Atticus* were he!

(193–214)

The clash of Atticus' contradictory actions and attitudes
in this portrait parallels the mixture of conflicting elements
in Sporus that revealed his satanic nature. This is not to
say that Atticus is as malignant as Pope's "vile Antithesis,"
but that every man of letters who misuses his talents is
to that same degree perverting a gift of God and joining
the devil's party. Pope makes this position clear when he
refers to Atticus as "Blest with each Talent." The linking
of "blessing" and "talent" points directly toward the biblical
parable of the talents, an obvious statement of the necessity
of good works for salvation.[13] It provides an exact analogue
to Atticus' case in the account of the servant who buried
his talent rather than use it. The entire parable, of course,

[83]

was interpreted as an *exemplum* of what God expects the faithful to do with his gifts: they are not to lie stagnant but to be used in charity and increased. The exegetes explained the talent itself to stand for *opes et facultates*,[14] so that Pope's application of the term and the parable at this point is hardly farfetched, and is certainly consistent with his view of the poetic life. The final irony of the passage lies in styling this worldly seeker after human praise Atticus: the eighteenth century knew the original Atticus, the correspondent of Cicero, as an exemplar of the retired life—an ideal of self-sufficiency and contemplation that this Atticus completely ignores.[15]

Poetasters and petty critics also share with Sporus the ubiquitous sin of pride and its consequent disordering effects:

> A man's true merit 'tis not hard to find,
> But each man's secret standard in his mind,
> That Casting-weight Pride adds to Emptiness,
> This, who can gratify? for who can *guess*?
> The Bard whom pilfer'd Pastorals renown,
> Who turns a *Persian* Tale for half a crown,
> Just writes to make his barrenness appear,
> And strains from hard-bound brains eight lines-a-year:
> He, who still wanting tho' he lives on theft,
> Steals much, spends little, yet has nothing left:
> And he, who now to sense, now nonsense leaning,
> Means not, but blunders round about a meaning:
> And he, whose Fustian's so sublimely bad,
> It is not Poetry, but Prose run mad:
> All these, my modest Satire bad *translate,*
> And own'd, that nine such Poets made a *Tate.*

(175–90)

The quality of the dunces' poetry is revealed succinctly by the scatological significance of "And strains from hard-bound brains eight lines-a-year," while the couplets imme-

[84]

diately following go on to record once again the familiar clash of discordant opposites and its resultant chaos. Poetic (and pecuniary) poverty outwardly shows their spiritual bankruptcy and disorder; through self-seeking pride, they too overreach themselves, imbalance the microcosm that is man and—in part at least—upset the world order. Pride tips the careful balance of opposites, here concisely represented in the metaphor of the scales (175–78). The minds of the dunces are discordant, unbalanced, and their works reflect the extremes into which their private hells have thrown them. This is analogous to the cosmic imbalance caused by original sin (in the world of Pope's poem, by the successful lies of Sporus); it is the defining characteristic of the fallen world and of unregenerate mankind. The dunces stand as Pope's image for this: they are the pseudo-elect, literary and religious "enthusiasts," who impute damnation to his active charity and label him one of the devil's agents.

> Pains, reading, study are their just pretence,
> And all they want is spirit, taste, and sense.
> Comma's and points they set exactly right,
> And 'twere a sin to rob them of their Mite.

(159–62)

Their proper scope lies in attending to commas and points, and Pope ironically provides employment for them by leaving them one to set right in the same line that tells them what their talents really are. This is their puny mite (the pun on "might" is, of course, operative); and it is all they possess. As with the phrase "Blest with each Talent" in the Atticus passage, the mention of "sin" and "Mite" here indicates a reference to the biblical widow's mite, the tiny sum of her possessions, which, given in charity, merited highly (Mark 12:41–44)—another meritorious work that returns the poem once again to its underlying argument. Consistent with the pattern of inversions of Scripture and

[85]

religion Pope has woven into the poem, the dunces selfishly retain their mite, just as Atticus has selfishly retained his talent instead of employing and increasing it. All of the literary offenders that Pope is concerned with, from Bentley and Theobald through to Sporus, sin in the same basic manner: they pervert the work they were meant to do. The dunces are lesser offenders because their abilities are slight; Atticus is a greater evil-doer because his talent is real and estimable. Such a dialectic of evil inevitably culminates in the concrete vision of the source of sin himself, dressed in human flesh, and, in keeping with the interests of the poem, in the guise of a totally depraved poet.

III

All this has been as true of those who flattered Pope as of those who reviled him: even these, because they praise insincerely and for the wrong reasons, share the essentially evil nature of Sporus: their works too are perverse.

> One Flatt'rer's worse than all;
> Of all mad Creatures, if the Learn'd are right,
> It is the Slaver kills, and not the Bite.
> A Fool quite angry is quite innocent;
> Alas! 'tis ten times worse when they *repent*.

> (104–8)

The "Slaver" is much the same poison as the "Half Froth half Venom" that Sporus spits abroad, and it links Pope's flatterers imagistically and ethically with Eve's tempter. Even their religion, in keeping with the pattern, is an inversion of orthodoxy: anger with them is innocence; real guilt enters with their repentence. Their interior disharmony is mirrored in their writings; in the confusion of genres of "high Heroic prose" (109); in the fact that a defense from one of them is an actual insult (111–12); in their selection of "All that disgrac'd my Betters" (120) for praise. They share fully in the essential discord that marks all who misuse the faculty of language and degrade the function of literature, and that is further adumbrated by their parallel perversion of man's religious condition.

This section of the *Arbuthnot* builds to a reverberating crescendo in Pope's adaptation of the Midas story, a passage that manages to concentrate and focus most of the major themes of the poem's *confirmatio*:

'Tis sung, when *Midas*' Ears began to spring,
(*Midas,* a sacred Person and a King)
His very Minister who spy'd them first,
(Some say his Queen) was forc'd to speak, or burst.
And is not mine, my Friend, a sorer case,
When ev'ry Coxcomb perks them in my face?
"Good friend forbear! you deal in dang'rous things,
"I'd never name Queens, Ministers, or Kings;
"Keep close to Ears, and those let Asses prick,
"Tis nothing"—Nothing? if they bite and kick?
Out with it, *Dunciad!* let the secret pass,
That Secret to each Fool, that he's an Ass:
The truth once told, (and wherefore shou'd we lie?)
The Queen of *Midas* slept, and so may I.

(69–82)

Pope frequently in this poem utilizes segments of classical works to establish effective and prestigious sanctions for his judgments. In this case, his lines imitate fairly closely, in form and content, the following passage from Persius:

Men' mutire nefas? nec clam, nec cum scrobe?—Nusquam!—
Heic tamen infodiam: Vidi, vidi ipse, libelle:
Auriculas asini quis non habet? Hoc ego opertum,
Hoc ridere meum, tam nil, nulla tibi vendo
Iliade.

(I. 119–23)[16]

[87]

These lines occur in Persius' own apology for writing satire. He has based his defense on the fact that the complete corruption of literature and taste demands satire: the Midas passage is the culmination of this argument. Everyone has ass's ears; no one can recognize true poetry. Pope's adaptation of this to his own circumstances, with specific mention of his *Dunciad*, places his own works in a direct line of descent from Persius' *libellus*, and shows them to be every bit as necessary: taste and literature in his time are fully as degenerate as in Persius'.

The Midas of fable won his ass's ears by preferring the music of Pan to that of Apollo, a fact that indicated far more to the Renaissance than mere bad taste. In his specific capacity as god of music, Apollo was closely identified with the music of the spheres, that universal harmony which, in Christian terms, is analogous to the harmony that constitutes God's essence.[17] It is this very same harmony of which Midas is oblivious that Sporus attempts to destroy and Bufo to subvert. As king, Midas' position in the human hierarchy parallels God's eminence in the spiritual, and the simple fact of his deafness to that universal harmony whose human exemplar he should be convicts him of the same sort of perversion of his role that marks all the other dunces. Like Bufo, Midas denies Apollo his rightful place and turns a deaf ear to true poetry.

This allusion also enables Pope to extend the scope of his attack beyond the confines of literature and ethics, by pointing to political and cultural disorder as well. The Renaissance firmly believed that Persius' satires contained many veiled strictures upon Nero (this accounts in large part for his reputation for obscurity), and that, in particular, Midas in this passage signified Nero himself.[18] Pope's own lines emphasize Midas' kingship—"*Midas, a sacred Person and a King*" (70)—and the mention, immediately following, of minister and queen would definitely pinpoint the Hanoverian court as the target of his stroke. The juxtaposition of George II with the despotic emperor and degenerate poetaster Nero is damning enough, but the commentary tradition provides yet more damaging indictments. It is practically a commonplace there that Midas represents the imprudence and arrogance of princes, their bad administration of state affairs, their avarice and ignorance.[19] Pope's note, which points to Dryden's retelling of the story in his modernization of the *Wife of Bath's Tale*, serves the same purpose: Dryden too emphasizes Midas' kingly failings:

> *Midas* the King, as in his Book appears,
> By *Phoebus* was endow'd with Asses Ears,
> Which under his long Locks, he well conceal'd,
> (As Monarch's Vices must not be reveal'd)
> For fear the People have 'em in the Wind,
> Who long ago were neither Dumb nor Blind;
> Nor apt to think from Heav'n their Title springs,
> Since *Jove* and *Mars* left off begetting Kings.[20]

In Dryden, this last is probably a gratuitous stroke at William; in Pope's context, it is undoubtedly a slap at the Hanoverians and their conspicuous lack of divine right to the throne. All the political connotations of the Midas figure enable Pope to imply quite strongly that political corruption and poetic degeneracy are as intimately related as the latter is to religious disorder, and that all three have their fountainhead in the fatuous, boorish king of England. Persius' Midas and England's George unite in a single symbol of total cultural depravity, with Nero's—and George's—minion, Sporus, as its vicious mouthpiece.

This all-pervasive disorder provides the background against which the drama of the poem is played out, and Pope recalls its presence from time to time to keep his situation in perspective. Immediately on the heels of the Midas passage, for instance, he presents what can only be described as a classical parody, designed to show that the dunces pervert culture and literature and classical ideals

in exactly the same way and to exactly the same degree
as they pervert religion.

> Let Peals of Laughter, *Codrus!* round thee break,
> Thou unconcern'd canst hear the mighty Crack,
> Pit, Box and Gall'ry in convulsions hurl'd,
> Thou stand'st unshook amidst a bursting World.
>
> (85–88)

Codrus is a type-name for a hack poet, drawn from Juvenal's third satire; but this is the least important aspect of the passage. As Pope's note points out, these lines allude to Horace's Od.III.iii.:

> Justum & tenacem propositi virum
>   Non civium ardor prava jubentium,
>   Non vultis instantis tyranni
>   Mente quatit solida, neque Auster
> Dux inquieti turbidus Hadriae;
> Nec fulminantis magna Jovis manus.
>   Si fractus illabatur orbis,
>   Impavidum ferient ruinae.
>
> (1–8)

Pope's adaptation of the lines follows closely Addison's translation, which he had already criticized in the *Peri Bathous* as an example of poetic vulgarity. But it is more than literary ineptitude that Pope is attacking, although that forms an important part of his satire. To understand the full significance of this allusion, it is necessary to have in mind the complete Horatian context. There "the Man resolv'd and steady to his trust" [21] in the name of virtue faces unperturbed "the rude rabble's insolence" and "the tyrant's fierceness," the might of aroused nature and even the ultimate dissolution of the world itself. Such "godlike arts" as these, Horace claims, have gained for Augustus "a place among the gods." In such a context, Pope's Codrus becomes a total perversion of Horace's man of firm resolve in righteous cause. Pope has turned upside down the traditional conception of the world as a stage, and has reduced the cataclysmic fall of nature that the virtuous man is to withstand to the petty compass of an audience's yawn and laugh at Codrus' theatrical inability. Codrus, steadfast only in complacency and incompetence, falls as far short of his classical prototype as George II does of the deified Augustus. Both destroy the good order of government and poetry and invert a classical ideal, in the same way that Bufo and Sporus corrupt the relations of poet and patron.

Pope exemplifies this once again in his picture of the spider-scribbler, which unites all three primary aspects of corruption—literary, religious, and political—in one image of universal evil.

> Who shames a Scribler? break one cobweb thro',
> He spins the slight, self-pleasing thread anew;
> Destroy his Fib, or Sophistry; in vain,
> The Creature's at his dirty work again;
> Thron'd in the Centre of his thin designs;
> Proud of a vast Extent of flimzy lines.
> Whom have I hurt? has Poet yet, or Peer,
> Lost the arch'd eye-brow, or *Parnassian* sneer?
> And has not *Colly* still his Lord, and Whore?
> His Butchers *Henley,* his Free-masons *Moor?*
> Does not one Table *Bavius* still admit?
> Still to one Bishop *Philips* seem a Wit?
>
> (89–100)

This spider obviously stems from the same breed as the one in Swift's *Battle of the Books,* a brash innovator whose compositions are spun out of his own internal venom.[22] The salient fact is that he sits "thron'd" and kinglike in the center of his evil works: like George, the spider symbolizes the outward spread of corruption from its radial center, the crown. Significantly enough, the first dunce named is the poet laureate Cibber, whose "Lord" is, of course, George. This citation identifies George indisputably as the ultimate source of political and cultural depravity. The remaining names show the extent of that depravity: the corruption of religion and taste, for instance, is revealed by the association of one poetaster with Masonry and another with a bishop. Taken together, all these are the "mad Creatures" (105) whose deadly slaver imagistically unites them with their spiritual kin, the totally evil Sporus. Like him, they also pander to the tastes of Midas-Nero-George.

As with morality and poetry, politics and poetry have in effect become interchangeable metaphors, so that mention of one implies the other, and none is ever really absent from the poem. Because of this, Pope can relegate politics itself to a background function in the *Arbuthnot,* touching on it lightly now and again as a sort of *leitmotif.* Of this nature are Pope's references to his own condescension to ministers (265–66), his refusal to flatter even kings (338), and George's obliviousness to poetry (222). The seemingly neutral allusion to the innocence of his own early poetry is also part of this pattern of political reference:

> Soft were my Numbers, who could take offense
> While pure Description held the place of Sense?
> Like gentle *Fanny*'s was my flow'ry Theme,
> A painted Mistress, or a purling Stream.

(147–50)

This last line is drawn, as Pope's note carefully indicates, from "a Verse of Mr. *Addison,*" and it is just as pertinent as his earlier use of Addison's Horatian translation. It echoes quite closely one of the closing lines of *A Letter from Italy,*[23] a verse epistle in which Addison praised English liberty and Britain's strong position in Europe—praise that, however valid in 1701 under the Stuart Queen Anne, must have sounded somewhat hollow in 1735 with George II on the throne and Walpole's peace policies undermining English prestige. And if the general referent of this whole passage is Pope's own praise (in *Windsor Forest*) of England's power in its harmonious, balanced condition under Anne, the satire then cuts even deeper. The process of deterioration since that time has ended in almost complete discord under George.

Like so many of the poem's concerns, the theme of political corruption also reaches its climax in the portrait of Sporus, where it merges with all the other aspects of contemporary degeneracy that caught Pope's attention. There the corruption that, in the cosmos of the poem, began with the symbolic identification of George, Midas, and Nero, concentrates itself in the person of Nero's—and George's— favorite. Sporus pours his poison into the queen's ear—like Midas', the external sign of her cultural depravity—which, in the reality of eighteenth-century politics, was the portal of actual power in the kingdom. Persius' Midas passage has served Pope as the starting point for an imagistic pattern that further unites the poetasters and links them in the bonds of a common boorishness, much as St. Paul's epistle has provided him with the chains that bind them in the common sin of pride. Ears—all of them lengthened by means of the Midas allusion—are gained, lost, pricked, and perked throughout the *Epistle to Arbuthnot*. Pope fears the whisper that "perhaps, yet vibrates on his Sovereign's Ear" (357). He unflinchingly damns the corrupt politician, whether "on a Pillory, or near a Throne,/ He gain his Prince's Ear, or lose his own" (366–67). Eve's ear, and these, and Midas', are all overt symbols of a literary and political corruption that cannot be hidden: the true poet, like Persius and like Pope, can discern it and must tell it— *auriculas asini quis non habet?*

[93]

IV

Just as the dunces have shown themselves anarchists in literature, religion, and government, Pope's defense of himself focuses on his cultural, political, and theological orthodoxy. The dialectic of the *Epistle to Arbuthnot* demands that an absolute distinction be drawn, at all points, at all stages of his life, between the products of the hacks and the accomplishments of the genuine poet. To a large extent, the *Arbuthnot*'s mode of procedure dictates how this must be done: since the poetasters offend against the canons of classical taste, Pope will have to prove his rightful place in his cultural and literary heritage; since their works reflect the disorder of pride, his will have to reveal the humility and charity of a rightly disposed Christian.

Surprisingly few lines of the main body of the *Arbuthnot* are actually assigned to presenting Pope's own defense, but he uses those few tellingly. Their concentration, their density of theme and reference, unmistakably confirms his case in the terms that he has chosen. He begins his defense of his literary career *ab ovo,* or almost so, by explaining his childhood propensity for verse:

> Why did I write? what sin to me unknown
> Dipt me in Ink, my Parents', or my own?
> As yet a Child, nor yet a Fool to Fame,
> I lisp'd in Numbers, for the Numbers came.
> I left no Calling for this idle trade,
> No Duty broke, no Father dis-obey'd.
> The Muse but serv'd to ease some Friend, not Wife,
> To help me thro' this long Disease, my Life,
> To second, ARBUTHNOT! thy Art and Care,
> And teach, the Being you preserv'd, to bear.
> But why then publish? *Granville* the polite,
> And knowing *Walsh,* would tell me I could write;
> Well-natur'd *Garth* inflam'd with early praise,
> And *Congreve* lov'd, and *Swift* endur'd my Lays;

The Courtly *Talbot, Somers, Sheffield* read,
Ev'n mitred *Rochester* would nod the head,
And *St. John*'s self (great *Dryden*'s friends before)
With open arms receiv'd one Poet more.
Happy my Studies, when by these approv'd!
Happier their Author, when by these belov'd!
From these the world will judge of Men and Books,
Not from the *Burnets, Oldmixons,* and *Cooks.*

(125–46)

These lines go far beyond the mere mention of Pope's natural aptitude for verse, and their argument implies far more about Pope's ethical attitude toward literature than the seeming innocence of their surface statement indicates. His dipping in ink constitutes a metaphoric baptism into literature and provides the ethical *incipit* for his whole career. Pope elaborates and clarifies his meaning by alluding, in the same lines, to a famous New Testament episode:

And as Jesus passed by, he saw a man which was blind from his birth. And his disciples asked him, saying, Master, who did sin, this man, or his parents, that he was born blind? Jesus answered, Neither hath this man sinned, nor his parents: but that the works of God should be made manifest in him. I must work the works of him who sent me, while it is day: the night cometh, when no man can work. (John 9:1–3)

The argument at this point is both complex and important. Pope has asked why he writes, what sin has forced him to this burdensome way of life; and the answer demanded is obviously the one Christ gives. He writes, not because of any sin, but that the works of God may be made manifest in him. Pope's echo of the apostles' question points to a conceptual linking of his poetry and the tribulations it brings him with the blind man's affliction. In both cases, a life of illness and affliction provides the means of showing forth the glory of God: in the case of the blind

[95]

man, his miraculous cure accomplishes this; Pope manages it through the agency of his poetry—at once his affliction, his cure, and his work.

The concept of works reverberates in the poem. The dunces impute to Pope's works damnation: their own reflect it. Now Pope claims specifically that his poetry is exactly what he implied it was in the *Fortescue*—a semisacramental act that mirrors the glory and holiness of God's own work of creation. This too comprises the ultimate significance of the dipping in ink: it is the fact of *baptism* into literature, of entering upon the craft of writing as a work of God rather than a deed of pride, that separates Pope immeasurably from the dunces. Every aspect of their lives, every action, reveals the enormity of the gulf between: Pope "No Duty broke, no Father dis-obey'd" (130); the clerk "fore-doom'd his Father's soul to cross, . . . pens a Stanza when he should *engross*" (17–18).[24] The Cornus whose wife elopes "curses Wit, and Poetry, and *Pope*" (25–26), but Pope's chaste Muse pointedly "but serv'd to ease some Friend, not Wife" (131). Just as Sporus incarnates a grotesque parody of God, the dunces enact a sad perversion of the real poet. The verse of the poetasters mirrors their pride: Pope's writings furnish the vehicle by which the works of God are made manifest to a fallen world.

Impressive as Pope's presentation of his ethical case is, it still amounts to only half of the task he has set himself, and absorbs only a small part of the two verse paragraphs of his concise *biographia literaria*. This section of the *Arbuthnot* fuses the two main concerns of Pope's defense—Christian ethics and classical literary or cultural standards—into one massive vindication of his conduct and character as poet. His allusions draw just as heavily on classical sources as on scriptural. He has modeled his lines on sections of Ovid's *Tristia* and *Ex Ponto*: the forms are identical—epistle—and, far more important, the passages Pope has chosen to imitate and integrate into the *Arbuthnot* are those wherein the exiled Ovid attempts to justify *his* poetic career and clear himself of the unjust charges brought against him. These allusions, combined with the significance of Pope's baptism in ink, serve to round out his portrait of himself as an ideal Christian writer firmly supported by classical tradition and precedent.

Pope's exclamation, "Why did I write?" (125), matches the banished Ovid's *cri de cœur* in the first book of the *Ex Ponto*:

> Cur igitur scribam miraris. miror & ipse:
> Et mecum quaero saepe, quid inde feram.
>
> (I.v.29–30)[25]

Pope is drawing just as heavily on the general context of Ovid's lines as on the significance of the lines themselves. Ovid bemoans the fact that he ever wrote poetry, because all his sufferings have sprung from that. "To the present moment," he says in the couplet preceding the one Pope echoes, "no work of mine has brought me any profit, even though you enumerate them all; would that none had harmed me!" Pope's troubles with favor-seekers and libelers, all of which are directly traceable to the fact of his writing, are severe enough and similar enough to validate his appropriation of Ovid's lament, and to enable him to capitalize on the Roman author's troubles.

The remainder of Pope's two verse paragraphs imitate several different passages from one of the elegies of Ovid's *Tristia*. The poem thus drawn upon is Ovid's autobiography and defense (simultaneously, a review of his poetic career), ending in a boast of his undying fame and an assertion of his innocence of any wrong-doing. It has, quite obviously, many thematic similarities to the *Epistle to Arbuthnot*, and Pope has carefully exploited them in three key instances. His mention of his youthful inclination to poetry (127–28) parallels (as Dr. Johnson pointed out) Ovid's account of his early vocation:

[97]

At mihi jam puero coelestia sacra placebant;
    Inque suum furtim Musa trahebat opus.
Saepe pater dixit, Studium quid inutile tentas?
    Maeonides nullas ipse reliquit opes.
Motus eram dictis: totoque Helicone relicto,
    Scribere conabar verba soluta modis.
Sponte sua carmen numeros veniebat ad aptos:
    Et, quod tentabam dicere, versus erat.

(IV.x.19–26)[26]

The role "the Muse" played in Pope's life as comforter, healer, and instructor (131–34) is likewise based on Ovid's description of the consolation poetry afforded him in his adversity:

Hic ego, finitimis quamvis circumsoner armis,
    Tristia, quo possum, carmina fata levo.
Quod, quamvis nemo est, cujus referatur ad aures;
    Sic tamen absumo decipioque diem.
Ergo, quod vivo, durisque laboribus obsto,
    Nec me sollicitae taedia lucis habent,
Gratia, Musa, tibi. nam tu solatia praebes;
    Tu curae requies, tu medicina mali:
Tu dux, tu comes es: tu nos abducis ab Istro;
    In medioque mihi das Helicone locum.

(IV.x.111–20)[27]

And the catalogue of friends and companions who loved him and his poems is modeled on Ovid's similar listing of his literary friends and the praise accorded his verses:

Temporis illius colui fovique poetas;
    Quotque aderant vates, rebar adesse Deos.
Saepe suas volucres legit mihi grandior aevo,
    Quaeque necet serpens, quae juvet herba, Macer.
Saepe suos solitus recitare Propertius ignes;
    Jure sodalitii qui mihi junctus erat.

[98]

Ponticus Heroo, Bassus quoque clarus Iambo
    Dulcia convictus membra fuere mei.
Et tenuit nostras numerosus Horatius aures;
    Dum ferit Ausonia carmina culta lyra.
Virgilium vidi tantum: nec avara Tibullo
    Tempus amicitiae fata dedere meae.
Successor fuit hic tibi, Galle; Propertius illi.
    Quartus ab his serie temporis ipse fui.
Utque ego majores, sic me coluere minores:
    Notaque non tarde facta Thalia mea est.
Carmina cum primum populo juvenilia legi;
    Barba resecta mihi bisve semelve fuit.
Moverat ingenium totam cantata per Urbem
    Nomine non vero dicta Corinna mihi.

(IV.x.41–60)[28]

Pope's manipulation of allusive materials from *Tristia* IV. x. has enabled him to demonstrate a classical precedent for almost every moment of his literary career, from his childhood through to his present difficulties. Besides the vindication of his true status that the similarities imply, Pope comes to share as well in Ovid's now well-proven boast that he will win immortality through his poetry. Pope's fusion of these ideas with his Christian conception of poetry as a religious life effects an elevation of the pagan's tribulations to the more lofty and more orthodox status of the just man's sufferings in a sinful world. Moreover, such a mingling of viewpoints tends to add a further dimension to the immortality the poet hopes to win by his pains.

The complaints and self-justifications that were wrung from Ovid by a harsh exile among a barbaric, uncultured people, Pope is forced to write in his own England—with consequent implications about Englishmen that appear intentional and highly unflattering. While Ovid suffered under the despotic Tiberius, Pope is maligned under the boorish and tyrannical (so, at least, the Tory polemicists would have it) George II. Ovid's exile in a barbarian land at the

[99]

whim of an absolute monarch serves as the classical analogue for Pope's spiritual exile in a land of universal discord
and corruption, ruled by a Midas-like and incompetent
Hanoverian despot. Its only saving graces are the few who
rise above the mob and preserve the true standards of judgment in literature, politics, and religion. These are, of course,
the Tory, High Church intelligentsia who formed the core
of Pope's friends—Granville, Garth, Swift, Atterbury, and
Bolingbroke—"great *Dryden*'s friends before." It is from
this viewpoint that Pope has worked out his apology for his
literary life; it is by these standards that he damns the
Hanoverian king, courtiers, literature, and influence.

Once these basic differences between himself and his
enemies have been established, all Pope must do to prove
his merit is to distinguish his own works from the doings of
the scribblers. In just such a manner, his picture of the abuse
of genuine talent in Atticus is followed immediately by an
autobiographical passage repudiating Atticus' worldliness
in favor of an ideal of restraint and self-sufficiency:

> What tho' my Name stood rubric on the walls?
> Or plaister'd posts, with Claps in capitals?
> Or smoaking forth, a hundred Hawkers load,
> On Wings of Winds came flying all abroad?
> I sought no homage from the Race that write;
> I kept, like *Asian* Monarchs, from their sight:
> Poems I heeded (now be-rym'd so long)
> No more than Thou! great GEORGE! a Birth-day Song.
> I ne'er with Wits or Witlings past my days,
> To spread about the Itch of Verse and Praise;
> Nor like a Puppy daggled thro' the Town,
> To fetch and carry Sing-song up and down;
> Nor at Rehearsals sweat, and mouth'd, and cry'd,
> With Handerchief and Orange at my side:
> But sick of Fops, and Poetry, and Prate,
> To *Bufo* left the whole *Castalian* State.

(215–30)

Atticus, "like the *Turk*," can brook no rivals; Pope, "like *Asian* Monarchs," keeps from public sight. Atticus gives his little senate laws; Pope "ne'er with Wits or Witlings past [his] days." The playwright Atticus sits attentive to his own applause, while Pope emphatically disowns the theater and all its appurtenances. In direct contrast to Atticus' concern for his reputation, Pope describes himself as so indifferent to public opinion that he does not in the least care whether his name is apotheosized (218 and Pope's note) or whether it becomes part of a phallic and slightly diseased obscenity (215–16).

So too the description of Bufo's abuse of the patron's position is matched by the significant mention of Pope's and the Duchess of Queensbury's loyalty to Gay (256–60), which is probably intended to serve as a model for the proper poet-patron relationship. Bufo's degradation of his poets into servile flatterers contrasts starkly with Pope's statement of stubborn independence and total integrity (261–66). He even ironically grants Bufo and his kind something of what they claim: if they wish to play God, he will be the righteous Job who suffers their whims patiently.

> Blest be the *Great!* for those they take away,
> And those they left me—For they left me GAY.
>
> (255–56)

This parody of Job's prayer[29] is of a piece with Bufo's other attempts to usurp God's prerogatives. In this case, Pope can make himself a party to it without compromising his religious position because the actual agent of the evil that befalls Job is Satan, not God. There is an even further irony in that the evil intended by "the *Great*" in their neglect of true poets actually becomes a boon to Pope: their ministrations at least relieve him of some of the dunces.[30]

The simple enumeration of Pope's works proves him in all circumstances the proponent of orthodoxy: "I pay my Debts, believe, and say my Pray'rs" (268)—a statement that alludes to and fulfils the requirements of the Lord's Prayer, and demonstrates in the compass of a single line Pope's moral excellence. Immediately before he presents his portrait of the libeler, he disowns any line that can "Give Virtue scandal, Innocence a fear" (285); and immediately after he has put the finishing touches on his sketch of Sporus, he launches a long *distinguo* that unequivocally marks off the differences between himself and Sporus and all the lesser offenders who have preceded Sporus. This passage (334–59) marks the end of the poem's *confirmatio* and sums up the progress of its argument. In it, he denounces worldly ambition, specifically denies that he is guilty of pride, and repudiates flattery. He claims

> That not in Fancy's Maze he wander'd long,
> But stoop'd to Truth, and moraliz'd his song,

$$(340-41)^{31}$$

and that for the sake of virtue he has endured all the slanders and calumnies that the Sporuses of this world have been able to heap upon him. This summing up links the end of the poem's argument with its beginning, and reveals just how far it has advanced. The poetasters have libeled Pope's person, defamed his morals, and "imputed" to him trash and dulness (346–53). This last charge brings the argument full circle, back to the Arthur who "Imputes to me and my damn'd works the cause" (24) of his son's hack poetry and disobedience. At this point in the poem, the success of Pope's defense can be measured by the reader's awareness of the irony of that charge in the light of the imputation of righteousness that his works have merited.

V

The final sections of the *Epistle to Arbuthnot*, its *refutatio* and *peroratio*, finally turn to the problem announced in the *Advertisement* and attempt to absolve Pope's "Person,

Morals, and Family" from the aspersions of the libelers. These charges are logically treated here, this late in the poem's progress, because they are *not* the primary concern of the *Arbuthnot*. That concern, the real conceptual center of the poem, is literature and the literary life. Only after Pope has proved that he is an authentic poet and his enemies merely degenerate hacks can he reasonably refute their personal slanders with any semblance or honor or expectation of belief.

Arbuthnot's question "But why insult the Poor, affront the Great?" (360) initiates this last movement of the poem and offers Pope the stimulus for his ultimate justification of his life. His immediate response details the ethical position from which he has acted throughout the poem: "A Knave's a Knave, to me, in ev'ry State" (361)—the servant of truth is unmoved by any of the criteria of worldly success, and the dunce remains in fact a dunce whether he be in appearance peer or poet. Pope carefully enumerates the virtues that mark him off from them: he is "Foe to [Dennis'] Pride, but Friend to his Distress"; he is humble, patient, and long-suffering (368–81).

Despite this readily apparent virtue, some still malign "His Father, Mother, Body, Soul, and Muse" (381). The position of his poetry in this list identifies it nicely as a function of his soul, a spiritual and religious work, and, of course, implies the wickedness and perversity of those who attack it. Pope's defense of his family accomplishes this same task. His own conduct and his later prayer to live up to his father's example strongly imply that he shared his father's pious opinion that "it was a Sin to call our Neighbour Fool" (383). The peculiar significance of this declaration to the context of the *Epistle to Arbuthnot* can be found in the contemporary explanations of the biblical pronouncement to which it refers:

But I say unto you, That whosoever is angry with his brother without a cause shall be in danger of the judgment: and whosoever shall say to his brother, Raca, shall be in danger of the council: but whosoever shall say, Thou fool, shall be in danger of hell fire. (Mat. 5:22)

For the exegetes, to say "Raca" is to commit the lesser sorts of insults or affronts; to call another "fool" signified all other sorts of slanders, curses, and calumnies, which were in themselves mortal sins.[32] Pope's incorporation of this idea here serves the dual purpose of clearing himself of the last vestiges of the charges of malignancy and libel that satire inevitably attracts, and of identifying those who have maligned him finally and irrevocably as unregenerate sinners. In the face of the idle slanders of his enemies, he celebrates the unselfish love and heroic virtue of his parents with the words Virgil uses to consecrate the deaths of Nisus and Euryalus:

> Unspotted Names! and memorable long,
> If there be Force in Virtue, or in Song.
>
> (385–86)[33]

So also Pope distinguishes his father's and his own actions from the religious factionalism of the dissenters and from their duncical subtleties. His father lived a "Stranger to Civil and Religious Rage" (394); "he knew no Schoolman's subtle Art" (398).

> Born to no Pride, inheriting no Strife,
> Nor marrying Discord in a Noble Wife,
> Stranger to Civil and Religious Rage,
> The good Man walk'd innoxious thro' his Age.
>
> (392–95)

Pope's father was quite pointedly "Born to no Pride"—which is not merely to say that he was of humble family, but that he escaped the all-pervasive pride of the scribblers. He inherits no strife; that is, he does not share in that discordant clash of extremes and opposites that characterizes Sporus and his party. Instead, he is himself a concordant individual, sharing in the harmony that is the nature of God and his rightly ordered and properly acting creatures. The elder Pope's marriage is metaphor for all this. Marriage is the great traditional symbol for the harmonic resolution of opposites on all levels of the theory,[34] and the clearly designated concordant match of line 393 is figurative shorthand for the poet's and his father's complete personal and social harmony. Pope's father and, by strong implications, Pope himself, are presented as virtuous and rational men who have discerned and followed God's plan, and who have in all instances preserved that proper concord that is the sign of his handiwork.

These lines are complicated by having another poetic pattern overlaid upon the rhetorical one into which they initially fit. This pattern functions alongside the rhetorical structure of this section, employing the same words and the same lines toward different, but complementary, ends. From line 380 to the end of the poem, Pope's verses form a coherent and complete miniature elegy, preserving all the details of the formal elegiac pattern.[35] This poem-within-a-poem opens with a lamentation, here specificaly adapted to the larger context of which the elegy is a part, by bemoaning not simply the death of Pope's father, but also the scribblers' defamation of his character. It then proceeds to describe his ancestry, that is, in formal elegiac terms, his *genos*:

> Of gentle Blood (part shed in Honour's Cause,
> While yet in *Britain* Honour had Applause)
> Each Parent sprung—"What Fortune, pray?"—Their own,
> And better got than *Bestia*'s from the Throne.
>
> (388–91)

The next section (392–95) presents the character (*phusis*) of Pope's father, in this case that of a regenerate and concordant Christian, who shunned both the pride of the dunces and the disorder of political and religious sectarian struggles.

[105]

Pope then recounts his father's education and accomplishments (*paideia* and *praxeis*), which are those of a man of retired and contemplative life—a consideration that has influenced even the preceding *phusis*.

> No Courts he saw, no Suits would ever try,
> Nor dar'd an Oath, nor hazarded a Lye:
> Un-learn'd, he knew no Schoolman's subtle Art,
> No Language, but the Language of the Heart.
>
> (396–99)

And all is concluded with the supreme moment of the Christian's existence, the quiet and holy deathbed:

> By Nature honest, by Experience wise,
> Healthy by Temp'rance and by Exercise:
> His Life, tho' long, to sickness past unknown,
> His Death was instant, and without a groan.
> Oh grant me thus to live, and thus to die!
> Who sprung from Kings shall know less joy than I.
>
> (400–405)

This last couplet concludes Pope's defense of his family. Its aspiration to emulate his father's example significantly echoes Horace:

> Non qui Sidonio contendere callidus ostro
> Nescit Aquinatem potantia vellera fucum,
> Certius accipiet damnum, propiusve medullis,
> Quam qui non poterit vero distinguere falsum.
> Quem res plus nimio delectavere secundae,
> Mutatae quatient. Si quid mirabere, pones
> Invitus. Fuge magna: licet sub paupere tecto
> Reges, et regum vita praecurrere amicos.
>
> (Ep. I. x: 26–33)

As can be seen, Horace's lines provide Pope with more than a verbal echo or simple precedent for his feeling. Occurring in such circumstances, in a poem devoted to the praise of the retired, temperate life, they provide in themselves a corroboration of the worth of the very attributes Pope has just eulogized in his father—his self-control, his withdrawal from public turmoil, his honesty and temperance.

In point of fact, this whole passage, beginning with line 391, is typical of the procedure of the *Arbuthnot*: it is a skilful fusion of classical and Christian motifs. Pope's father is described as a regenerate Christian, concordant and temperate; at the same time, and in the same terms, he is portrayed as fulfilling a classical ideal. His conduct (and, by extension, his son's) bears the justifying and ennobling marks of tradition and orthodoxy from whatever point of view it is examined. And it is, of course, no accident that the final, Horatian lines of the passage refer to the lesser happiness of those "sprung from Kings," since the entire pattern of the poem has educated the reader to recognize in England's king the source and fount of all the disorder to which the poet is here contrasting his father.

The final verse paragraph of the poem is both the *Epistle*'s peroration and this miniature elegy's *consolatio*. Turning again to Arbuthnot, Pope comforts himself with the thought that his mother still survives. The ultimate Christian consolation is, of course, the reward of heaven. It is precisely this that Pope implies his father has received:

> Me, let the tender Office long engage
> To rock the Cradle of reposing Age.
>
> .   .   .   .
>
> Explore the Thought, explain the asking Eye,
> And keep a while one Parent from the Sky!
>
> (408–9, 412–13)

The fullest statement of that solace comes in the final two lines of the poem, after Pope's prayers for his friend, his mother, and himself, in the Christian poet's hopeful assertion of divine approval, and in his faithful acquiescence to his Redeemer's will:

Whether that Blessing be deny'd, or given,
Thus far was right, the rest belongs to Heav'n.

(418–19)

This elegy of the pious death and holy reward of Pope's father is yet another piece in the mosaic of proof that demonstrates Pope's virtue and condemns his libelers. Its poetic and rhetorical efficacy as the conclusion of the *Arbuthnot* are indisputable. It welds together all of the various fragments of proof that have grown out of Pope's initial description of his argument with the poetasters as one about the relative merits of their works; it shows quite clearly the goal for which Pope himself was striving. The reward that the poet's father has won by a life of quiet and devotion is the one that his son seeks by a life of literature and suffering. Heaven's benign approval blesses the elder and younger Pope alike.

VI

If there is any validity to the contention that the argument of the *Epistle to Arbuthnot* centers around a dialectic of works, it then remains to examine the total poem as a work in itself, a final proof *in se* of Pope's merit. The role of Arbuthnot in the poem illuminates this: he functions as a rhetorical *adversarius* much in the manner of Fortescue in Pope's Imitation of Sat.II.i. Like Fortescue, Arbuthnot is Pope's means of incorporating his audience into the poem and leading it to the conclusion he wants drawn. Arbuthnot is prudent and cautious, and shows a sensible man's fear at Pope's indiscreet mention of court figures:

"Good friend forbear! you deal in dang'rous things,
"I'd never name Queens, Ministers, or Kings;
"Keep close to Ears, and those let Asses prick,
"Tis nothing"

(75-78)

He hurriedly interrupts when it appears Pope's anger is carrying him beyond safe limits:

> "Hold! for God-sake—you'll offend:
> "No Names—be calm—learn Prudence of a Friend:
> "I too could write, and I am twice as tall,
> "But Foes like these!"

(101-4)

In both these instances, his caution bows before Pope's righteous anger, and his long silence during the major part of Pope's harangue thus becomes a sign of at least respectful neutrality, if not outright agreement. The crucial turning point in his attitude occurs at Pope's mention of Sporus; even Arbuthnot's prudence shatters before his disgust at "that mere white Curd of Ass's milk" (306). Since he is the representative in the poem of responsible opinion, his interjection at this point vindicates Pope's satire and his satiric judgments, and tenders him a carte blanche for past, present, and future activities. This agreement to the justice of Pope's pronouncements accounts for the distinctly altered tone of Arbuthnot's next interruption: "But why insult the Poor, affront the Great?" (360). The simple fact that his former frightened pleas for Pope to desist have now become a much milder and more traditional question about his satiric practice is in itself significant, and once more his prolonged and submissive silence as Pope takes a high moral line and demolishes his objection indicates his substantial agreement with Pope's position. Given this pattern of increasing approval on Arbuthnot's part, coupled with the similar use Pope has made of his former *adversarius*, Fortescue, it seems more than likely that Warburton had Pope's authority for, and was correct in, assigning the last two lines of the poem to Arbuthnot.[36] As with Fortescue's final lines in Sat.II.i., these indicate the *adversarius'* complete conversion to Pope's point of view, his total approbation of Pope's conduct and, particularly, of the final work Pope has set himself, that of extending "With lenient Arts . . . a Mother's breath"

(410). From the standpoint of oratorical theory, they demonstrate the final suasion of the poem's audience that it is the function of the art of rhetoric to accomplish. If they are pronounced by Arbuthnot, rather than by Pope, they constitute the Epistle's internal validation of itself: the audience that it contains has been moved to assent to the propositions it contains, and to submit itself and its reason to the final judgment of that providential order that Pope has espoused throughout the poem.

Pope's major effort, throughout the Epistle, has been to present himself as a regenerate, concordant individual, in contrast to the depravity and disorder that mark the dunces and their works. Given this argument, it follows that it is absolutely crucial that his own works reflect the harmony he claims to possess. Pope has managed to balance one broad section of the poem against another, and to effect in himself as *persona* and in the poem a reconciliation of opposite concepts that makes of the poem itself a miniature of the divine harmony and a perfect expression of his own internal harmony, an ordered and self-contained world in small. First he deals with the favor-seekers, in the first part of his *confirmatio;* and then, in the second part, he treats the libelers. Immediately after this follows the *Arbuthnot's refutatio,* in which Pope depicts himself as the concordant mean between these extremes, avoiding both lying and flattery, presumptuous pride and ignoble self-abasement. Even within these larger sections, the poem proceeds by a balancing of opposites: after each passage descriptive of a particular dunce's faults, there follows a section presenting Pope's contrasted abhorrence of these errors. Classical allusion balances Christian reference; the orthodoxy of the public poet parallels the probity of the private man. By these means, the poem's structure is made to corroborate Pope's arguments, and his works—the very subject of the dispute—are molded into an integral part of the evidence that resolves the question incontestably in Pope's favor. The poem mirrors the divine plan and manifests the works of God. True poet is shown forth by true poem, and all ends with the imputation of righteousness that Pope's work has fairly merited: "Thus far was right, the rest belongs to Heav'n."

1. The two poems are also much alike in their basic rhetorical structure. Lines 1–6 form the succinct *exordium* of the *Arbuthnot,* introducing Pope's plight. The *narratio* (7–26) details specifically the situation under which Pope suffers and presents the ethical terms of the poem's argument. The *partitio* is based firmly on the *narratio* and flows logically from it: Pope simply divides his concern, the plague of poetasters, into its two natural groups, would-be friends and actual enemies, favor-seekers and libelers:

> What *Drop* or *Nostrum* can this Plague remove?
> Or which must end me, a Fool's Wrath or Love?
> A dire Dilemma! either way I'm sped,
> If Foes, they write, if Friends, they read me dead.
>
> (29–32)

The first section of the *confirmatio* deals with the favor-seekers (33–124). Pope then initiates, at line 125, a justification of his own literary career, from which he modulates easily into the long catalogue of his enemies, running through to line 359, which is the second half of the *confirmatio* and corresponds to the other half of his division of the poem's subject. The poem's *refutatio* (360–405) is devoted to absolving Pope, his family, and his writings from the slanders of the libelers. The final lines of the poem (406–19) are at once its *peroratio* and a concluding prayer.

2. Juvenal III.9. Here is Dryden's translation:

> But worse than all the clatt'ring Tiles; and worse
> Than thousand Padders, is the Poet's curse.
> Rogues that in Dog-days cannot Rhime forbear;
> But without Mercy read, and make you hear.
>
> (13–16)

3. Martial XIII.lxii:

> Versus, & breve, vividumque carmen
> In te ne faciam times, Ligurra,
> Et dignus cupis hoc metu videri:
> Sed frustra metuis, cupisque frustra
> In tauros Libyci ruunt leones,
> Non sunt papilionibus molesti.
> Quaeras censeo, si legi laboras,
> Nigri fornicis ebrium poetam,
> Qui carbone rudi, putrique creta
> Scribit carmina, Quae legunt cacantes.
> Frons haec stigmate non meo notanda est.

The text of Martial quoted is the Delphine, ed. Vincentius Collesso (Paris, 1680).

4. *Ars Poetica* 457: "Hic dum sublimes versus ructatur, & errat. . . ."

5. See Romans 3:20, 27–28; 4:1–8, 20–25; 5:11–15; 8:12–14, 28–30, and the commentaries on these passages, e.g., Cornelius à Lapide, *Commentarius in Sacram Scripturam* (Amsterdam, 1681–84), pt. 12, pp. 1–196, and Matthew Poole, *Synopsis Criticorum Aliorumque Sacrae Scripturae Interpretum* (London, 1676), V, cols. 1–330. Paul's purpose in Romans was to refute the doctrines of a body of Judaizing Christians who would have subjected proselytes to circumcision and the obligations of the Mosaic code. To this end, he emphasized the primary importance, for salvation, of faith in Christ, and pointed to Abraham as an example of one who was justified through faith rather than through the works of the Law; because of his belief, God imputed righteousness to him. The purpose of the Law, according to the apostle, was to convict mankind of sin, "for until the law sin was in the world: but sin was not imputed when there was no law" (5:13). It was to save mankind from the curse of original sin that Christ entered the world; through faith in him men are adopted as children of God and are freed from the bondage of sin. The biblical exegetes, of course, built upon this foundation. They point out that sin entered the world through Satan's and Adam's fall, and they insist upon the necessity of baptism to cleanse the faithful from the stains of original sin. They further argued that St. Paul opposed only the merely mechanical performance of the works of the Old Law, not good works done in charity. Pointing to the Epistle of St. James, they explained that the apostle's concept of faith included hope, charity, and good works done in charity; and it is by these that righteousness is imputed and salvation merited. Roman Catholic and Anglican interpretations of this epistle are in all essential points alike. See Martin C. Battestin, *The Moral Basis of Fielding's Art* (Middletown, Conn., 1959), pp. 14–25, for the perpetuation of this controversy in the 1730's, its contemporary importance because of the advent of Methodism, and the orthodox emphasis on good works.

6. See Earl R. Wasserman, *Pope's Epistle to Bathurst* (Baltimore, 1960). For Pope's use of this theme in *Windsor Forest*, see Wasserman, *The Subtler Language*, pp. 101–68.

7. *PL.X.175–81* and X.504–17; Genesis 3:14–15.

8. Pope's use of the toad-snake metaphor enjoys a rhetorical efficacy distinct from, but complementary to, the effectiveness it gains from its biblical and Miltonic reverberations. This particular image occurs in the *Rhetorica ad Herennium* as an example of the proper use of simile in censure: "Simile is the comparison of one figure with another, implying a certain resemblance between them. This is used either for praise or censure. . . . For censure, so as to excite hatred, as follows: 'That wretch who daily glides through the middle of the Forum like a crested serpent, with curved fangs, poisonous glance, and fierce panting, looking about him on this side and that for some one to blast with venom from his throat—to smear it with his lips, to drive it in with his teeth, to spatter it with his tongue.' "—IV.lxix.62 (translation by Harry Caplan in the "Loeb Classical Library" edition, pp. 385–87). Pope's adaptation and use of this image here thus becomes an exemplification of his familiarity with classical theory and his ability to employ it, and a further condemnation of Sporus through his likeness to this handbook figure of the libeler.

9. Here is Pope's expression of the idea in the *Essay on Man:*

> In Pride, in reas'ning Pride, our error lies;
> All quit their sphere, and rush into the skies.

> Pride still is aiming at the blest abodes,
> Men would be Angels, Angels would be Gods.
> Aspiring to be Gods, if Angels fell.
> Aspiring to be Angels, Men rebel;
> And who but wishes to invert the laws
> Of ORDER, sins against th'Eternal Cause.
>
> (I. 125–30)

The relevance of this formulation to Pope's use of these same ideas in the *Arbuthnot* should be abundantly obvious. See also Maynard Mack's Introduction to the *Essay*, TE, III, pt. i, pp. lxx–lxxi.

10. Many of the points of Pope's description of Bufo—his avarice, his willingness to listen and applaud, but not to pay, his own penchant for poetry, his infrequent distribution of meals—are ultimately drawn from Juvenal's archetypal picture of the bad patron, Satire VII.36–49.

11. That this is the general conception with which Pope was working is suggested by a couplet deleted from the final version of the poem: "To bards reciting he vouchsafed a nod,/ And snuffed their incence like a gracious God" (noted by Courthope, *The Works of Alexander Pope,* eds. Whitwell Elwin and W. J. Courthope [London, 1871–86], III, 259 n. 3).

12. The essential identity of Bufo and Sporus is further indicated by the presence of characteristics of both in the portrait that forms a bridge between their sections of the poem. It is the character of the libeler as distinguished from Pope as true poet, and is imitated from Horace's similar sketch in Sat.I.iv., another apologia. The lines are *Arbuthnot,* 287–304, and Horace, Sat.I.iv.81–85.

13. Matthew 25 :14–30. This reference is made even more likely by the fact that the English word "talent" is derived from the Greco-Roman weight and coin *talentum,* and has come to have its present meaning only through the metaphoric significance of this parable.

14. See, for example, Cornelius à Lapide, *Commentarius,* pt. 14, pp. 457–61.

15. See, for instance, Pope's own use of the example in *Windsor Forest,* 235–58.

16. Here is Dryden's translation of the passage:

> Cou'd he do this, and is my Muse controll'd
> By Servile Awe? Born free, and not be bold?
> At least, I'll dig a hole within the Ground;
> And to the trusty Earth commit the sound:
> The Reeds shall tell you what the Poet fears,
> *King* Midas *has a Snout, and Asses Ears.*
> This mean conceit, this darling Mystery,
> Which thou think'st nothing, Friend thou shalt not buy:
> Nor will I change, for all the flashy Wit,
> That flatt'ring *Labeo* in his Iliads writ.
>
> (239–48)

17. See, for example, Francisco Pomey's *Pantheum Mythicum, seu Fabulosa Deorum Historia* (Amsterdam, 1730), p. 33: "Quartum, Musica fuit [Apollo], a sole etiam non aliena: Nam medias inter planetas, numeroso motu, quasi quendam concentum efficit; cytharaque septem nervis constante canere creditus, pari numero planetis consonantibus."

18. See Casaubon's scholion on line 121 (p. 113). Dryden's note on line 244 of his translation is quite to the point: after briefly recounting the Midas story, he adds, "By *Midas*, the Poet meant *Nero*" ([Kinsley] II, 751, n. 15). It is important to recall in this connection that Sporus was the court favorite of Nero, a fact that supplies yet another link in the chain that binds the *Arbuthnot's* culprits together.

19. See, for example, Natali Conte's *Mythologiae* (Padua, 1637), pp. 521–22.

20. (Kinsley) IV, 1707–8, 157–64.

21. The quoted passages are from Addison's translation; see *The Miscellaneous Works of Joseph Addison*, ed. A. C. Guthkelch (London, 1914), I, 179–80.

22. This is the general tenor of Warburton's annotation of the line in his edition, IV, 16: "This *metamorphosing*, as it were, the *Scribler* into a *Spider* is much more poetical than a comparison would have been. But Poets should be cautious how they employ this figure; for where the likeness is not very striking, instead of giving force, they become obscure. Here, everything concurs to make them run into one another. They both *spin*; not from the *head* (reason) but from the *guts* (passions and prejudices) and such a *thread* that can entangle none but creatures weaker than themselves."

23. Addison, pp. 61, 163–68:

> But I've already troubled you too long
> Nor dare attempt a more advent'rous song.
> My humble verse demands a softer theme,
> A painted meadow, or a purling stream;
> Unfit for Heroes; whom immortal lays,
> And lines like *Virgil's*, or like yours, shou'd praise.

There is an interesting gradation to Addison's appearances in the *Arbuthnot*, ranging from his unacknowledged but real presence in the Codrus passage (85–88), to his noted authorship here, to his full presence as the primary target of the Atticus passage.

24. Like much else in the poem, Pope's father and the concept of fatherhood have been wrenched into ambivalence: they are at once facts in themselves and metaphors for higher realities. Naturally enough, the attitudes of Pope and the dunces toward their parents and his also crystallize into the basic dichotomy that separates God's party from Satan's. The poetasters disobey their own fathers and revile Pope's, while his own proper respect and compliance to both his spiritual and his earthly father is demonstrated by the parental approval of his writings and by his final, elaborate defense of his father's reputation and character at the conclusion of the poem. Ultimately, this may all relate once again to the predestinarian controversy and to St. Paul's remarks about the spiritual paternity of God and the predestined conformity of the elect to the image of his Son. See Romans 8:14–30.

25. All quotations from Ovid will be taken from *P. Ovidii Nasonis Opera Omnia Cum Notis selectissimis Variorum studio B. Cnippingii* (Amterdam, 1683).

26. "But to me even as a boy service of the divine gave delight and stealthily the Muse was ever drawing me aside to do her work. Often my

father said, 'Why do you try a profitless pursuit? Even the Maeonian left no wealth.' I was influenced by what he said and wholly forsaking Helicon I tried to write words free from rhythm, yet all unbidden song would come upon befitting numbers and whatever I tried to write was verse." —Arthur Leslie Wheeler, (trans.), ("Loeb Classical Library" [London, 1959]), p. 199.

27. *Ibid.*, p. 205: "Here, though close around me I hear the din of arms, I lighten my sad fate with what song I may; though there be none to hear it, yet in this wise do I employ and beguile the day. So then this living of mine, this stand against the hardness of my sufferings, this bare will to view the daylight's woes, I owe, my Muse, to thee! For thou dost lend me comfort, thou dost come as rest, as balm, to my sorrow. Thou art both guide and comrade: thou leadest me far from Hister and grantest me a place in Helicon's midst. . . . "

28. *Ibid.*, p. 201: "The poets of that time I fondly reverenced: all bards I thought so many present gods. Ofttimes Macer, already advanced in years, read to me of the birds he loved, of noxious snakes and healing plants. Ofttimes Propertius would declaim his flaming verse by right of the comradeship that joined him to me. Ponticus famed in epic, Bassus also, famed in iambics, were pleasant members of that friendly circle. And Horace of the many rhythms held in thrall our ears while he attuned his fine-wrought songs to the Ausonian lyre. Vergil I only saw, and to Tibullus greedy fate gave no time for friendship with me. Tibullus was thy successor, Gallus, and Propertius his; after them came I, fourth in the order of time. And as I reverenced older poets so was I reverenced by the younger, for my Thalia was not slow to become reknowned. When first I read my youthful songs in public, my beard had been cut but once or twice. My genius had been stirred by her who was sung throughout the city, whom I called, not by a real name, Corinna."

29. Job 1:21–22: "And [Job]said, Naked came I out of my mother's womb, and naked shall I return thither: the Lord gave, and the Lord hath taken away; blessed be the name of the Lord. In all this Job sinned not, nor charged God foolishly."

30. Lest this allusion to Job be thought too gratuitous for the theology of even this poem to bear, it is important to note that biblical commentators had linked the blind man of St. John's gospel with Job through the similarity of their sufferings for meritorious ends: see Cornelius à Lapide, pt. 15, p. 390, col. 2. Pope's identification of himself with Job is a further elaboration of an already present theme, and yet another point of distinction between himself and the dunces.

31. Pope's stooping to truth constitutes the second half of a hawking metaphor that began when the dunces were whistled off his hands (254). The movements imaged in these two instances are precisely those moral directions of the parties to which they attributed: the dunces rise—the ascent of pride—and Pope stoops—the lowliness of humility.

32. See Cornelius à Lapide, pt. 14, p. 137, and Matthew Poole, IV, cols. 143–51. That Pope deliberately intended to echo this warning is suggested by its manuscript version, "It was a Sin to call our Brother Fool," which employs more exactly the words of the gospel account. In spite of the revision, however, the reference is still both recognizable and pertinent. See John Butt, *Pope's Poetical Manuscripts*, British Academy Lecture (London,

1954), plate iv, which is a photographic reproduction of Huntington MS 6006. The earlier reading of the line is clearly discernible.

33. *Aeneid* IX. 446–47: "Fortunati ambo! si quid mea carmina possunt,/ nulla dies unquam memori vos eximet aevo. . . . "

34. The history and significance of this image has been thoroughly documented in Brendan O Hehir's unpublished doctoral dissertation, "Balanced Opposites in the Poetry of Pope" (The Johns Hopkins University, 1959), pp. 201–21.

35. For a clear and concise analysis of the traditions and conventions of the elegy, see D. C. Allen, *The Harmonious Vision* (Baltimore, 1954), pp. 41–47.

36. The Twickenham editor rejects Warburton's authority here, although he has accepted it in all other similar instances in this poem.

Chapter IV

The Rules of Poetry and the Laws of Life
*The Second Epistle of the Second Book of Horace,
Imitated*

T HE EPISTLE TO ARBUTHNOT marks a change
in Pope's couplet style. The taut, line-by-line,
couplet-by-couplet progression of the *Fortescue* is
there altered toward a more expansive flow of language, a
more—if the adjective is allowable—Miltonic movement
from verse paragraph to verse paragraph, from topic to
topic, within the poem. While the character sketches of
Bufo, Sporus, and Atticus still retain the smaller con-
trapuntal units of the *Fortescue*, the remainder of the poem
is primarily constructed of these larger blocks of verse—
most notably, Pope's noble culminating defense of his
family and heritage. The *Second Epistle*, dedicated to an
anonymous colonel, refines that style to a high level of
excellence: it captures beautifully the easy movement and
slow but insistent current of conversation of the colloquial,
yet gentlemanly, Horatian verse it imitates. This loose,
broad progression accurately embodies the thematic materials of the poem. Logically as well as physically, the epistle
advances by large steps from one concern to another,[1] each
one in turn building upon and incorporating its predecessor.
As it proceeds from fable to fable, its interests grow from
human law to the laws of art to the laws of life, finally
to embrace, within the expansive boundaries of the *ars
moriendi* tradition, the confrontation of human and divine
justice.

I

The ostensible interest of a major part of this Imitation is the problem of worldly possessions and what one ought to do with them. Pope contends, here as elsewhere, that real ownership is impossible on earth, and that temporary use of objects is all that man can attain.[2] Implicitly, this argument draws upon perennial Christian teachings about temperance and the use of worldly goods, and it presupposes God's ultimate ownership of all the objects man calls his own. Explicitly, Pope here employs the Roman legal distinction of *dominium* and *usufructus*[3] to secure these points:

> If there be truth in Law, and *Use* can give
> A *Property,* that's yours on which you live.
> Delightful *Abs-court,* if its Fields afford
> Their Fruits to you, confesses you its Lord:
> All Worldly's Hens, nay Partridge, sold to town,
> His Ven'son too, a Guinea makes your own:
> He bought at thousands, what with better wit
> You purchase as you want, and bit by bit;
> Now, or long since, what diff'rence will be found?
> You pay a Penny, and he paid a Pound.
>
> (230–39)

In quite orthodox fashion, Pope points out that all property, all worldly belongings, are the gifts of Fortune and, like her, are bound to time and mutability. They can never be held, and the certainty of death reveals their final futility.

> Estates have wings, and hang in Fortune's pow'r
> Loose on the point of ev'ry wav'ring Hour;
> Ready, by force, or of your own accord,
> By sale, at least by death, to change their Lord.
> *Man?* and *for ever?* Wretch! what wou'dst thou have?

Heir urges Heir, like Wave impelling Wave:
All vast Possessions (just the same the case
Whether you call them Villa, Park, or Chace)
Alas, my BATHURST! what will they avail?
Join *Cotswold* Hills to *Saperton's* fair Dale,
Let rising Granaries and Temples here,
There mingled Farms and Pyramids appear,
Link Towns to Towns with Avenues of Oak,
Enclose whole Downs in Walls, 'tis all a joke!
Inexorable Death shall level all,
And Trees, and Stones, and Farms, and Farmer fall.

(248–63)

This much of Pope's argument is commonplace and unexceptional. It is the pattern of associations he has built around these ideas that accounts for the distinctive character of this Imitation. From the very beginning of the poem, the conception of property and possession has been intimately connected with its opposite, theft, and with that which mediates between them, law. All three tend, throughout the poem, to lose their individual character and to merge into one another. Theft becomes a mode of possession, property a form of theft, and law ambiguously either and neither:

If there be truth in Law, and *Use* can give
A *Property,* that's yours on which you live.

(230–31)

The course of the poem is largely the pattern of the modulation of these ideas. The fable that opens the epistle has been altered from Horace's to bring these conceptions into play at the very outset: where the fault of the Roman slave was a childish attempt at running away (2–16), that of Pope's French servant is theft (3–20). Pope's explanation of this tale immediately casts it into a legal context, and simultaneously calls the nature of law into question by hopelessly fogging the basis of equity:

[119]

If, after this, you took the graceless Lad,
Cou'd you complain, my Friend, he prov'd so bad?
Faith, in such case, if you should prosecute,
I think Sir Godfrey should decide the Suit;
Who sent the Thief that stole the Cash, away,
And punish'd him that put it in his way.

(21–26)

The poem as a whole turns upon the four key fables imbedded in it.[4] Pope's application of this one to his own case puts the poet's profession in the same sort of quasi-legal light, and even makes a tentative move toward identifying equity as rules to which all parties agree.

Consider then, and judge me in this light;
I told you when I went, I could not write;
You said the same; and are you discontent
With Laws, to which you gave your own assent?

(27–30)

The concerns of theft and possessions are developed even further in the tale of the soldier who captured a fortress in anger because he was robbed, and then refused to endanger himself again because he had won a sufficiency (33–51). Pope's personal application of this makes law—or at least laws to which he had not given his "own assent"—the thief, and poetry the means of regaining his stolen patrimony:

But knottier Points we knew not half so well,
Depriv'd us soon of our Paternal Cell;
And certain Laws, by Suff'rers thought unjust,
Deny'd all Posts of Profit or of Trust:
Hopes after Hopes of pious Papists fail'd,
While mighty WILLIAM's thundring Arm prevail'd.
For Right Hereditary tax'd and fin'd,
He [Pope's father] stuck to Poverty with Peace of Mind;

And me, the Muses help'd to undergo it;
Convict a Papist He, and I a Poet.
But (thanks to *Homer*) since I live and thrive,
Indebted to no Prince or Peer alive,
Sure I should want the Care of ten *Monroes,*
If I would scribble, rather than repose.

(58–71)

Pope's moderation in preferring quiet to further gain
parallels the soldier's proper "temperance" in spurning the
prospect of greater rewards, and represents the appropriate
ethical response to the lure of worldliness. That is, of course,
a mean that neither despises earthly goods nor values them
too highly. Pope elaborates this position at even greater
length later in the poem.

Yes, Sir, how small soever be my heap,
A part I will enjoy, as well as keep.
My Heir may sigh, and think it want of Grace,
A man so poor wou'd live without a *Place*:
But sure no Statute in his favour says,
How free, or frugal, I shall pass my days:
I, who at some times spend, at others spare,
Divided between Carelessness and Care.
'Tis one thing madly to disperse my store,
Another, not to heed to treasure more;
Glad, like a Boy, to snatch the first good day,
And pleas'd, if sordid Want be far away.

(284–95)

Once again the doctrine of the mean is presented in the
language of *concordia discors*: Pope's orthodox moral stance
nicely balances thrift and liberality, carelessness and care.
But the mention of statutes (288) draws even this conception of temperance into the pale of the laws that haunt
the poem by recalling (as Warburton's note indicates)[5]
the restrictions upon papists' inheritance rights. This links

any laws that oppose proper moderation with "certain Laws, by Suff'rers thought unjust" (60), and makes of law itself a mode of immorality.

But there are other laws than those of England, and other thieves than the kings of England. Pope's use of these first two fables has associated his poetry with both law and property. In the first case, his *not* writing is apparently one of those laws, parallel to the law against theft, to which the unnamed colonel has assented (27–32); and in the second, it is the means by which he has earned his fortune (64–72). Both these applications rather surprisingly tend to describe poetry as a worldly pursuit of much the same order as the acquisition of wealth. Pope firmly cements this identification by the use he makes of the poem's third fable:

> The *Temple* late two Brother Sergeants saw,
> Who deem'd each other Oracles of Law;
> With equal Talents, these congenial Souls
> One lull'd the *Exchequer*, and one stunn'd the *Rolls*;
> Each had a Gravity wou'd make you split,
> And shook his head at *Murray,* as a Wit.
> 'Twas, "Sir your Law"—and "Sir, your Eloquence"—
> "Yours *Cowper*'s Manner—and yours *Talbot*'s Sense."
>   Thus we dispose of all poetic Merit,
> Yours *Milton*'s Genius, and mine *Homer*'s Spirit.
> Call *Tibbald Shakespear,* and he'll swear the Nine
> Dear *Cibber!* never match'd one Ode of thine.
> Lord! how we strut thro' *Merlin*'s Cave, to see
> No Poets there, but *Stephen,* you, and me.
> Walk with respect behind, while we at ease
> Weave Laurel Crowns, and take what Names we please.
> "My dear *Tibullus!*" if that will not do,
> "Let me be *Horace,* and be *Ovid* you.
> "Or, I'm content, allow me *Dryden*'s strains,
> "And you shall rise up *Otway* for your pains."
> Much do I suffer, much, to keep in peace

This jealous, waspish, wrong-head, rhiming Race;
And much must flatter, if the Whim should bite
To court applause by printing what I write:
But let the Fit pass o'er, I'm wise enough,
To stop my ears to their confounded stuff.

(127–52)

Not only are poets compared to lawyers, but their actions are pictured as exact analogues of each other: both strive "to court applause" (150) and to aggrandize themselves. This fact explains poetry's association with worldly pursuits: like law, poetry is a public concern, and unavoidably involves the poet in all the distractions of business.

As the references to Theobald, Cibber, and Stephen Duck demonstrate, the writers involved in this sort of poetic popularity contest could scarcely be called first-rate, and a place in Queen Caroline's Merlin's Cave could only with heavy irony be described as a distinction Pope might envy. His opinion of this whole state of affairs is contained in the witty adaptation, in line 146, of Dryden's translation of Virgil, "Tell that, and rise a *Phoebus* for thy pains." [6] The line is taken from the third eclogue (162), which is a traditional shepherds' composition and singing contest that ends, equally traditionally, in a draw. The application of this convention to these decidedly unpastoral circumstances produces a complete distortion of the poet's role and character, and finally results in a gross travesty of the shepherd-poets' customary rivalry for excellence.

Pope has distinguished himself as true poet from these worldly scribblers by indicating his active repugnance for just such "business" as these others profess. This is embodied poetically in his derisive scorn for the locus of these distractions, London.

But grant I may relapse, for want of Grace,
Again to rhime, can *London* be the Place?
Who there his Muse, or Self, or Soul attends?

[123]

In Crouds and Courts, Law, Business, Feasts, and Friends?
My Counsel sends to execute a Deed:
A Poet begs me, I will hear him read:
In Palace-Yard at Nine you'll find me there—
At Ten for certain, Sir, in Bloomsb'ry-Square—
Before the Lords at Twelve my Cause comes on—
There's a Rehearsal, Sir, exact at One.—
"Oh but a Wit can study in the Streets,
"And raise his Mind above the Mob he meets."
Not quite so well however as one ought;
A Hackney-Coach may chance to spoil a Thought,
And then a nodding Beam, or Pig of Lead,
God knows, may hurt the very ablest Head.
Have you not seen at Guild-hall's narrow Pass,
Two Aldermen dispute it with an Ass?
And Peers give way, exalted as they are,
Ev'n to their own S–r–v—nce in a Carr?
Go, lofty Poet! and in such a Croud,
Sing thy sonorous Verse—but not aloud.

(88–109)

These lines describe a ladder of increasing earthliness and alienation not only from the pursuit of true poetry but from anything of spiritual worth whatever. Beginning with the impossibility of cultivating, in town, one's "Muse, or Self, or Soul" (90), they pass gradually through the petty distractions of poetasters and lawyers to the more weighty interference of a "Pig of Lead" (102)—wittily transformed from Horace's *hac lutulenta ruit sus* (75)—to end dramatically in the vision of absolute corporeality of noblemen, "exalted as they are," balked by their own excrement borne by in a triumphal chariot. (106–7). Woven into this scale of degradation are words and phrases that associate the whole process with the law, and that in turn bind the concept of legality firmly to the idea of materiality. This is the significance of the mention of "Courts, Law, Business" (91) and "Two Aldermen" in "Guild-hall's narrow Pass"

(104–5). For the same reason, two of the affairs that con-
sume the poet's time are the execution of a deed with his
lawyer (92) and the hearing of his case before the House
of Lords (96). The beginning of this passage acutely characterizes this whole process as a "relapse, for want of Grace"
(88), a repetition of Adam's original fall from grace. Entering the public life and losing one's self in business are viewed
as a second fall: in themselves, they alienate man from the
things of the spirit and tie him to the ephemera of the
world.

Opposed to the self-aggrandizement of the scribblers and
the unsettling distractions of worldly concerns is the calm,
rigorous, and ordered practice of the true poet:

> In vain, bad Rhimers all mankind reject,
> They treat themselves with most profound respect;
> 'Tis to small purpose that you hold your tongue,
> Each prais'd within, is happy all day long.
> But how severely with themselves proceed
> The Men, who write such Verse as we can read?
> Their own strict Judges, not a word they spare
> That wants or Force, or Light, or Weight, or Care,
> Howe'er unwillingly it quits its place,
> Nay tho' at Court (perhaps) it may find grace:
> Such they'll degrade; and sometimes, in its stead,
> In downright Charity revive the dead;
> Mark where a bold expressive Phrase appears,
> Bright thro' the rubbish of some hundred years;
> Command old words that long have slept, to wake,
> Words, that wise *Bacon,* or brave *Raleigh* spake;
> Or bid the new be *English,* Ages hence,
> (For Use will father what's begot by Sense)
> Pour the full Tide of Eloquence along,
> Serenely pure, and yet divinely strong,
> Rich with the Treasures of each foreign Tongue;
> Prune the luxuriant, the uncouth refine,
> But show no mercy to an empty line;

[125]

Then polish all, with so much life and ease,
You think 'tis Nature, and a knack to please:
"But Ease in writing flows from Art, not Chance,
"As those move easiest who have learn'd to dance.

(153–79)

The most salient fact about this passage is that it casts the craft of poetry, even in its highest reaches, into that ambiguous legal context that has pervaded the poem. It is not simply that poetry has rules or laws that must be fulfilled, but that good poets are in fact judges—"Their own strict Judges" (159). Composition and creation are described in the same sort of jargon: poets do not "spare" (159) words; they "degrade" (163) them even though they find favor at Court; they "command" (167) and "bid" (169) the reformation of the language; they "show no mercy" (175) to a bad line.

Its relation to law, of whatever nature that may be, does little to define poetry, and certainly provides nothing at all in the way of an ethical evaluation of the vocation. If anything, its connection with judging and law would indicate that a vague immorality, a taint of worldliness, clings to even the finest practitioners of an art at best ethically ambivalent. This problem is resolved by the unmistakable presence in Pope's text of verbal reference to a pair of biblical events, either or both of which serve to illuminate Pope's conception of the poetic act.

Such they'll degrade; and sometimes, in its stead,
In downright Charity revive the dead;

. . . .

Command old words that long have slept, to wake.

(163–64, 167)

The entire metaphor of the passage, the resurrection of the dead, as well as its significant coupling with the command

[126]

to sleepers to wake (a simple extension of the basic metaphor), points directly to Christ's raising of Lazarus or of
the daughter of Jairus. Since both episodes work toward
the same end and function equally well in Pope's allusive
context, I here quote the better known instance of the
reviving of Lazarus:

> These things said he: and after that he saith unto them,
> Our friend Lazarus sleepeth; but I go, that I may awake
> him out of sleep. Then said his disciples, Lord, if he sleep,
> he shall do well. Howbeit Jesus spake of his death: but they
> thought that he had spoken of taking of rest in sleep. Then
> said Jesus unto them plainly, Lazarus is dead. And I am glad
> for your sakes that I was not there, to the intent that ye may
> believe; nevertheless let us go unto him. . . . And when he
> had thus spoken, he cried with a loud voice, Lazarus, come
> forth. And he that was dead came forth. (John 11 : 11–15;
> 43–44)[7]

Christ's act is a deliberate demonstration of his Messianic
role, accomplished through a free gift of grace—Pope's
"downright Charity"—to give glory to God. Pope's application of this incident and its significance to his own profession is entirely consistent with the idea of poetry he has
promulgated in other Horatian Imitations. Poetry becomes,
once again, the semisacramental act of a morally good man,
an almost divinely ordained messenger. Its ultimate purpose
is to adumbrate the essential, God-appointed order of the
world, and to thereby show forth the glory of God. That
glory and that order are demonstrated by the harmony of
true poetry and by its concord of opposite elements—in
this case, accomplished through a river metaphor that has
elsewhere served Pope well as the vehicle for the theme of
concordia discors:[8]

> Pour the full Tide of Eloquence along,
> Serenely pure, and yet divinely strong.
>
>   (171–72)

In such a context, it is almost redundant for Pope to point out that poetry's strength is "divine."

Despite this essentially virtuous character, poetry is still colored and tainted by its connection with legality. Like the concept of property, with which it shares a common touchstone in the theme of law, poetry, too, is bound to time. In Pope's view of the matter—at least in this poem— poetry retains the aspect of temporality. Like all man's other works in this world, it exists *sub specie temporis* rather than *sub specie aeternitatis*. The further allusive content of the passage discussed above makes this clear. Many of the commentators on the corresponding section of Horace's epistle (106–25) refer to a similar locus in the *Ars Poetica* (46–72) that discusses much the same aspects of poetry—that is, usage, neologisms and antique words, and literary refinement.[9] Pope fleshes out his Imitation with materials borrowed from this source. The influence is most readily discernible in his description of the use of old words as a revival or a rebirth (a metaphor that is present in the *Ars Poetica* passage but absent in Ep. II.ii.) and in line 173, "Rich with the Treasures of each foreign Tongue," for which there is no authority whatever in Horace's epistle. The significance of the occurrence of this allusion at this point is, as usual, provided by context of the *Ars Poetica* passage as a whole, rather than merely the parts of it that Pope incorporates into his poem to consolidate the reference. In this case, the *Ars Poetica* section drawn upon ends with a heavy emphasis on the transience of all mortal works, including poetry. Here is Creech's translation:

> As *Leaves* on Trees do with the turning Year,
> The former fall, and others will appear;
> Just so it is in *Words,* one Word will rise,
> Look green, and flourish, when another dyes.
> All We, and Ours, are in a changing State,
> Just *Nature*'s Debt, and must be paid to Fate:
> Great *Caesar's Mole,* that braves the furious Tides,

Where now secure from Storms, his Navy rides:
E'en that *drain'd Lake,* where former Ages row'd,
A great *unfruitful Wast,* tho now 'tis plough'd,
Bears Corn, and sends the neighboring Citys food:
Those new *Canales,* that bound fierce *Tiber's* force,
That teach the Streams to take a better Course,
And spare the Plough-man's hopes: e'en these must waste,
Then how can *feeble Words* pretend to last?[10]

Such sentiments explain the association of poetry with the much denigrated laws: they are alike in that both are ultimately things of this world, inextricably bound to the evanescence of passing time.

Pope's allusion to the *Ars Poetica* has also defined another subdivision of the poem's general theme of property. Its concern, and that of the passage as a whole, is with words, new and old, and their usage—that is, with literary property and with the literary implications of the doctrines of *dominium* and *usufructus*. What Pope is defending is the poet's right to employ language—all language of all peoples —for his own ends: "Use will father what's begot by Sense" (170). This is particularly the point of his remarks about reviving dead words and commanding "old words that long have slept, to wake" (163). These amount to a succinct justification of this imitation of Horace specifically and of his imitative mode generally. Pope's use of the materials of classical poets and poems involves a question of the ownership and use of literary property. His lines declare that it is the right and duty of the true poet to take possession of the works of his predecessors and to transmit to his age as a living thing the legacy of the past. Because of this, and because poetry and language are so inextricably bound to time, the poet's task in every age inevitably becomes what Pope has described—a resurrection, a raising of dead words, dead thoughts, dead cultures, to life.

This is the real significance of Pope's appropriation to himself of "*Homer's* Spirit" (136); it is for this reason,

[129]

also, especially fitting that he has claimed to live and thrive "thanks to *Homer*" (68) immediately after utilizing a line from the *Iliad* to characterize William III pejoratively.[11] His request that he be considered Horace (144) must also be viewed in this light. He is not only donning for his age the guise of the Roman poet, but actually assuming his character and poetic rights, commanding his old words to wake into eighteenth-century English. Pope's subsequent plea to be allowed "*Dryden's* strains" (145) accomplishes exactly what it asks by incorporating and adapting to his own context one of Dryden's lines (146). To increase still further the depth of the application of concepts of property to poetry, the line in question is drawn from Dryden's translation of Virgil, yet another example of a poet's proper assumption of *usufructus* and of the transmission of a cultural inheritance.

Pope even extends this practice and these concepts to his own early poetry by his insertion of two lines—carefully marked as a quotation—from the *Essay on Criticism*:

"But Ease in writing flows from Art, not Chance,
"As those move easiest who have learn'd to dance.

(178–79)

He has appropriately revived these words in his present context by altering the original verb "comes" to "flows," thus linking the couplet closely with his use of the river metaphor and fitting it coherently into the passage. This entire process he summarizes in the final line of the triplet that describes the concordant nature of true poetry; it is, among other things, "Rich with the Treasures of each foreign Tongue" (173). The etymological connection of "treasure" and "thesaurus" defines precisely the nature of language and consequently the limitations of the poet's materials and craft. Words and poems are considered as plunder to be taken and used by the talent of the individual poet; with them as with all other earthly things, "*Use* can give/ A *Property*" (230–31).

[130]

If language and poetry are varieties of property and subject to all the laws that govern possessions, then they are also subject to the ravages of time. Pope's argument in this entire section of the epistle has made clear that not even the sacramental nature of true poetry is sufficient to save it from the fate of all mortal works. Pope has made this attitude explicit in the lines that introduce the entire disquisition on poetry.

> Years foll'wing Years, steal something ev'ry day,
> At last they steal us from our selves away;
> In one our Frolicks, one Amusements end,
> In one a Mistress drops, in one a Friend:
> This subtle Thief of Life, this paltry Time,
> What will it leave me, if it snatch my Rhime?
> If ev'ry Wheel of that unweary'd Mill
> That turn'd ten thousand Verses, now stands still.
>
> (72–79)

Time too is a thief that, governed by its own inexorable law, steals away all human accomplishments. It is against this background of futility in the face of inevitable death that Pope has chosen to place his vocation; it is because of this that his otherwise much honored craft is in this poem degraded to the level of worldliness.

This point is reinforced by means of a rather obvious scriptural allusion imbedded in Pope's description of the plight of the scholar or poet:

> The Man, who stretch'd in Isis' calm Retreat
> To Books and Study gives sev'n years compleat,
> See! strow'd with learned dust, his Night-cap on,
> He walks, an Object new beneath the Sun!
> The Boys flock round him, and the People stare:
> So stiff, so mute! some Statue, you would swear,
> Stept from its Pedestal to take the Air.
>
> (116–22)

The "Object new beneath the Sun" (119) recalls the ultimate source behind the cliché, the famous dictum from Ecclesiastes about human life:

> The thing that hath been, it is that which shall be; and that which is done is that which shall be done: and there is no new thing under the sun. (1:9)

This expressed for the Renaissance the utter instability and transience of human life and of the things of earth; the whole of Ecclesiastes belabors this concept to urge men to faith in God and reliance upon him rather than upon corruptible creatures.[12] In Pope's context, the phrase becomes ironic: the poet is *not* a new object, but shares the common ephemerality of all other created beings.

All this tends to leave poetry in a rather paradoxical light. At once it is, and it is not, worldly; it is, and it is not divine. It is a sacramental act, revealing and sharing in God's harmonious order; yet at the same time it is an essentially human work, limited and ultimately overcome by the power of common mortality. The explanation of this contradiction lies in human nature itself, of which poetry is the mirror. Man too shares this paradoxical character, being both mortal and immortal, flesh and spirit. Since, as the poem has been at great pains to prove, the flesh and the works of the flesh perish, the resolution of the problem of temporality and the allaying of the paradox depend upon the cultivation of the spirit. For this very purpose, Pope has slighted his own profession; it is only in contrast with works tending immediately toward salvation that poetry is in any way unworthy.

II

Like everything else in the poem, the concept of salvational works is also brought in contact with the touchstone of legality. Pope's fourth fable, once again crucially altered from the Horatian original, introduces this whole topic into the poem and sets it also in a legal or governmental light.

> If such the Plague and pains to write by rule,
> Better (say I) be pleas'd, and play the fool;
> Call, if you will, bad Rhiming a disease,
> It gives men happiness, or leaves them ease.
> There liv'd *in primo Georgii* (they record)
> A worthy Member, no small Fool, a Lord;
> Who, tho' the House was up, delighted sate,
> Heard, noted, answer'd, as in full Debate:
> In all but this, a man of sober Life,
> Fond of his Friend, and civil to his Wife,
> Not quite a Mad-man, tho' a Pasty fell,
> And much too wise to walk into a Well:
> Him, the damn'd Doctors and his Friends immur'd,
> They bled, they cupp'd, they purg'd; in short, they cur'd:
> Whereat the Gentleman began to stare—
> My Friends? he cry'd, p-x take you for your care!
> That from a Patriot of distinguish'd note,
> Have bled and purg'd me to a simple *Vote*.
>
> (180–97)

Pope employs this story as an allegory or analogy of his own case. Poetry, like law or politics, is an ephemeral worldly activity, a delusion from which he must be awakened into ultimate reality. As the lord (who has been ubiquitously present in the poem as a symbol of worldly-mindedness)[13] cursed his doctors, Pope also curses his spiritual doctor, Wisdom.

> Well, on the whole, *plain* Prose must be my fate:
> Wisdom (curse on it) will come soon or late.
> There is a time when Poets will grow dull:
> I'll e'en leave Verses to the Boys at school:
> To Rules of Poetry no more confin'd,
> I learn to smooth and harmonize my Mind,

Teach ev'ry Thought within its bounds to roll,
And keep the equal Measure of the Soul.

(198–205)

The entire presentation of spiritual activity fuses the concerns of poetry and of law. It is depicted as a turning from the "Rules of Poetry" to the laws of life, but those two disciplines are discovered to be identical in formulation. The activity that Pope describes in lines 203-5 and posits of the soul is exactly the same activity he has depicted at greater length in lines 159-79 and attributed to poetry; they present the same process of polishing and refinement, but what had been originally the concern of language and of poets is now realized to be the proper business of the soul and of men generally. The passages are even more closely linked by their common use of the river metaphor to describe the concord of their respective objects (see lines 171-72 and 204). What this means is that the rules of poetry are also the rules of morality: they differ only in the object to which they are applied. Inevitably, the results of this process are identical. They end again in concord, the harmony that Pope here explicitly states is the object of such labor—"I learn to smooth and harmonize my Mind" (203). Such a conception of spirituality has been almost inescapable: very early in this epistle, when Pope first introduced his dual theme of poetry and ethics, he presented them both as arts.

Bred up at home, full early I begun
To read in Greek, the Wrath of Peleus' Son.
Besides, my Father taught me from a Lad,
The better Art to know the good from bad.

(52–55)

Poetry's own sacramental nature makes such a correlation even easier, and renders the application of what are essentially the terms of literary criticism to the work of the soul highly appropriate.

[134]

Poetry and morality share a setting as well as a set of rules. Both are best accomplished within the quiet and retirement of the country. The "Grottos and Groves" (110) to which Pope's poets run to compose their songs recur in the more significant guise of an aid to self-collection and as an escape from the distractions of the town.

> Soon as I enter at my Country door,
> My Mind resumes the thread it dropt before;
> Thoughts, which at Hyde-Park-Corner I forgot,
> Meet and rejoin me, in the pensive Grott.
> There all alone, and Compliments apart,
> I ask these sober questions of my Heart.
> If, when the more you drink, the more you crave,
> You tell the Doctor; when the more you have
> The more you want, why not with equal ease
> Confess as well your Folly, as Disease?
> The Heart resolves this matter in a trice,
> "Men only feel the Smart, but not the Vice."
>
> (206–17)

The significance of the retired country seat as a place of genuine spiritual activity must not be underestimated in eighteenth-century poetry.[14] Pope's seemingly casual mention of it here would serve sufficiently to call to mind the major ramifications of the *topos,* which would in turn illuminate not only the following section of this epistle (the disquisition on property and temporalia), but would also provide a perspective for the poem as a whole. Viewed in the light of the retired as opposed to the active or public life, the Imitation can be seen to compose a lengthy encomium of the virtues and morality of the private life of meditation. It takes the law in all its various manifestations as the concrete exponent of the business of the public life that distracts man from the care of his soul. Its condemnation of all these annoyances, particularly embodied in the symbol of London (the site of Pope's "relapse," and of the perverted pastoral singing contest), is then to be understood as the traditional eschewing of the worldliness of cities that comprises one of the main facets of retired-life poetry. Conversely, Pope's articulation and praise of the doctrine of temperance are the logical sequels of such a moral position, and are equally at home within the confines of the literature of the retired life.

It is against this background that Pope's numerous references to English law and English government must be placed. They are the concrete manifestations of both the distractions and immorality of the world, and of the irrational and often unjust workings of Fortune as well. For this reason, the fables Pope has adapted from Horace's poem have been given specific temporal and political locations ("In ANNA's Wars" [33], "While mighty WILLIAM's thundering Arm prevail'd" [63], "*in primo Georgii*" [184]), and Pope's development of them has involved a semiauto-biographical history of the maladministration of England's affairs. Chronologically, the whole process begins in 1688, the year of Pope's birth and the "Glorious Revolution."

> Bred up at home, full early I begun
> To read in Greek, the Wrath of Peleus' Son.
> Besides, my Father taught me from a Lad,
> The better Art to know the good from bad:
> (And little sure imported to remove,
> To hunt for Truth in *Maudlin's* learned Grove.)
> But knottier Points we knew not half so well,
> Depriv'd us soon of our Paternal Cell;
> And certain Laws, by Suff'rers thought unjust,
> Deny'd all Posts of Profit or of Trust:
> Hopes after Hopes of pious Papists fail'd,
> While mighty WILLIAM's thundring Arm prevail'd.
> For Right Hereditary tax'd and fin'd,
> He stuck to Poverty with Peace of Mind;
> And me, the Muses help'd to undergo it;
> Convict a Papist He, and I a Poet.
>
> (52–67)

Since this passage is intended as an explanation and application of the fable that preceded it (the tale of the soldier), William III must inescapably be recognized as the counterpart of the thief who stole the soldier's money. Moreover, the "knottier Points" (58) that "Depriv'd us soon of our Paternal Cell" (59) correspond to the confiscation of Horace's property after the final victory of the usurper Augustus (Ep.II.ii. 46–52), and thus set up a broad analogy between the Roman civil war, the reign of Augustus, and his subsequent reprisals, on one hand, and the "Glorious Revolution," the kingship of William, and the antipapist laws on the other. This is all designed quite obviously to cast William's title and that of his Hanoverian successors into as poor a light as possible, and to further undermine their weak claim by demonstrating the gross injustice of their subsequent conduct. To reinforce this last point, Pope deviates significantly from his original: where Horace can simply say that he now possesses a sufficiency and imply the generosity of Maecaenas and Augustus, Pope pointedly remarks that it is due to his translations that he can "live and thrive,/ Indebted to no Prince or Peer alive" (68–69). The character Pope would fit upon William is perhaps best defined by the line that he adapts to him out of the *Iliad,* "While Meleager's thundring arm prevail'd (ix. 666).[15] In the *Iliad,* it occurs in Phoenix's speech likening Achilles to Meleager and warning him of the consequences of his implacability. Pope's own note to the *Iliad* passage points out the similarity of the two in the unswerving nature of their anger and resentment. In our immediate context, the line picks up and develops a suggestion contained in the mention of "the Wrath of Peleus' Son" ([53] which at least one commentator had seen as oblique satire on Augustus' reprisals),[16] and defines the antipapist laws passed in William's reign as the same sort of irrational anger and revenge as that of Achilles, which did so much harm to the Greeks.

Pope's own political allegiance is made plain in the lines describing his father's sufferings for "Right Hereditary"

(64), that right—or rather, those rights—being the Stuart succession and the Roman faith. Pope carefully links himself with his father: "Convict a Papist He, and I a Poet" (67). The alliteration, the noun-pronoun chiasmus, the zeugma, the ever-present pun on Pope's surname, all work to equate the two charges, to make Pope's poetic profession a religious commitment, and to link that commitment to the "Right Hereditary" of the Jacobite cause. Such an allegiance places Pope on the side of divine right and freedom of conscience as opposed to usurpation, tyranny, and the abuse of law.

It is for this reason that Pope can speak without irony of the reign of Anne, the last Stuart monarch, and apply to himself straightforwardly the story of the "temperate" soldier's service "In ANNA's Wars" (33). It is merely metaphor for Pope to speak of himself and his Tory friends as soldiers in such political wars, and it is quite accurate for him to claim that it was then that he and they gained their worldly sufficiency. The glory, honors, and rewards that are offered the soldier as an incentive for further action are all part of the traditional gifts of Fortune, and imply a necessary thralldom to the things of the world. Such a servitude, indeed, is the lot of the lord who, "*in primo Georgii,*" (184), was "a Patriot of distinguish'd note" (196). Pope very clearly implies that political activity (or, in fact, public activity of any kind) under the Hanoverians can only be madness and delusion. Even his satire, virtuous and public-spirited as it may be, is only another such deception, which must be abandoned for the wisdom of self-possession and the cultivation of one's soul. The reason for this is that the Hanovers have so utterly perverted the public life, both in church and state, that it no longer offers a viable means of government or of salvation.

> When golden Angels cease to cure the Evil,
> You give all royal Witchcraft to the Devil:
> When servile Chaplains cry, that Birth and Place

Indue a Peer with Honour, Truth, and Grace,
Look in that Breast, most dirty Duke! Be fair,
Say, can you find out one such Lodger there?
Yet still, not heeding what your Heart can teach,
You go to Church to hear those Flatt'rers preach.

(218–25)

The debasement of an angelic spirit to a golden coin is as
emblematic of the avarice and worldliness for which Pope
holds the Hanovers responsible as their failure to cure the
King's Evil is of their want of divine right and legitimate
succession. Their lack of God's sanction, Pope intimates,
has been filled by a diabolical right, a complete perversion
of the source of kingly authority. This is shown by Pope's
description of "touching" as "royal Witchcraft" (219), and
by his attribution of it to the "Devil" who then possessed
it—George II. Even the church is an obstacle rather than
an aid to salvation, since its function is only to flatter its
auditors into complacent self-satisfaction with their worldliness. This pattern of perversion was even reflected in the
court's reaction to poetry: a word the true poet spurns
and condemns might—ironically—"find grace" (162) at
court.[17] It is because of this total corruption of the public
avenues of justice and salvation that Pope is forced to
choose the life of retirement in a quiet country house—and
even this fact takes an ironic and perverse turn from the consideration that it also was dictated by those same antipapist laws whose injustice Pope has made paradigmatic
of the government of England.[18]

III

Because of the failure of human law and human government, Pope must seek stability and justice in the divine
laws of God's universal dominion. According to the pattern
of associations that gathered around the idea of the retired

[139]

life, the country seat provided, besides an escape from the sinful attractions of the world, an unexcelled opportunity to discern the workings of God in nature. Pope's Imitation is faithful to the tradition in this point as well: God is discovered animating, inspiring, and governing, not in nature generally, but in human nature specifically.

> Talk what you will of Taste, my Friend, you'll find,
> Two of a Face, as soon as of a Mind.
> Why, of two Brothers, rich and restless one
> Ploughs, burns, manures, and toils from Sun to Sun;
> The other slights, for Women, Sports, and Wines,
> All *Townshend*'s Turnips, and all *Grovenor*'s Mines:
> Why one like *Bu*—with Pay and Scorn content,
> Bows and votes on, in Court and Parliament;
> One, driv'n by strong Benevolence of Soul,
> Shall fly, like *Oglethorp*, from Pole to Pole:
> Is known alone to that Directing Pow'r,
> Who forms the Genius in the natal Hour;
> That God of Nature, who, within us still,
> Inclines our Action, not constrains our Will;
> Various of Temper, as of Face or Frame,
> Each Individual: His great End the same.

(268–83)

The conception underlying this verse paragraph is Pope's favorite one of the "Ruling Passion," that individual appetite that, governed by reason, "the God within the Mind," [19] impels man to his proper end. The idea—or rather, the complex of ideas—is a very involved one, and has implications affecting Pope's total theologicophilosophical view of the world. The Ruling Passion is implanted in the mind by God to provide the stimulus without which all action, whether morally good or bad, would be impossible. This passion is ideally to be governed by reason, and if so used will maintain man in a proper, balanced state of virtuous activity. Even if abused, however, its effects still tend to good in the over-all scheme of creation, since God's careful balancing of opposites inevitably draws good out of evil and reconciles divergent extremes to its one great end:

> Virtuous and vicious ev'ry Man must be,
> Few in th' extreme, but all in the degree;
> The rogue and fool by fits is fair and wise,
> And ev'n the best, by fits, what they despise.
> 'Tis but by parts we follow good or ill,
> For, Vice or Virtue, Self directs it still;
> Each individual seeks a sev'ral goal;
> But HEAV'N's great view is One, and that the Whole:
> That counter-works each folly and caprice;
> That disappoints th' effect of ev'ry vice:
> That happy frailties to all ranks apply'd,
> Shame to the virgin, to the matron pride,
> Fear to the statesman, rashness to the chief,
> To kings presumption, and to crowds belief,
> That Virtue's ends from Vanity can raise,
> Which seeks no int'rest, no reward but praise;
> And build on wants, and on defects of mind,
> The joy, the peace, the glory of Mankind.
>
> (*Essay on Man*, II. 231–48)

Perhaps the most apposite analogue of Pope's present text can be found in his *Epistle to Bathurst*, where he explains the doctrine of the Ruling Passion more fully and exactly than is usually his wont:

> "The ruling Passion, be it what it will,
> "The ruling Passion conquers Reason still."
> Less mad the wildest whimsey we can frame,
> Than ev'n that Passion, if it has no Aim;
> For tho' such motives Folly you may call,
> The Folly's greater to have none at all.
> Hear then the truth: " 'Tis Heav'n each Passion sends,
> "And diff'rent men directs to diff'rent ends.

[141]

"Extremes in Nature equal good produce,
"Extremes in Man concur to gen'ral use."
Ask what makes one keep, and one bestow?
That POW'R who bids the Ocean ebb and flow,
Bids seed-time, harvest, equal course maintain,
Thro' reconciled extremes of drought and rain,
Builds Life on Death, on Change Duration founds,
And gives th' eternal wheels to know their rounds.

(155–70)

This is the long way about to Pope's adaptation of Horace's *Naturae Deus humanae* (188), but all these ideas are contained in essence in the lines from which we began. "That Directing Pow'r" (278) is God as creator and providential governor of the universe; "That God of Nature . . . within us still' (280) is God as sustainer and preserver of his own creation and system. The "Genius" (279) is then the soul of man, formed and biased from birth by the divergent attractions of the Ruling Passion and of Reason. "His great End" (283), which is the same for all, is not only the harmony of the total scheme of creation, but also that individual concord within each soul that will win for its possessor the greater and more perfect harmony of heaven. This harmony, which has been depicted earlier in the rules of poetry and of life, is here exemplified in its cosmic aspect by Pope's balancing of opposite personalities against each other: the two brothers, one of whom labors while the other dallies (270–73), the avaricious and contemptible Bubb Doddington, and the generous and admirable Oglethorp (274–77). The entire section ends on a note of unity and harmony in the singleness and coherence of God's one "great End".

What all this means for Pope's poem should now be apparent. The Imitation of Ep.II.ii. has proceeded from its very beginning by means of a series of modifications of the concept of law: the paragraph we have been discussing presents the ultimate manifestation of that legality in a

description of the laws of the universe and of the God whose
will is the law of all things. Pope has advanced from earthly,
human law to the laws of art and the soul to, finally, the
great *Nomos* that governs the created world. All human
laws have been denigrated because they are as nothing in
the face of the fiat that originally ordered and still continues to sustain the harmony of the conflicting elements of
the universe. Human law is partial and imperfect, and
depends inevitably on the forceful coercion of conscience—
as is glaringly apparent from the "Laws, by Suff'rers thought
unjust" (60) of the poem's beginning. Even the rules of art,
although they approximate the principles and harmony of
God's order, are mutable, marred by their inescapable link
to time and man's mortality. It is only God's government
that is eternal, unchangeable, and everywhere alike, forever
reconciling the opposing elements of his creation into a harmonic whole, whether it is in the mind of man, or the order
of society, or the revolutions of the spheres. Only
God's laws operate without interfering with the freedom of man's will, fitting his choices, whatever they are, into
the balanced pattern: God "Inclines our Action, not constrains our Will' (281).

It is to this vision of ultimate law and perfect justice that
Pope's references to English law have led. The imperfection
and injustice of earthly laws, their pettiness and futility,
have been counterpointed against God's serene government
of the universe. The only point at which they have cor-
responded is in their mutual insistence on the evanescence
of this world, a fact that renders earthly laws by their own
decree absurd:

> The Laws of God, as well as of the Land,
> Abhor, a *Perpetuity* should stand.
>
> (246–47)

The particular Law of God referred to in this case I take to
be Leviticus 25: 23:

[143]

> The land shall not be sold for ever: for the land is mine; for
> ye are strangers and sojourners with me.

The commentators explain this passage in a manner quite
appropriate to Pope's present theme. God, they pointed out,
is the Lord of all things, and man has use of them only for
his lifetime: in effect, a capsule version of the poem's theme
of God's *dominium* and man's temporary *usufructus*.[20] The
very fact that a perpetuity cannot stand has been the moti-
vating force behind the entire epistle: the imposition of
impermanence as the condition of man's existence in the
world has forced Pope to expand his field of vision and to
seek after enduring laws and those lands in which he will be
more than a mere stranger and sojourner. Such ideas naturally culminate in the metaphor of the passage that concludes this whole section of the *confirmatio*, wherein man's
condition in the world is expressed in terms of the Christian
symbol of the body as the bark or ship of the soul.[21] This
same passage serves Pope as a brief summation by permit-
ting him to announce his personal freedom from the domination of Fortune:

> What is't to me (a Passenger God wot)
> Whether my Vessel be first-rate or not?
> The Ship itself may make a better figure,
> But I that sail, am neither less nor bigger.
> I neither strut with ev'ry fav'ring breath,
> Nor strive with all the Tempest in my teeth.
> In Pow'r, Wit, Figure, Virtue, Fortune, plac'd
> Behind the foremost, and before the last.
>
> (293–303)

This quest for permanence explains the poem's concern
with imminent and unavoidable death and with prepared-
ness for it; for Christians, final stability is attainable only
after death. This idea returns the poem to some of its very
first considerations, and resumes finally the thread of argu-

ment that was hinted in Pope's "Nay worse, to ask for Verse at such a Time!/ D'ye think me good for nothing but to rhime" (31–32). Everything in the epistle up to this point has been a prelude to this: the insufficiency of earthly laws, the impossibility of earthly permanence, the discernment of the government of God in the universe—all have led naturally to the idea of a holy preparation for death, and all are appropriately subsumed into that theme. Pope is carefully exploiting for poetic purposes the basic materials of the *ars moriendi* tradition, an almost codified formulation of the preparations for death.[22]

The major points of this pattern are easily discernible in the conclusion of Pope's Imitation. His insistence on the transience of human things has led him inevitably to consideration of his own death: the reference to his heir (286) makes clear that this is his concern. Throughout most of the poem, he has sought to show the instability and untrustworthiness of man's life in the world; and, in the later part of the poem especially, he has labored to dispel the false attractions of temporal objects. This in itself constitutes the dissuasion from avarice that looms so large in *ars moriendi* tradition, and it is formally identified as such by the poem's interlocutor: "But why all this of Av'rice? I have none" (304). Immediately after this, Pope launches a volley of questions that combine the interests of the remaining four temptations with the interrogations on points of faith and confession of sins.

> I wish you joy, Sir, of a Tyrant gone;
> But does no other lord it at this hour,
> As wild and mad? the Avarice of Pow'r?
> Does neither Rage inflame, nor Fear appall?
> Not the black Fear of Death, that saddens all?
> With Terrors round can Reason hold her throne,
> Despise the known, nor tremble at th' unknown?
> Survey both Worlds, intrepid and entire,
> In spight of Witches, Devils, Dreams, and Fire?

[145]

> Pleas'd to look forward, pleas'd to look behind,
> And count each Birth-day with a grateful mind?
> Has Life no sourness, drawn so near its end?
> Can'st thou endure a Foe, forgive a Friend?
> Has Age but melted the rough parts away,
> As Winter-fruits grow mild e'er they decay?
> Or will you think, my Friend, your business done,
> When, of a hundred thorns, you pull out one?
>
> (305–21)

And the last verse paragraph of the poem corresponds quite closely to the *ars moriendi* pattern's final injunctions about personal conduct, even down to the specific advice to make a will:

> Learn to live well, or fairly make your Will;
> You've play'd, and lov'd, and eat, and drank your fill:
> Walk sober off; before a sprightlier Age
> Comes titt'ring on, and shoves you from the stage:
> Leave such to trifle with more grace and ease,
> Whom Folly pleases, and whose Follies please.
>
> (322–27)

These two sections also serve as the final rhetorical divisions of the epistle. The series of questions and counterquestions (304–21) forms a succinct and effective *refutatio* that anticipates and silences the auditor's possible objections to Pope's thesis. The brief *peroratio* (322–27) follows, bringing the poem's legal theme to its inevitable close in the advice to "fairly make your Will" (322) and concluding the whole epistle with the omnipresent and ever-ambiguous concept of grace (326–27). These last lines in particular gather great strength and solemnity from their correspondence to the final steps of the *ars moriendi* tradition's preparations for death. They are the inescapable conclusion of the poem's emphasis on time; they expand the theme of law and judgment to that ultimate law and final judgment that await dying man. Beyond the art of poetry lay the art of life, both in their perfection embodying that rule and measure, that balance and harmony, which transcend and finally absorb them. Now, at the very last, Pope—man—must abandon both in the face of universal concord and the justice he has longed for.

1. The distribution of the index guides to the Latin and English texts bears this out: the relationships indicated are almost entirely between whole paragraphs of verse rather than between individual lines and phrases.

2. See, for instance, Thomas Aquinas, *Summa Theologica*, II.II.q.66.a.1 and II.II.q.141.a.6. Pope utilizes these and similar ideas intensively in his Imitation of Ep.I.vi and his Paraphrase of Sat.II.ii.

3. Most succinctly stated in Lucretius' *De Rerum Natura* (Dryden's translation), III.971:

> For life is not confin'd to him or thee;
> 'Tis giv'n to all for use; to none for Property.

For a typical discussion of this idea, see the lengthy article on *Possessio* in Jean Pontas' *Dictionarium Casuum Conscientiae* (Venice, 1757), III, 91–98.

4. Built around these four fables is the standard rhetorical structure of the epistle. The first fable and its application (1–32) constitute the *exordium*; they introduce the general theme of worldiness and hint at its opposite, retirement. The second fable and its accompanying application (33–72) comprise the *narratio* and *partitio* of the epistle, introducing into the poem the themes of temperance and Fortune, and dividing its interests in two by the bifurcation of Pope's education into the art of poetry and the art of life (with the implied correspondence of those two arts to the active and contemplative lives.) The first part of the *confirmatio* tallies with the first division: it discusses the craft of poetry and associates it with worldly pursuits and the limitations of time and death. The second part of the *confirmatio* extends from line 180 to line 303, and is concerned with Pope's mastering of the rules of life and preparing for the end of his mortal career. From line 304 to the end is the poem's *refutatio* and *peroratio*.

5. Here is his note in its entirety: "*But sure no statute*] Alluding to the statutes made in England and Ireland, to regulate the Succession of Papists, *etc.*" Many of Warburton's notes of this poem call attention to its legal theme and to the important changes Pope has made from his Horatian original. By and large, that much maligned editor's observations show a perceptivity and awareness of Pope's design that belies his reputation for obtuseness.

6. This allusion was first noted by Wakefield, and is contained in the annotations of the TE.

7. See also the accounts of the raising of the daughter of Jairus, Mat. 9:24-25, Mark 5:39-42, and Luke 8:52-55.

8. See Wasserman's explanation of Pope's use of the Thames and of the myth of Lodona, *Subtler Language*, pp. 163–68. Interesting precedents for such conceptualization of rivers can be found, of course, in Denham's *Cooper's Hill*, in Spenser's fable of the marriage of the Thames and the Medway (*FQ*, IV.xi), and in the marriage of the Mulla and Allo in *Colin Clouts Come Home Again* (104–55).

9. Desprez cites the *Ars Poetica* passage in connection with lines 115 and 119 (p. 595), and Dacier mentions it in connection with line 119 (VII, 480–81).

10. Creech, *The Odes, Satyrs, and Epistles of Horace*, p. 550.

11. See below, p. 137.

12. See, for instance, Cornelius à Lapide, pt. VII, pp. 50–51 and Matthew Poole, II, col. 1819, for interpretations of this particular pronouncement. It is again interesting to note, as a further indication of the potential interconnections that the Renaissance recognized between the ideas that Pope is here working with, that Cornelius here quotes several lines from the *Ars Poetica* passage that Pope has incorporated into his poem, for the purpose of proving the inevitability of common mortality. Page 2 of his volume also gives a general statement of the argument of the whole of Ecclesiastes: earthly affairs are vain, and man must turn to the spiritual for the permanent and true.

13. Cf. the Lord of the opening section (14), the Lords of the London passage (96 and 106); the Patriot Lord (185); the "most dirty Duke" (222); the "Lords of fat E'sham" (241) who claim to own "Half that the Dev'l o'erlooks from Lincoln Town" (245); Bathurst himself and his worldly accomplishments (256–63), and finally the avarice that becomes a tyrant and "lord[s] it" (305–6).

14. For the peculiar importance of this tradition to Pope, see Röstvig, II, 223–28. Miss Röstvig's two volumes on the metamorphoses of this theme in English literature are invaluable, and my conclusions here are based primarily on her findings.

15. Noted by Butt, TE, IV, 169.

16. The commentator was the scholiast Porphyrion (in Landino's edition, p. 263ᵛ).

17. An ambiguity about the word "grace," an ever-present pun on its social and theological senses, has reticulated itself throughout the poem: see lines 18, 21, 88, 162, 221, 286, and 326.

18. Papists were forbidden to reside within ten miles of London or Westminster.

19. *Essay on Man*, II.204. My discussion of the Ruling Passion is drawn primarily from *Essay on Man*, II.133–248.

20. See Cornelius à Lapide, pt. I, p. 750. Cornelius also quotes a passage from Philo that enumerates the gifts of Fortune and urges independence of them.

21. The bark of the soul is ubiquitous in Christian iconology and literature, but a handy condensation of its significance can be found in Michael Lloyd's "The Fatal Bark," *MLN*, LXXV (1960), 102–8, and in D. C. Allan's "Donne and the Ship Metaphor," *MLN*, LXXVI (1961), 308–12. It is important to note at this point that the corresponding lines of Horace's

poem (199–202) occur in Van Veen's *Emblemata Horatiana* (p. 92) accompanied by the following verses:

> La vie cachée est la meilleure.
> Cesse de te ronger des soins ambitieux;
> Foule aux pieds les grandeurs qu'en vain tu te proposes:
> Vi pauvre, mais content. Ceux-la sont presque Dieux
> Qui n'ont besoin d'aucunes choses.

The associations are obviously with the temperate, retired life, which is one of the aspects of this poem that Pope has chosen to exploit; it appears once again that he is working with familiar materials in a manner well known to his audience.

22. This tradition was occasionally utilized in literary works before Pope: see Kathrine Koller, "Falstaff and the Art of Dying," *MLN*, LX (1945), 383–86, and B. Langston, "Marlowe's Faustus and the Ars moriendi Tradition" (in *A Tribute to George C. Taylor* [Chapel Hill, 1952]). For information about the *ars moriendi* tradition, see Sister Mary C. O'Connor, *The Art of Dying Well: The Development of the Ars moriendi* (New York, 1942), esp. pp. 24–41. I have also made use of Miss Koller's convenient summary, *op. cit.*, pp. 384–85. The pattern is essentially as follows: consideration of the nature of death and fortitude in the face of it are urged; the five temptations that assail the dying man—disbelief, despair, impatience, pride, and avarice (which stands for all wordly appetite)—are examined so that they may be withstood; the dying man is questioned about points of faith and about a confession of sins, and finally is given positive instructions as to prayers, worship, and the making of his will. The most significant features of this pattern were identical for Catholics and Protestants alike.

Chapter V

Human Maker and Divine:
The First Epistle of the First Book of Horace, Imitated

HORACE'S first epistle is a clever protest to his friend and patron, Maecaenas, to explain why he no longer has time for poetry. With characteristic good humor, he points out that he is too old for such trifles; his time must now be spent on the far more important pursuit of truth—"Quid verum atque decens, curo & rogo, & omnis in hoc sum" (11). In the Renaissance, this noble aim won almost universal praise for Horace's poem. Christoforo Landino, for instance, takes this epistle as the occasion for an effusive dedication to Guido Feltri, in the course of which he praises philosophy and wisdom, links Horace's name with such figures as Socrates, Orpheus, and Amphion, and extravagantly lauds him as a great teacher and the wisest of poets—"omnium poetarum sapientissimum." [1] Badius Ascensius introduces the epistle by stating that in it Horace urges the pursuit of virtue and holy wisdom ("sapienta sancta"); that is, what pertains to decent actions and a holy life. [2] Such criticisms as these are the spiritual parents of Pope's poem. Horace had to depend for the formulation of his ethical norms on reason alone; Pope had both reason and faith—more specifically, in the case of this Imitation, he had both Horace and the Bible, and a commentary tradition, culminating in Dacier, that united the two.

Dacier's commentary may be viewed as the end product of the entire Renaissance effort to understand and assimilate the art of ancient Rome. Pope's reliance on it here, [3] his exploitation of its ideas, places him directly in the main channel of Renaissance thought and makes of this Imitation not only a brilliant poem but a major statement of that culture's view of the role of poets and poetry.

At the center of the poem lies the core conception of the religion of avarice, a worldly belief that detail by detail parodies orthodox Christianity. Enveloping this are the presence and persona of Pope as true poet and true Christian, now bidding farewell to that perverse world, preparing himself for death and judgment, and, under the guidance of Wisdom, adding the final touches to his last and best work, his own soul. The poem progresses from the carnality of the worldly to the spirituality of those "whom Wisdom calls her own," and closes with the merging of human and divine creators.

I

Horace's valediction to trifles becomes in Pope's hands a careful assessment of, and farewell to, a world inhospitable to virtue and to poets. The poem's *partitio* indicates clearly the direction the body of the epistle is going to take. Its subject matter is sin, its recognition and its cure.

> Say, does thy blood rebel, thy bosom move
> With wretched Av'rice, or as wretched Love?
> Know, there are Words, and Spells, which can controll
> (Between the Fits) this Fever of the soul:
> Know, there are Rhymes, which (fresh and fresh apply'd)
> Will cure the arrant'st Puppy of his Pride.
> Be furious, envious, slothful, mad or drunk,
> Slave to a Wife or Vassal to a Punk,
> A Switz, a High-dutch, or a Low-dutch Bear—
> All that we ask is but a patient Ear.
>
> (55–64)

The passage catalogues all seven of the deadly sins— pride, anger, lust, envy, gluttony, sloth, and avarice. The corresponding Horatian passage (32–40) contains the same list, which had been traditionally recognized as the counterpart of the Christian deadly sins;[4] Ascensius, for example, notes simply and tersely that they are "septem peccata mortalia."[5] The first listed sin, avarice, is the subject of Pope's attention in this epistle. As in previous poems, it becomes symbolic of all earthly desire and representative of all sin. Pope is on sound theological ground in attributing such importance to avarice; there is a divergent tradition that viewed it rather than pride as the chief of deadly sins,[6] and Pope appears to be manipulating that body of opinion for his own ends in this epistle.

This same section not only proposes the poem's theme, but it also singles out the person who is to be the exponent of the sin of avarice. Pope has by means of his index guides linked Horace's *Amator* (38) with "Slave to a Wife or Vassal to a Punk" (62)—both of which characters fit George II precisely. Queen Caroline's ascendency over her husband was common knowledge, and provided much political fodder for the opposition.[7] Equally notorious was George's infatuation for Madame de Walmoden, with whom he spent several politically costly months in 1737. Pope has slyly hit at this peccadillo earlier in the poem; he has carefully altered the gender of the betrayed in the line "Long as the Night to her whose love's away" (36) so that it points to Caroline and her erring husband rather than to Horace's generalized and male lovers (20). Lest there be any doubt at whom Pope is here directing his satire, the concluding nationality of the very next line unequivocally fixes the barb to George: "A Switz, a High-dutch, or a Low-dutch Bear" (63). The linking (by means of the index guides) of this last phrase with Horace's emphatic "Nemo adeo ferus" (39) places it beyond all question that George is the sinner intended. The coupling of avarice at the head of a list of the deadly sins and George II at its foot reveals that Pope is employing avarice as metaphor for all the sins, and his king as their prime human exponent. George's somewhat questionable political pre-eminence wins him a corresponding moral "bad eminence."

[153]

The process approximates that of the other Imitations in thereby equating political and moral offenses, and in viewing George as the appropriately sinful king of a worldly and avaricious society.

The central portion of Pope's poem is concerned with investigating and detailing the mores of the world governed by George II. It posits a strict opposition between the ideal life of wisdom and the practices of a people corrupted by greed.

> Here, Wisdom calls: "Seek Virtue first! be bold!
> "As Gold to Silver, Virtue is to Gold."
> There, London's voice: "Get Mony, Mony still!
> "And then let Virtue follow, if she will."
> This, this the saving doctrine, preach'd to all,
> From low St. James's up to high St. Paul;
> From him whose quills stand quiver'd at his ear,
> To him who notches Sticks at Westminster.
>
> (77–84)

This passage is typical of the poem's method and texture; its smooth and apparently straightforward surface statement is enriched and strengthened by its allusional content and by the commentary tradition that lies behind it. Its very first lines incorporate biblical references that expand the dichotomy far beyond the Roman poet's range and define Wisdom in a way far more significant than pagan prudential knowledge.

> Get Wisdom because it is better than gold: and purchase prudence, for it is more precious than silver. (Prov. 16:16)[8]

And again:

> Get wisdom, get understanding: forget it not; neither decline from the words of my mouth. Forsake her not, and she shall preserve thee: love her, and she shall keep thee. Wisdom is the principal thing; therefore get wisdom: and with all thy getting get understanding. (Prov. 4:5-7)

[154]

The specific mention of Wisdom, as well as Pope's obvious parody of the scriptural "Get wisdom, get understanding" in his "Get Mony, Mony still" (79), firmly secures the presence and effectiveness of the allusion.

The Wisdom in question is not merely the human attainment; rather it is that female figure (Sapientia, Sophia) who haunts the pages of the Old Testament, and whom the biblical commentators identified with the Son, the Logos, the second person of the Trinity. She represents, in one aspect, *Sapientia increata,* the indwelling wisdom of God, and in this guise she is equivalent to the Logos, the creating Word of God. In her other aspect, she apears as *Sapientia creata,* that ray of divine wisdom which is imparted to the faithful, and is so linked with Christ, the incarnate God-man. The wisdom she personifies is the specifically Christian knowledge that transcends the limited human wisdom of the pagans; she is the higher wisdom that Christ imparted to men, the wisdom that is attained only through the *imitatio Christi,* the conforming of oneself to the life of Christ. Wisdom is thus both a model and a goal for men. In life, she was to be formed in the soul as *Sapientia creata*; after death, she would be seen and comprehended in the beatific vision as *Sapientia increata.*[9] She is the spotless mirror of the *Fortescue,* of which Pope's life and art were partial reflections. Her overt presence in this poem provides a norm for judging the activities of the worldly that goes well beyond Horace's rational ethic and damns them far more completely. It calls into play one of the central metaphors of the poem, the opposition of spiritual and material wealth, and insures, by the simple strength of biblical authority, that the greedy citizens of London be recognized as totally depraved sinners, who have perversely chosen to gain the world and lose their souls. All this is the logical continuation of the moral stance implied in Pope's initial classification of their aberrations as sins rather than as breaches of decorum.

Once more, it is important to recognize that these are essentially commonplace ideas that Pope is dealing with, ideas that the eighteenth century felt entirely congruent to its conception of Horace. Dacier's commentary is at this point especially relevant; he makes the same distinction Pope makes, in almost the same terms that Pope uses, and in addition provides the biblical parallel that the English poet incorporates.

> Vilius argentum est auro, virtutibus aurum] C'est ce que la Sagesse crie aux hommes: Vous courez les mers pour gagner de l'or & de l'argent, & vous ne voulez rien faire pour acquerir la vertu; cependant la vertu est plus precieuse que tout l'argent & que tout l'or du monde. C'est que Salomon dit dans le même sens, & en suivant la même figure: *Melior est acquisitio ejus negotione argenti & auri primi & purissimi; fructus ejus pretiosior est cunctis opibus, & omnia quae desiderantur huic non valent comparari.* "L'acquisition de la sagesse est meilleure que tout l'or & l'argent que l'on gagne dans de commerce; ses fruits sont plus utiles & plus purs, elle est plus precieuse que toutes les richesses: & tout ce qui peut être l'objet des desirs des hommes ne fauroit lui être comparé."
>
> O cives, cives, quaerenda pecunia primum est] si la Sagesse crie d'un côté aux hommes, *la vertu vaut mieux que l'or;* la Folie leur crie d'un autre côté, *l'or vaut mieux que la vertu.* Et comme la Sagesse est seule, & que la Folie a toûjours après elle une foule de gens qui repetent ce qu'elle dit, il ne faut pas s'étonner si la voix de la premiere n'est pas entenduë, & si celle de l'autre est suivie. Tout ce passage est fort beau, mais le tour, qui en est fort brusque, a été cause qu'on ne l'avoit pas bien éclairci.[10]

Dacier's opposing voices are Wisdom and Folly, Pope's are Wisdom and London; but they amount to the same thing, and what they are respectively urging is identical. The savant's mention of *la Sagesse* and his citing of the passage from Scripture bring to bear upon Horace's poem the very same ideas about Wisdom that Pope calls into play in his own epistle. There can be no doubt about the nature of the Wisdom to which Dacier refers; in an earlier note, he has already identified her as "l'esprit de Dieu."[11] She is unquestionably the same figure in exactly the same guise that she

wears in Pope's Imitation. The biblical exegetes provide even
further evidence of the eighteenth century's readiness to
view Horace in this specifically Christian light, and of the
traditional nature of the concepts Pope is employing. Cornelius à Lapide, in his commentary on the biblical pasages
Pope utilizes, contrasts their counsels with the worldly-
minded of whom Horace speaks, and quotes directly the pertinent lines—"quaerenda Pecunia primum est,/ Virtus post
nummos."[12] The Protestant commentator Matthew Poole
makes exactly the same association and quotes the same
Horatian lines.[13]

The presence of the Wisdom figure and the ideas she
personifies provides Pope's poem with the stable point necessary on which to turn a neat and logical inversion. If to
heed Wisdom's voice, to assimilate oneself to her, is the
proper duty of a Christian, then those who choose to follow
the opposite, London's way, are not merely un-Christian,
but arrantly anti-Christian. This conception informs Pope's
entire treatment of the avaricious. They are all seen within
the context of a coherently developed antireligion that per-
verts point by point the tenets of orthodox Christianity.
The beginnings of this pattern may be seen even in the cataloguing of George II as an eighth deadly sin; instead of
kingship by divine right, he seems to hold his crown by some
sort of diabolical succession. So it is in this section of the
poem, where London's advice is pointedly opposed to divine
Wisdom's and revealed as a complete inversion of the
scriptural counsel, that the sources of that corruption are
closely associated with the court—"From low St. James up
to high St. Paul;/ . . . /To him who notches Sticks at
Westminster" (82–84). And to describe that corruption
itself, Pope ironically borrows terminology from orthodox
religion; it becomes a "saving doctrine, preach'd to all" (81),
yet another inversion of the proper pattern of salvation. It
seems even, by its inclusion of St. James and St. Paul, to pervert the doctrinal content of the New Testament epistles.
Of a piece with all this is the fact that all three indicated loci

[157]

in the paragraph not only link this inversion to the court, but further show its extent in that they also have orthodox religious connotations, either by name or by past or present function.[14]

This conception is further elaborated by the succeeding verse paragraphs, and additional details of the extent and nature of the process of inversion are given.

> BARNARD in spirit, sense, and truth abounds.
> "Pray then what wants he?" fourscore thousand pounds,
> A Pension, or such a Harness for a slave
> As Bug now has, and Dorimant would have.
> BARNARD, thou art a *Cit,* with all thy worth;
> But wretched Bug, his *Honour,* and so forth.
>   Yet every child another song will sing,
> "Virtue, brave boys! 'tis Virtue makes a King."
> True, conscious Honour is to feel no sin,
> He's arm'd without that's innocent within;
> Be this thy Screen, and this thy Wall of Brass;
> Compar'd to this, a Minister's an Ass.
>   And say, to which shall our applause belong,
> This new Court jargon, or the good old song?
> The modern language of corrupted Peers,
> Or what was spoke at CRESSY and POITIERS?
>
> (85–100)

Pope's satiric assault is now continued against the court by name rather than by intimation. The virtuous king of the children's song (92) stands out in glaring contrast to the actual king of England and his sinful affiliations. The same is true of the perverse "Honour" of "wretched Bug" (90), which amounts to the complete antithesis of "True, conscious Honour" (93); the adjective that describes Bug links him succinctly with the "wretched Av'rice" (56) that is the root of all this sin. The honest song of the children (and the "song" that is Pope's poem?) is further contrasted with what had been previously named "London's voice" (79),

[158]

and is now recognized as "The modern language of corrupted Peers" (99). England's political corruption is revealed by the difference between that speech and "what was spoke at CRESSY and POITIERS" (100). George's reign and Walpole's controversial peace policies show but poorly alongside the victories of England's hero kings. Pope's own attitude toward Henry V and Edward III is made clear in his *Epistle to Augustus*, where George is ironically declared their superior.

> Edward and Henry, now the Boast of Fame,
> And virtuous Alfred, a more sacred Name,
> After a Life of Gen'rous Toils endur'd,
> The Gaul subdu'd, or Property secur'd,
> Ambition humbled, mighty Cities storm'd,
> Or Laws establish'd, and the World Reform'd;
> Clos'd their long Glories with a sigh, to find
> Th' unwilling Gratitude of base mankind!
>
> (7–14)

Edward and Henry had connotations for the political battles of the 1730's that make their presence here extremely telling. In contrast to opposition charges that George was a tyrant, Edward and Henry were held up as careful protectors of English freedoms and rights.[15] By calling attention to them here, Pope has once again invoked his persistent equation of moral and political offense, and shown that George's inversion of orthodox religion and the king's divine commission is paralleled by his destruction of traditional English liberties. It is for this very reason that Bug is pictured as possessing a "Harness for a Slave" (87); under a tyrant king, all Englishmen are slaves.

Naturally enough, other prominent members of the government of which George is the spiritual head are also allotted their share of the satire. Walpole particularly is singled out for censure; the mention of minister, the easily made Wall-Walpole pun, and particularly the use of the word

[159]

"Screen" (95), all point directly to the chief functionary of George's government. In the opposition press, Walpole was frequently saddled with the charge of protecting or screening those involved in public swindles, particularly with regard to the abortive attempt to investigate the doings of the South Sea Company.[16] This and Walpole's notorious practice of bribery have obvious relation to the poem's insistence upon avarice as the besetting sin of England and upon George's court as the source of it. Sir Robert's unconcealed and often unashamed actions in these and similar matters are more than sufficient to warrant a pun on "Wall of Brass" (95); his conduct was nothing if not brazen, and his protection depended on brass—money. More scathing satire than this, however, is called into play by those words. Just as George is the antithesis of a virtuous and divinely ordained king, Walpole is the complete perversion of a holy and divinely ordained minister. Pope's adaptation of Horace's "murus aheneus" (57) incorporates the correspondence between that phrase and an identical one in Scripture—a correspondence that, once again, the biblical commentators both recognized and noted:

> For behold I have made thee this day a fortified city and a pillar of iron and a wall of brass, over all the land, to the kings of Juda, to the princes thereof and to the priests and to the people of the land. (Jer. 1:18)[17]

As Jeremiah was the God-appointed prophet and minister to the king and people of Judah, so Walpole, in the world-turned-upside-down that Pope has delineated, is the diabolical prophet and minister to the sinful king and people of England. By virtue of the biblical allusion, Walpole is revealed to be the anti-prophet of an anti-king in an anti-Christian society; he is dedicated to preaching the doctrine of avarice rather than the counsel of Wisdom. This is why his protection is so pointedly contrasted with the innocence of those who "feel no sin" (93). The words of the scriptural passage are God's announcement to Jeremiah of his destined mission; the words of Pope's epistle are his description of Walpole's evil task in a degenerate England.

The same sort of gross inversion takes place in the verse paragraph that treats of Barnard and "wretched Bug" (90). Such commentators as Landino had taught the Renaissance to see in Horace's listing of *animus, mores, lingua,* and *fides,* (54) the possession of *sapientia* and *virtutes morales.*[18] Pope's translation of these as "spirit, sense, and truth" (85) seems to owe its wording to Christ's prediction that "the true worshippers shall worship the Father in spirit and in truth" (John 4: 23), which exegetes are unanimous in judging to be the essence of proper devotion to God.[19] Barnard, although abounding in these virtues, simply because he lacks the money necessary to buy respect and place, is doomed to be a vulgar "*Cit*" (89), while Bug is deemed "his *Honour,* and so forth" (90). In the world's view, true worship and true worth are not simply insufficient; they are nothing at all. Money is the measure of all things, and honor follows it, even to ornament "such a Harness for a slave/As Bug now has" (87-88). A materialistic England consistently follows its own sinful will in preferring mere riches to spiritual and moral wealth.

Pope's satiric attack on George and the court culminates in a fierce and explicit denunciation of both as the epitome of evil.

> Who counsels best? who whispers, "Be but Great,
> "With Praise or Infamy, leave that to fate;
> "Get Place and Wealth, if possible, with Grace;
> "If not, by any means get Wealth and Place."
> For what? to have a Box where Eunuchs sing,
> And foremost in the Circle eye a King.
> Or he, who bids thee face with steddy view
> Proud Fortune, and look shallow Greatness thro':
> And, while he bids thee, sets th' Example too?
> If such a Doctrine, in St. James's air,
> Shou'd chance to make the well-drest Rabble stare;

If honest S*z take scandal at a spark,
That less admires the Palace than the Park;
Faith I shall give the answer Reynard gave,
"I cannot like, Dread Sir! your Royal Cave;
"Because I see by all the Tracks about,
"Full many a Beast goes in, but none comes out."
Adieu to Virtue if you're once a Slave:
Send her to Court, you send her to her Grave.

(101–19)

The court is the grave of virtue. What should be God's ordained king is a beast who devours the virtuous and makes
of his depraved followers slaves of the order of Bug—whose
name, like the metaphor "lion" applied to George, indicates
his fall from the human to the animal. In point of fact,
George and Bug are even more closely linked by Pope's
Bear-bugbear-Bug pun, which extends over some twenty
lines of the poem. George is initially referred to as "a Low-
dutch Bear" (63); shortly after this, while pointing out
which constitutes the greatest offense in the eyes of the
world, Pope phrases it so:

But to the world, no bugbear is so great,
As want of figure, and a small Estate.

(67–68)

I would suggest that the specific "bugbear" referred to
here is once again George II; "want of figure" captures
exactly George's own corpulence, and the "small Estate"
in question characterizes Hanover nicely, particularly since,
in 1737–38, George's partiality for that duchy made it quite
a formidable bugbear for the English portion of the world.[20]
    Pope's theological punning on the words "Grace" (103),
"scandal" (112), and "Doctrine" (110) exploits the implications of the antireligion he has posited. The inversion
is made apparent by the fact that the proper doctrine of
temperance and freedom from thralldom to the world gives

"scandal" to an ironically "honest S*z" (112), whose position as Keeper of the Privy Purse would naturally render him one of the most influential promulgators of the avaricious gospel of George and Walpole. Even the goal of all this sinful striving, "to have a Box where Eunuchs sing,/ And foremost in the Circle eye a King" (105–6), reflects far more than Pope's simple conviction that opera is a degenerate art form. Given the terms of the inverted religion, these lines imply a gross parody of the orthodox Christian's final reward, the vision of the harmony of the heavenly king. The idea is, of course, a homiletic commonplace, but perhaps Milton's poetic formulation of it is most pertinent:

> Speak yee who best can tell, ye Sons of Light,
> Angels, for yee behold him, and with songs
> And chorale symphonies, Day without Night,
> Circle his Throne rejoicing, yee in Heav'n;
> On Earth join all ye Creatures to extol
> Him first, him last, him midst, and without end.
>
> (*PL*, V. 160–65)

And, from Milton again, the Son's words to the Father:

> Then shall thy Saints unmixt, and from th' impure
> Far separate, circling thy holy Mount
> Unfeigned *Halleluiahs* to thee sing,
> Hymns of high praise, and I among them chief.
>
> (*PL*, VI. 742–45)

Such a reference appears all the more possible in the light of Christ's own contrasting of the "eunuchs, which were made eunuchs of men" with those "which have made themselves eunuchs for the kingdom of heaven's sake" (Mat. 19:12). Pope's *castrati* are obviously of the first sort, as is everyone else who is in any way connected with the Hanoverian court; they are thus appropriately contrasted

[163]

with the wise man who, recalling the lessons taught Boethius
by his Lady Philosophy, rejects the false values of the
world and "bids thee face with steddy view/ Proud Fortune,
and look shallow Greatness thro'" (107–8). Pope's personal repudiation of the ways of the court cleverly turns
his exclusion from Queen Caroline's Merlin's Cave into a
voluntary escape from the lair of the king of beasts and
into a consequently virtuous quest for wisdom (115–19).

Having thus categorically disposed of the source of England's corruption and perversion, Pope is now free to turn
his attention to the recipients of it, the English public:

> Well, if a King's a Lion, at the least
> The People are a many-headed Beast:
> Can they direct what measures to pursue,
> Who know themselves so little what to do?
> Alike in nothing but one Lust of Gold,
> Just half the land would buy, and half be sold:
> Their Country's wealth our mightier Misers drain
> Or cross, to plunder Provinces, the Main:
> The rest, some farm the Poor-box, some the Pews;
> Some keep Assemblies, and wou'd keep the Stews;
> Some with fat Bucks on childless Dotards fawn;
> Some win rich Widows by their Chine and Brawn;
> While with the silent growth of ten per Cent,
> In Dirt and darkness hundreds stink content.
>
> (120–33)

The distinction between ruler and ruled does not exist in
Horace's poem; his diatribe is against a generalized "Populus
Romanus" (67), and the section (73–77) that corresponds
to the lines quoted from Pope is merely a continuation
of it. The separation of the government from the people
is directly traceable to the commentators' expansions:

Olim quod vulpes aegroto cauta leoni] . . . L'application
qu'Horace fait de cette fable est très-ingenieuse et très-
solide. Le Lion c'est la Republique, & le Gouvernement;

[164]

les animaux ce sont les particuliers; le Renard c'est le Sage. Le peuple se laisse étourdir par les grandes promesses qu'on lui fait de le rendre heureux, & il croit que les richesses & les honneurs font le souverain bien de l'homme; il suit donc ces faux biens, & neglige le veritable; mais la fin de cela est qu'il se trouve dans abime de maux dont il ne sauroit plus se retirer.[21]

Pope has followed this distinction and its logical consequent in Dacier's succeeding note[22] by making George the lion and the people the many-headed beast. These metaphors further associate them quite specifically with George's sinful character; the "many-headed Beast" that they are described as inescapably links them with the apocalyptical beast with many heads:

And I stood upon the sand of the sea, and saw a beast rise up out of the sea, having seven heads and ten horns, and upon his horns ten crowns, and upon his heads the name of blasphemy. And the beast which I saw was like unto a leopard, and his feet were as the feet of a bear, and his mouth as the mouth of a lion: and the dragon gave him his power, and his seat, and great authority. (Rev. 13:1-2).

The image is a conventional one, and had been similarly used by many poets and pamphleteers before Pope. He himself had previously, and more explicitly, so characterized the mob in his *Epistle to Augustus*:

> There still remains to mortify a Wit,
> The many-headed Monster of Pit.
>
> . . . .
>
> While all its throats the Gallery extends,
> And all the Thunder of the Pit ascends!
>
> (304-5; 326-27)

This satanic beast is associated with George qua devil not only through its possession of aspects of both bear and lion but also through such other biblical images as the

[165]

Petrine "devil, as a roaring lion . . . seeking whom he may
devour" (Peter 5:8)—which, of course, has been precisely
George's role in lines 115–18 of the poem. George and his
subjects are united even more definitively in their diabolical
natures by the exegetes' interpretation of the beast's seven
heads as symbolizing the seven deadly sins.[23] Just as George
was earlier described as the epitome and exponent of those
vices, so now the people, in an ever-widening circle of
corruption, assume that same role, and with it its consequent guilt and apostasy. Like George, they too become
primarily characterized by avarice: "Alike in nothing but
one Lust of Gold" (124). Within the confines of that one
representative vice, they are depicted, as are all of Pope's
sinners, as the exemplification of total discord by the
divergence of their pursuits, a fact that is emphasized by
Pope's careful repetition of the word "some" with varying
verbs (128–31). Warburton's note provides the key to the
political corruption that consistently accompanies this moral
degeneracy:

> *Their Country's wealth our mightier Misers drain,*] The
> undertakers for advancing Loans to the Public on the Funds.
> They have been commonly accused of making it a job. But
> in so corrupt times, the fault is not always to be imputed to
> a Ministry: it having been found, on trial, that the wisest
> and most virtuous citizen of this or any other age, with every
> requisite talent in such matters, and supported by all the
> weight an honest Administration could afford him, was, they
> say, unable to abolish this inveterate mystery of iniquity.[24]

The remainder of the paragraph employs a familiar Popean
technique; it forms a scale of increasing depravity, starting
with the materialism and immorality of those who "wou'd
keep the Stews" (129), proceeding on to the corporeality
of those who "with fat Bucks on childless Dotards fawn"
(130) and the literal flesh-trading of those who "win rich
Widows by their Chine and Brawn" (131), to end in the
fungous insensibility of sinners who "In Dirt and darkness

. . . stink content" (133). All these are the chaotically confused citizens of England whose opinions Pope must reject because they "know themselves so little what to do" (123).

The next verse paragraph develops all these ideas even further through an elaborate satiric inversion of the scriptural Job:

> Of all these ways, if each pursues his own,
> Satire be kind, and let the wretch alone.
> But show me one, who has it in his pow'r
> To act consistent with himself an hour.
> Sir Job sail'd forth, the evening bright and still,
> "No place on earth (he cry'd) like Greenwich hill!"
> Up starts a Palace, lo! th' obedient base
> Slopes at its foot, the woods its sides embrace,
> The silver Thames reflects its marble face.
> Now let some whimzy, or that Dev'l within
> Which guides all those who know not what they mean
> But give the Knight (or give his Lady) spleen;
> "Away, away! take all your scaffolds down,
> "For Snug's the word: My dear! we'll live in Town."
>
> (134-47)

Here, as in his other use of a satiric anti-Job figure in the *Epistle to Bathurst*, Pope is playing his satiric creation against the traditional image of Job. The Old Testament character had become almost identified with patience, charity, and contempt for wealth; in addition, he was one of the few Gentile worshippers of the true God.[25] Like Sir Balaam of the *Bathurst*, whom Satan "tempts by making rich, not making poor," Sir Job reverses the pattern of the biblical Job by allowing himself to be corrupted by wealth. He is a paradigm of the interior disharmony of the rich, a man who finds it impossible "to act consistent with himself an hour" (137). His changing fancy clashes tellingly with the steadfastness and patience of the biblical Job; like him,

[167]

Sir Job is described as a rich man (Horace's *Dives* [81]),
but the English sinner distinctly lacks the spiritual wealth
of the Old Testament saint. His corruption is mirrored not
only in his inconsistency but also in the fact that he aban-
dons the country ("Greenwich Hill" [139]) to "live in
Town" (147); in the light of Pope's exploitation of the
town-country opposition in his Imitation of Ep.II.ii, this
must be viewed as yet another in the series of sinful inversions of man's proper duties, the deliberate choice of
the occasion of maximum temptation and sin over the best
possible locus for proper cultivation of the soul. Pope carefully defines both the source and the nature of Sir Job's
perversion and discord (and, consequently, that of all the
poem's other sinners) in the triplet that describes his
motivation (143–45). The Horatian original of this is the
succinct "Cui si vitiosa Libido/ fecerit auspicium" (82–83),
and the commentaries on these lines are helpful in illumi-
nating Pope's adaptation:

> Cui si vitiosa libido fecerit auspicium] On ne sauroit trouver
> d'expression plus heureuse, ni qui contienne plus de sens &
> plus de raison. Mais il faut la bien faire entendre. *Vitiosa
> libido, un desir vicieux,* c'est-à-dire un desir corrompu, qui
> vient du caprice, du dégoût & du déreglement, & non pas de
> la necessité. Celui qui a ce desir, *laborat suo vitio,* & non pas
> *vitio rerum,* comme Horace s'explique dans la Satire II, du
> Livre I. Par exemple, ce Riche, dont il est ici question,
> cherche un beau lieu pour bâtir: on lui parle de Baïes, il est
> ravi: il va donc retressir la mer par les fondemens d'un Palais
> magnifique. Ces fondemens ne sont pas plûtôt jettez, que son
> inconstance & le déreglement de son esprit le portent à se
> dégoûter de la mer, & à souhaiter d'avoir dans la terre
> ferme. Voilà un desir vicieux, parce qu'il ne vient pas de la
> nature. Et comme tous les desirs, qui viennent de nôtre
> corruption, nous sont plus chers, & ont plus de force que ceux
> qu'excite la vertu, l'amour propre nous les déguise sous
> des apparences trompeuses, & nous leur obeïssons comme
> à une necessité, ou plûtôt comme à une autorité absoluë qui
> prend dans nôtre coeur la place de la Religion. C'est pourquoi

Horace dit, *fecerit auspicium,* que ces desirs corrumpus sont les auspices que suit cet inconstant, & qui reglent toute sa conduite. Ses desirs sont le Dieu auquel il obeït. Virgile, qui étoit aussi grand Philosophe que grand Poëte, a expliqué admirablement les deux principes de toutes nos actions, dans ces vers du IX. Livre de l'Eneïde, où Nisus dit:

> —*Diine hunc ardorem mentibus addunt,*
> *Euryale, an sua cuique Deus fit dira cupido?*

"Eurylus, sont-ce les Dieux qui nous inspirent cette ardeur? ou nos propres desirs prennent-ils dans nôtre coeur la place d'un Dieu"? [26]

Dacier thus identifies the action of Horace's *Dives* as a parody of religion, an immoral substitution of the dictates of his own will for the will of God. Pope's reference to "that Dev'l within" (143), which the index guides link with *vitiosa Libido* (82), shows that he is working in terms of the same conception; Sir Job is inspired by Satan rather than resisting his devices as did his biblical original; where the Gentile Job followed the true God, his English anti-type obeys Satan and falls into the idolatry of avarice. The extent of the perversion becomes clearer when the promptings of "that Dev'l within" are contrasted with the virtuous dictates of "That God of Nature, who, within us still,/ Inclines our Action, not constrains our Will" (Ep.II.ii., 280–81). God urges man toward stability; the world and the devil call him to multiplicity and confusion. Warburton's note on these lines enters into the spirit of the satire and ironically points out what Pope is doing by denying that he has done it:

> *Now let some whimsy, & c.*] This is very spirited, but much inferior to the elegance of the original,
>
> > Cui si vitiosa Libido
> > Fecerit auspicium
>
> which alluding to the religious manners of that time, no modern imitation can reach.[27]

[169]

Pope elaborates this inversion even beyond its explicit attribution to the devil. His very next line echoes Christ's last words and couples the avaricious with those who crucified him: "that Devil within/ Which guides all those who know not what they mean" (143–44). Their guiding principles flow from the same source, the Satan who was traditionally recognized as attempting to imitate God and who achieved only a grotesque parody of him. George and his subjects are the disciples of Satan, and their earthly kingdom is consequently in all points a travesty of God's spiritual dominion.

The final paragraph of the *confirmatio* adds one more element to the antireligion—a "martyr" (151) who is just as much an inversion as the "saving doctrine" of London— before going on to apply all of its previous charges to the poor:

> At am'rous Flavio is the Stocking thrown?
> That very night he longs to lye alone.
> The Fool whose Wife elopes some thrice a quarter,
> For matrimonial Solace dies a martyr.
> Did ever Proteus, Merlin, any Witch,
> Transform themselves so strangely as the Rich?
> "Well, but the Poor"—the Poor have the same itch:
> They change their weekly Barber, weekly News,
> Prefer a new Japanner to their shoes,
> Discharge their Garrets, move their Beds, and run
> (They know not whither) in a Chaise and one;
> They hire their Sculler, and when once abroad,
> Grow sick, and damn the Climate—like a Lord.
>
> (148-60)

All the inconsistency and discord of the rich are concentrated in the comparison of their actions to the transformations of "Proteus, Merlin, any Witch" (152): all three references agree in attributing their vagaries to satanic influence.[28] The final line of the triplet that contains this charge applies it *in toto* to the poor: "the Poor have the same itch" (154). The paragraph then goes on to catalogue their inconsistencies and disharmony and to link them morally with the anti-Christian wealthy by a mutation of Christ's words—"They know not whither" (158) they go. Just as the rich have substituted their own whims for God's law, so too the poor usurp God's final prerogative and take their own will for his judgment; they "damn . . . like a Lord" (160). The ambiguity of the final word is quite pertinent. The poor are like earthly lords in their sin and their discord; they are like them also in their identical attempt to emulate their heavenly lord in exercising absolute dominion in themselves. What they achieve is only a further elaboration of the already established satanic parody of God's order, which has been the central concern of the poem thus far.

All these various details of the anti-religion have been present in the poem by implication from the very first paragraph of the *confirmatio.*

> 'Tis the first Virtue, Vices to abhor ;
> And the first Wisdom, to be Fool no more.
> But to the world, no bugbear is so great,
> As want of figure, and a small Estate.
> To either India see the Merchant fly,
> Scar'd at the spectre of pale Poverty !
> See him, with pains of body, pangs of soul,
> Burn through the Tropic, freeze beneath the Pole !
> Wilt thou do nothing for a nobler end,
> Nothing, to make Philosophy thy friend ?
> To stop thy foolish views, thy long desires,
> And ease thy heart of all that it admires ?
>
> (65-76)

This passage obviously opposes the views of the world and those of Wisdom in exactly the same way that its successors contrast Wisdom's voice with London's.[29] In point of fact,

"Wisdom" (66) and "Philosophy" (74) here are probably the very same female figure that appears in lines 77–78; Lady Philosophy was but another one of her many guises.[30] Even beyond this, however, it is quite significant that Pope alters the tribulations of his greedy merchants from Horace's "Per mare . . . fugiens, per saxa, per ignes" (46) to the contents of his lines 71–72. "Pains of body, pangs of soul," burning and freezing—these summarize the punishments of hell in orthodox Christian tradition. Pope's argument appears to be equally orthodox; sinners constitute their own hell, and are able to make for themselves a hell on earth. Implied in this is the whole satanic inversion of heaven and heaven's rule that Milton has elaborated throughout *Paradise Lost* and that Pope here adapts to his own needs.

In the *Bolingbroke,* Pope has pictured his England as very nearly a miniature Inferno: the concentric rings of corruption spread outward from a vicious and devil-like king, through court and nobles, through rich and poor, to encompass the entire life of the nation. Beast-king, the incarnation of sin, rules the Hydra-mob. Against this stand only the calm disengagement of the *nil admirari* argument of this paragraph's last lines (75–76) and the saving counsels of Wisdom.

II

Pope himself appears in the poem as the embattled champion of those counsels, as a man struggling in a hostile world to form in himself the image of Wisdom. From the very beginning of the poem, he has opposed himself to the chaos of the Hanoverian world and has taken pains to specify the nature of the alternative he has chosen. The poem's *exordium* presents his general situation.

ST. JOHN, whose love indulg'd my labours past
Matures my present, and shall bound my last!
Why will you break the Sabbath of my days?
Now sick alike of Envy and of Praise.
Publick too long, ah let me hide my Age!
See modest Cibber now has left the Stage:
Our Gen'rals now, retir'd to their Estates,
Hang their old Trophies o'er the Garden gates,
In Life's cool evening satiate of applause,
Nor fond of bleeding, ev'n in BRUNSWICK's cause.
　　A voice there is, that whispers in my ear,
('Tis Reason's voice, which sometimes one can hear)
"Friend Pope! be prudent, let your Muse take breath,
"And never gallop Pegasus to death;
"Lest stiff, and stately, void of fire, or force,
"You limp, like Blackmore, on a Lord Mayor's horse."
　　Farewell then Verse, and Love, and ev'ry Toy,
The Rhymes and rattles of the Man or Boy:
What right, what true, what fit, we justly call,
Let this be all my care—for this is All:
To lay this harvest up, and hoard with haste
What ev'ry day will want, and most, the last.

(1-22)

In Horace's rendering, this epistle falls somewhere between the categories of praise of the retired, contemplative life and denunciation of materialistic values. In Pope's hands, these themes are basically unchanged, but they are substantially reoriented. This can be seen initially in the substitution of Bolingbroke, the self-exiled leader of the opposition, for Horace's Maecaenas, the firm adherent of the court and trusted friend of Augustus. Pope's work, as he defiantly asserts, has been and will continue to be produced under Bolingbroke's aegis; thus from the beginning he identifies his Imitation as an anticourt poem. This emphasis is lightly carried through the remainder of the

[173]

paragraph by a series of careful citations. Line 6 touches on "modest Cibber," George's laureate, and, as many of Pope's poems claim, the king in wit as he in state. The mention of English generals' "old Trophies" (8) is a none too subtle thrust at Walpole's peace policy; and the final, pointed mention of "BRUNSWICK's cause" (10) constitutes a direct slap at George's German origins and leanings. Lest the point of this last be missed, Warburton has appended a somewhat heavy-handed note calling attention to it:

> *ev'n in Brunswick's cause*] In the former Editions it was *Britain's cause*. But the terms are synonimous.[31]

Needless to say, very few Englishmen in the 1730's would have found either the names or the interests of Brunswick and Britain identical.

All this, however, is submerged beneath the overriding concern of this first paragraph, which is the idea of retirement, after a long and active life, to prepare for death. This emphasis is present in several places—"shall bound my last" (2), "the Sabbath of my days" (3), "retir'd" (7), "In Life's cool evening" (9)—but most explicitly in Pope's cry, "Publick too long, ah let me hide my Age" (5). His mention of "the Sabbath of my days" (3) is important both for the religious connotations of the Sabbath (traditionally and scripturally, of course, the day completely devoted to the worship of God) and for other implications that Warburton's note somewhat clarifies:

> *Sabbath of my days?*] i.e. The 49th year, the age of the Author.[32]

Warburton's remark is to be understood, I think, in the light of the doctrine of the climacteric years, the belief that man's life fell into crucial periods determined by multiples of seven and nine: the forty-ninth and the sixty-third years were the most dangerous, both physically and morally, since body and soul were then more susceptible to destruction through disease and through the agency of the passions.[33] Pope's concentration on the ideas of retirement and preparation for death takes on particular relevance when viewed from this standpoint and, linked with the Imitation's interest in the sin of avarice, fits the entire poem into the context of the *ars moriendi* pattern of holy preparation for death and judgment. The tension between Pope's desire for this quiet and Bolingbroke's implied request that he re-enter a Hanoverian world of political and moral corruption supplies the stimulus for the whole epistle.

The second paragraph then elaborates one half of this conflict by presenting Reason as the poet's counselor, urging him to abandon poetry and the active life for the sake of retirement and meditation (11–16). Pope remains strongly within the commentary tradition by identifying Horace's unnamed voice as Reason,[34] and at the same time introduces into his Imitation the personification who is in various manifestations (as Philosophy, as Wisdom) to embody the values he endorses. Her naming of Blackmore as the antithesis of proper poetic conduct serves as the poem's first identification of its villains with the Whig, mercantile, city interests, who will be characterized as the exponents of avarice. The contrast of Pope's "Pegasus" (140) with Blackmore's "Lord Mayor's horse" (16) is also the first indication of the poem's mode of argument, that overmuch attention to the active life is in itself almost sinful and leads inevitably to an inversion of the proper order of things, to the production of discord rather than harmony. Thus Blackmore's verse is described as discordant, "stiff, and stately, void of fire, or force" (15)—a fact that Pope's note emphasizes by paraphrasing his own line as "stiff, and not strong; stately and yet dull. . . . "[35]

The remainder of the exordium is devoted to summing up Pope's general position: he will abandon poetry and the other "rhymes and rattles" (18) of the active life, and devote himself to "What right, what true, what fit, we justly call" (19). Significantly, many commentators had identified the Horatian original of this line ("Quid verum atque decens" [11]) with moral philosophy and ethics, some even making the specific distinction between theory and practice with reference to the active and contemplative lives;[36] this provides a piece of background valuable for its indications of the already close association of Horace's poem with the ideas Pope grafts onto it. Pope's list of interests, however, seems to draw both its content and its relevance from a Pauline chapter that he employs again later in the epistle:

> Finally, brethren, whatsoever things are true, whatsoever things are honest, whatsoever things are just, whatsoever things are pure, whatsoever things are lovely, whatsoever things are of good report; if there be any virtue, and if there be any praise, think on these things. (Phil. 4:8)

But more important than this is Pope's expansion of Horace's simple statement of concern for the pursuit of philosophy into an elaborate harvest metaphor that draws upon what must be termed a scriptural commonplace. Here is a New Testament instance of it:

> And I will say to my soul, Soul, thou hast much goods laid up for many years; take thine ease, eat, drink, and be merry. But God said unto him, Thou fool, this night thy soul shall be required of thee: then whose shall those things be, which thou hast provided? So is he that layeth up treasure for himself, and is not rich toward God. (Luke 12:19-21) [37]

Pope's intention clearly, is to "hoard" that "harvest" (21) that will render him "rich toward God." The opposition between material and spiritual wealth presents the basic thematic conflict of the epistle, and links it closely with the *ars moriendi* tradition's resistance of the temptation to avarice, and with the general pattern and concern of that tradition, the eradication of earthly appetite and concentration on man's heavenly goal.

[176]

The poem's *narratio* (23–54) goes on from this point to explain Pope's specific circumstances and to indicate in greater detail his intentions.[38]

> Long, as to him who works for debt, the Day;
> Long as the Night to her whose love's away;
> Long as the Year's dull circle seems to run,
> When the brisk Minor pants for twenty-one;
> So slow th'unprofitable Moments roll,
> That lock up all the Functions of my soul;
> That keep me from Myself; and still delay
> Life's instant business to a future day:
> That task, which as we follow, or despise,
> The eldest is a fool, the youngest wise;
> Which done, the poorest can no wants endure,
> And which not done, the richest must be poor.
>   Late as it is, I put myself to school,
> And feel some comfort, not to be a fool.
> Weak tho' I am of limb, and short of sight,
> Far from a Lynx, and not a Giant quite,
> I'll do what MEAD and CHESELDEN advise,
> To keep these limbs, and to preserve these eyes.
> Not to go back, is somewhat to advance,
> And men must walk at least before they dance.
>
> (35-54)

Pope identifies his concern as an explicitly spiritual activity; he seeks to release and use "all the Functions of my soul" (40). He returns once again to the theme of riches, this time phrasing it in seemingly paradoxical terms:

> That task, which as we follow, or despise,
> The eldest is a fool, the youngest wise;
> Which done, the poorest can no wants endure,
> And which not done, the richest must be poor.
>
> (43-46)

[177]

The paradox resolves itself in terms of the conflict between earthly riches and spiritual wealth around which the poem revolves. Once again, Pope is making use of a biblical commonplace, although he appears at this point to be utilizing a specific formulation of it from Proverbs:

> There is that maketh himself rich, yet hath nothing; there is that maketh himself poor, yet hath great riches. (Prov. 13:7) [39]

The exegetes make the obvious point that the riches in question are spiritual ones; it is equally clear that these are the only riches for which Pope is striving.

Pope has fitted his personal desire for spiritual growth into the context of *concordia discors* by comparing the duration of his delay to the progress of day, night, and year for various impatient hopefuls (35–40); the alternation of day and night and of the seasons of "the Year's dull circle" (37) were understood as manifestations in nature of the immutable law of the reconciliation of opposites. What he seeks to attain by cultivation of the soul is Wisdom, which is itself a concord. Wisdom is both the mirror of God's perfection and the pattern for his creation; since God's being embraces and reconciles all contradictions, and since the structural and sustaining principle of the universe is the harmonious contention of opposing elements, Wisdom of necessity constitutes in herself a harmony. In conformity with his attempt to make himself "That Man divine whom Wisdom calls her own" (180), Pope has, at the opening of his epistle's *narratio*, described himself as an exemplar of that harmony.

> But ask not, to what Doctors I apply?
> Sworn to no Master, of no Sect am I:
> As drives the storm, at any door I knock,
> And house with Montagne now, or now with Lock.
> Sometimes a Patriot, active in debate,
> Mix with the World, and battle for the State,

Free as young Lyttleton, her cause pursue,
Still true to Virtue, and as warm as true:
Sometimes, with Aristippus, or St. Paul,
Indulge my Candor, and grow all to all;
Back to my native Moderation slide,
And win my way by yielding to the tyde.

(23-34)

Pope is the properly concordant man who is capable of reconciling in himself points of view as divergent as those of Montaigne and Locke, Aristippus and St. Paul; he transcends contradictions and "grow[s] all to all" (32). The harmony of his mind embraces natural knowledge in Aristippus and supernatural revelation in St. Paul (with consequent implications for the content of an epistle imitated from a poet writing according to the light of unaided reason). The reasons for the presence of Montaigne and Locke, of Lyttleton and St. Paul, can ultimately be found in Horace's own vacillation between Stoic and Cyrenaic, and in the commentators' understanding of that phenomenon. Landino is most explicit; he seizes upon Horace's lines 14 through 19 as the opportunity for a brief disquisition on the active and contemplative lives, with general reference to the biblical Martha and Mary, who were the traditional exemplars of those two states.[40] Pope's "As drives the storm, at any door I knock,/ And house with Montagne now, or now with Lock" (25-26) presents these conflicting ways of life in the guise of a concord already achieved in his own practices. Warburton's note quite plainly bears this out:

And house with Montagne now, and now with Locke,] i.e. Chuse either an active or a contemplative life, as is most fitted to the season and circumstances.—For he regarded these Writers as the best Schools to form a man for the world; or to give him a knowledge of himself: Montagne excelling in his observations on social and civil life; and Locke, in developing the faculties, and explaining the operations of the human mind.[41]

[179]

The rest of the paragraph elaborates this basic idea. Lyttleton and the opposition represent the virtues of the active life; and while he is with them, it is Pope's task to "Mix with the World, and battle for the State" (28). Balanced against this is the life of retirement and contemplation, here represented by the moderation, passivity, and adaptability of Aristippus and St. Paul. The juncture of these two in Pope's own person defines him as a harmonic, properly ordered individual who is, moreover, fully discharging the Christian's duty to imitate Christ in leading the mixed life, combining the virtues of both active and retired states.[42]

Pope's intention, announced at tne beginning of the Imitation, is to abandon the active, public career he has pursued up to this point in favor of the retired life of meditation; thus his final choice of opinions in this paragraph is that of St. Paul, to

> Indulge my Candor, and grow all to all;
> Back to my native Moderation slide,
> And win my way by yielding to the tyde.
>
> (32-34)

These lines detail more than the passivity and quiet of the contemplative state. They allude to and incorporate three related Pauline pronouncements, all describing his apostolic mission and the duty of the faithful:

> I am made all things to all men, that I might by all means save some. (I Cor. 9:22)

> Even as I please all men in all things, not seeking mine own profit, but the profit of many, that they may be saved. (I Cor. 10:33)

> Let your moderation be known unto all men. The Lord is at hand. (Phil. 4:5)[43]

The submerged portions of the two texts from Corinthians, those parts of them that are not directly stated in Pope's poem but are nevertheless implied by the nature of allusion, both refer to Paul's apostolic role, his task of bringing salvation to the sinful world. Pope is assimilating this also to the ideal character he is building for himself; his proposed retirement will not only be a simple life of contemplation, but will also directly concern itself with the work of salvation. So too is the Pauline moderation fitted into the context of the poem. Moderation demands temperance in all earthly appetites, and the Imitation of Ep.I.i. is heavily and precisely concerned with the disordering effects of avarice, the symbol of excess in all earthly desires. Furthermore, in the opinion of the exegetes, St. Paul's moderation constituted a mean that avoided both excess and defect,[44] and the mean is normal human manifestation of the divine concord.[45] Thus Pope's backsliding to his "native Moderation" (33), besides adding a facet to the apostolic persona he is establishing for himself, contributes yet another element to the concordant character he has described. It is this harmony, self-containment, and moderation that place Pope in such stark contrast to the avaricious and discordant world he depicts in the central section of his poem.

That discord is confined behind as well as before by the harmony of Pope's persona. This character Pope resumes, immediately after the epistle's *confirmatio*, in the lightly ironic bantering of the *refutatio*.

> You laugh, half Beau half Sloven if I stand,
> My Wig all powder, and all snuff my Band;
> You laugh, if Coat and Breeches strangely vary,
> White Gloves, and Linnen worthy Lady Mary!
> But when no Prelate's Lawn with Hair-shirt lin'd,
> Is half so incoherent as my Mind,
> When (each Opinion with the next at strife,
> One ebb and flow of follies all my Life)
> I plant, root up, I build, and then confound,
> Turn round to square, and square again to round;
> You never change one muscle of your face,

[181]

You think this Madness but a common case,
Nor once to Chanc'ry, nor to Hales apply;
Yet hang your lip, to see a Seam awry!
Careless how ill I with myself agree;
Kind to my dress, my figure, not to me.

(161-76)

In its rhetorical aspect, this passage functions as a humorous refutation of Bolingbroke's errors and misconceptions about his friend, and as a rebuke to him for concentrating upon the surface appearances only. It links up with Pope's opening demur at Bolingbroke's implied request for more poetry and a consequent return to the active life. Thematically, it continues, now in a jocular vein, the representation of Pope's character as a harmonization of opposites; he is "half Beau half Sloven" (61), even his clothing varies. The disorder is only the surface appearance by which Bolingbroke is misled; beneath lies a concordant reality. This is graphically revealed with regard to his "incoherent" (166) mind. The "strife" (167) and the "ebb and flow of follies" (168) are only seeming discords; actually, they express the underlying harmony of Pope's soul. The "strife" is that concordant strife that is proper nature of man, who is himself, as Pope has explained in the *Essay on Man*,[46] a concord of the opposed principles of passion and reason. Horace's "Aestuat" (96), as the commentators point out[47] and as Pope has adapted it, properly refers to the motion of the tides, which were themselves a natural manifestation of the workings of *concordia discors;* Pope's use of this as metaphor for the processes of his thought brings them to share in that concord.

The line "I plant, root up, I build, and then confound" (169) also makes a superficial reference to his gardening and grotto at Twickenham as an example of the chaos of his life, but, at the same time, has submerged significance as an example of a divinely established harmony. It alludes to God's commission to Jeremiah:

See, I have this day set thee over the nations and over the kingdoms, to root out, and to pull down, and to destroy, and to throw down, to build, and plant. (Jer. 1 : 10)

This sets Pope in stark contrast to Walpole, the poem's antiprophet, and the government and doctrine he represents. Pope is the divine poet, a prophet sent to warn the world of its sins and to recall it to its true goal. It is significant, and quite fitting to Pope's theme, that the exegetes construed Jeremiah's rooting up and destroying as a divine command for the extirpation of carnal appetite in general and avarice in particular;[48] this opposes Pope even more pointedly to Walpole and his mercantile world. St. Augustine glosses this passage in *De Doctrina Christiana* in the course of a discussion of figurative expression in the Bible that provides a dual relevance for his comments:

Therefore whatever is read in the Scriptures concerning bitterness or anger in the words or deeds of the person of God or of his saints is of value for the destruction of the reign of cupidity. . . . But it is said of Jeremias, "Lo, I have set thee this day over kingdoms, to root up, and to pull down, and to destroy." There is no doubt that this whole expression is figurative and is to be referred to that end of which we have spoken.

Those things which seem almost shameful to the inexperienced, whether simply spoken or actually performed either by the person of God or by men whose sanctity is commended to us, are all figurative, and their secrets are to be removed as kernels from the husk as nourishment for charity.[49]

It is more than appropriate to Pope's context that his allusion should express "the destruction of the reign of cupidity"; it is also very fitting that Augustine should explain the biblical use of metaphor in almost exactly the same way Pope employs this one. The "almost shameful" surface statement of this line is one of confusion. It is ostensibly a confession of misdirection and error that, upon examination, reveals as its metaphoric kernel a declaration of the harmony and holiness for which the poet is striving.

This allusion has important implications for Pope's conception of his own role as poet. He has already, by means of allusions to the Pauline epistles, endowed his poetic persona with some of the sanctity of the apostle. Now, in direct contrast to the false prophet Walpole, to whom a similar biblical passage was ironically applied, Pope has proclaimed himself God's own ordained poet, set "over nations and over kingdoms" to preach a Jeremiad to a fallen and hellish England and to announce to those who will listen the true goal and the proper concordant pattern for life. This ideal of concord is his own end also:

> Is this my Guide, Philosopher, and Friend?
> This, He who loves me, and who ought to mend?
> Who ought to make me (what he can, or none,)
> That Man divine whom Wisdom calls her own,
> Great without Title, without Fortune bless'd,
> Rich ev'n when plunder'd, honour'd while oppress'd,
> Lov'd without youth, and follow'd without power,
> At home tho' exil'd, free, tho' in the Tower.
> In short, that reas'ning, high, immortal Thing,
> Just less than Jove, and much above a King,
> Nay half in Heav'n—except (what's mighty odd)
> A Fit of Vapours clouds this Demi-god.
>
> (177-88)

Sapientia, who has punctuated the poem as the virtuous alternative to "London's voice" (79), appears here in Pope's *peroratio* in the guise she has had in Western literature ever since, as Lady Philosophy, she rescued Boethius from his servitude to Fortune.[50] Her role here is to save Pope from exactly the same fate, that slavery to earthly appetite for which avarice has been his metaphor; thus the list of achievements that Wisdom can produce includes all the gifts of Fortune—honor, wealth, power, love, freedom—

[184]

paradoxically without their contingent dependence upon mutable sublunary nature. The individual "whom Wisdom calls her own" is "That Man divine" (180) because he is concordant and, consequently, like Wisdom herself, mirrors the harmony of God; thus the characteristics that Pope seeks to attain and that Wisdom can give are presented as a *concordia discors,* a series of linked and reconciled opposites —greatness without position, wealth without material possessions, freedom even in prison. It is for this reason also that Pope here refers to Bolingbroke by the titles he gave him in the fourth epistle of the *Essay on Man,* "Guide, Philosopher, and Friend" (177). That work, and the fourth epistle of it in particular, had devoted itself to defining the nature of human happiness, and Pope's conclusions there were exactly the same as they are here. Happiness does not consist in any sublunary good nor in any of the gifts of Fortune; rather "*the* perfection of Virtue *and* Happiness *consists in a* conformity *to the* Order *of* Providence *here, and a* Resignation *to it here and hereafter. . . .* " [51] Since, as must be abundantly clear, Pope conceived of the order of Providence as the harmonic reconciliation of opposites, it is highly appropriate at this point in his Imitation, where he defines his goal as complete concord, to recall by means of this allusion that this concord constitutes the highest and truest reach of human happiness. As he states it in the final lines of this poem, the goal of all this striving is to make man "that reas'ning, high immortal Thing,/ Just less than Jove . . . / Nay half in Heav'n" (185–87); that is to say, to make him a proper, spiritually oriented human being, as opposed to the animality of George and his followers. Man's dual nature, both corporeal and spiritual, is capable of development in either direction, according to the ends the individual chooses to serve. Pope's decision to follow Wisdom has resulted in his becoming a reflection of the concord of God's nature, in total contrast to the inverted satanic order that the adherents of avarice reflect. Unlike George and the worldly, who by their sin

[185]

have become literally demonic, Pope has made himself a
"Demi-god" (188), and has triumphed completely over the
material world that holds them in thrall. This is the
"Candor" (32)—in its root meaning—that Pope wished to
indulge: the brightness of the Wisdom who, as he said in
the *Fortescue*, reflects the beauty of God in creation and
art, the Wisdom who is "the brightness (*candor*) of eternal
light, and the unspotted mirror of God's majesty."

Viewed in this light, the final line of the *Bolingbroke*
becomes richly ambiguous. Its surface statement is completely Horatian in spirit, poking fun at the grandiose
ambitions of mere man, who remains forever tightly bound
by the limitations of his bodily self; in this respect, it refers
obviously to Pope's own infirmities and weaknesses. Perhaps
it also jokingly alludes to the clouds and vapors that fog
the comings and goings of Homeric gods and goddesses.
More seriously, it describes the Old Testament and Miltonic
God whose brightness is hidden by a veil of cloud. Most
seriously, and most certainly, it points directly to the biblical descriptions of Wisdom:

> I [Wisdom] made that in the heavens there should rise light
> that never faileth, and as a cloud I covered all the earth. I
> dwelt in the highest places, and my throne is in a pillar of a
> cloud. (Ecclus. 24:6-7)

And again:

> For she is a vapour of the power of God and a certain pure
> emanation of the glory of almighty God: and therefore no
> defiled thing cometh into her. For she is the brightness of
> eternal light, and the unspotted mirror of God's majesty, and
> the image of his goodness. And being but one, she can do all
> things: and remaining in herself the same, she reneweth all
> things and through nations conveyeth herself into holy souls.
> She maketh the friends of God and prophets. (Wisdom of
> Solomon 7:25-27)

In the same ironic, self-deprecating mode as the previous
part of this paragraph, this final line constitutes a state-

ment of the goal for which Pope is working and of the mission he has undertaken. Wisdom has made him a friend and a prophet of God; he seeks now to perfect her image in himself, and consequently to assimilate himself completely to God. The *Bolingbroke* completes the journey begun in the *Fortescue*: there Pope sought to realize the image of Wisdom in his art; here, in his valediction to poetry, he finds her in himself.

Like the allusions to St. Paul and to Jeremiah, Pope's present incorporation of sapiential theology has far-reaching implications for his theory of poetry. Just as those references cast the poet into the role of the Christian preacher, the idea of Sapientia, as Pope uses it, transforms the poet into a creator of God's own order, a "Demi-god" who reproduces in himself and his works the pattern of God's own creation.[52] The entire poem, like one of Pope's antithetical couplets, resolves itself into a harmonious balance of conflicting opposites, ending in a vision of the creator-poet's final assimilation into the being of the God who is the reconciliation of all contradictions and the allaying of all paradoxes. Pope's opening reference to "the Sabbath of my days" (3) is not a chance choice of phrase, but a deliberate approximation, within the conventions of *ars moriendi* and the retired life, of the creator-poet's character to that of the divine creator. Both have labored and seen that their creations were good; the rest from active life that Pope now seeks is that period of final preparation for the ultimate confrontation of human maker and divine.

From this perspective, even the St. John whose love presided over the beginning of the poem grows richly multivalent, recalling that other St. John whose Love was God, and whose God was the Word through whom all things were made. Perhaps it is this conception that underlies Pope's whole view of the craft of poetry: the idea that God too is a poet, a creator through the agency of the Word. Clearly, this is no mere truism for him, but a living truth that clothes his calling with the mantle of divinity. His references to poets as prophets, apostles, as the Messiah himself, are too frequent, too consistent, to be mere rhetoric. Both poetry and poets, he insists, are formed by Wisdom: the artifact mirrors God's creation, and the artist mirrors God.

III

Pope's final attempt at direct imitation of Horace thus links itself coherently with the poem from which he began. *To Bolingbroke* is the inevitable conclusion of the themes and theories of his Imitation of Sat.II.i., the final condemnation of his degenerate times, the fullest statement of the Christian poet's goal, and the inescapable culmination of his idea of poetry. In the seriousness of its view of Augustan England, it marks the penultimate stage in a progression from the bantering at folly of the *Fortescue* and the early *Dunciad* to the sombre, apocalyptical tones of *Dunciad* IV. Pope seems to have seen clearly that his art was among the fullest expressions of Renaissance culture and, as such, was simultaneously among the final expressions of that culture: the high tide of Renaissance classicism must inevitably be followed by the ebb. The perfection of Pope's forms, the clarity and richness of his verse, achieve in the face of oncoming chaos a posture of stability; they create of the materials of complete disorder a shapely illusion of tragic beauty that, in our time, Yeats would have understood.

Eighteenth-century neoclassicism, at least as it is manifested in Pope, is no more a matter of mere form, and no nearer a return to paganism, than was the Renaissance rediscovery of classical culture. Both are the process and the result of the interpenetration of Christian idea and classical motif, ancient form and modern meaning. The roots of Pope's poetry, and particularly of his use of classical matter in verse, stretch deep into the Renaissance and into the culture and spirit the Renaissance fostered. Even his idea of poetic composition is essentially a Renaissance one, which can be found formulated in someone as distant in time and space as Torquato Tasso:

> Yet for all that, the world, which includes in its bosom so many and so diverse things, is one, one in its form and essence, one the knot with which its parts are joined and bound together in discordant concord; and while there is nothing lacking in it, yet there is nothing there that does not serve either for necessity or ornament. I judge that in the same way the great poet (who is called divine for no other reason but that, because he resembles in his works the supreme architect, he comes to participate in his divinity) is able to form a poem in which as in a little world can be read in one passage how armies are drawn up, and in various others there are battles by land and sea, attacks on cities, skirmishes, duels, jousts, descriptions of hunger and thirst, tempests, conflagrations, prodigies; there are a variety of celestial and infernal councils, and the reader encounters seditions, discords, wanderings, adventures, incantations, works of cruelty, audacity, courtesy, and generosity, and actions of love, now unhappy, now happy, now pleasing, now causing compassion. Yet in spite of all, the poem that contains so great variety of matter is one, one is its form and its soul; and all these things are put together in such a way that one has relation to the other, one corresponds to the other, the one necessarily or apparently so depends on the other that if one part is taken away or changed in position the whole is destroyed. And if this is true, the art of composing a poem is like the nature of the universe, which is composed of contraries, such as appear in the law of music, for if there were no multiplicity there would be no whole, and no law, as Plotinus says.[53]

This, manifestly, is what Pope has accomplished. For this purpose, the Renaissance Horace has served him well, providing a concordant mixture of rational knowledge and supernatural revelation, reason and faith in harmonious balance, and offering as well all the advantages of applying ancient rules to modern actions. Within the expansive

[189]

bounds of his traditions, Pope has built the various, yet one, universe of great poetry; it is entirely fitting that the last Imitation should close with his own acknowledgement of his accomplishment on the Sabbath of that creation.

1. P. 232 verso.

2. P. 67 recto, second pagination.

3. Dacier's commentary looms far larger in this poem than that of any other critic. Consequently it is a fact of great significance that in this poem alone information is provided indicating some of the sources Pope utilized. Warburton's note to line 95, quoted in chapter I, needs to be repeated here: "Dacier laughs at an able Critic, who was scandalized, that the antient Scholiasts had not explained what Horace meant by *a wall of brass*; for, says Dacier, 'Chacun se fait des difficultez à sa mode, et demande des remarques proportionées à son goût:' he then sets himself in good earnest about this important inquiry; and, by a passage in Vegetius, luckily discovers, that it signified an *old veteran* armed cap-a-pie in brass, and placed to cover his Fellow. Our Poet has happily served himself of this impertinence to convey a very fine stroke of satire." Warburton is, of course, quite clearly stating that Pope has taken advantage of one of Dacier's suggestions to embellish his poem. Beyond this, however, there is a Scriblerus-like quality to his comment which would have been readily apparent to an age well acquainted with both Horace and Dacier. Not only is the point Warburton annotates so minor and so self-evident that the reference to Dacier seems gratuitous, but he has also garbled (I would suggest deliberately) the note he purports to be reproducing: "Un habile Critique a trouvé mauvais qu'on n'eût pas recherché pourquoi Horace avoit dit, *une muraille d'airain:* car chacun se fait des difficultez à sa mode, & demande des remarques proportionées à son goût. Il a donc voulu faire lui-même cette penible recherche; & aiant lû heureusement un passage de Vegece, qui appelle *une muraille d'airain* des Soldats armez de pied en cap, qui couvrent les autres, il a crû que c'étoit son veritable fait, & que la muraille d'airain de Vegece étoit la même que celle d'Horace. Mais rien n'est plus éloigné. Il ne faloit pas beaucoup creuser pour trouver que les Anciens disoient des murailles d'airain ou de fer, pour des murailles tres-fortes. C'est ainsi que Virgile a dit:—*Cyclopum educta caminis/Moenia. Des murailles sorties des fourneaux des Cyclopes.* Et dans un autre endroit:—*stat ferrea turris ad auras.*" Dacier's actual opinion coincides with Warburton's, and Warburton has in reality translated a good part of Dacier's note and passed it off as his own. It appears obvious from the accuracy of that portion of this note that Warburton quotes, as well as from the part of it that he has silently incorporated into his commentary, that he had his edition of Dacier near at hand, if not open before him. The confusion cannot then be attributed to slipshod scholarship, but rather to the intimate knowledge of an editor-friend who is using this self-evident fraud to call the reader's attention to an important influence on Pope's poem.

4. In point of fact, Horace's was closely associated with the Christian formulation, and may have influenced it. See Morton W. Bloomfield, *The Seven Deadly Sins* (East Lansing, Michigan, 1952), pp. 37, 45-46, and 72.

See also Gregory the Great, *Morales sur Job*, translated by André de Gaudemaris, with an Introduction by Robert Gillet (Paris, 1950), pp. 89–90.

5. P. 68 verso, second pagination.

6. Pope had already utilized this tradition in the *Epistle to Bathurst*; see Wasserman, *Bathurst*, p. 21.

7. See *Craftsman*, no. 499, and Lord Hervey's *Memoirs*, ed. Romney Sedgwick (London, 1952), pp. 44–45.

8. I here quote the Douai translation, since it more closely approximates Pope's phrasing. See also in this connection Prov. 3 : 14 and Prov. 8 : 10–11; in the latter chapter, Wisdom is depicted as crying "at the gates, at the entry of the city" (Prov. 8 : 3).

9. For a helpful discussion of Sapienta, see Charles S. Singleton, *Dante Studies 2 : Journey to Beatrice* (Cambridge, Mass., 1958), pp. 122–34.

10. VI, 372–73.

11. VI, 363.

12. *Commentaria*, pt. VI, p. 87.

13. *Synopsis*, II, col. 1470.

14. Acron, Porphyrion, and Cruquius' *Vetus Commentator*, all agree in pointing out that the forum of Janus formerly stood on the site now occupied by the Basilica of St. Paul. In light of this fact, Pope's assigning to its English counterpart, St. Paul's Catherdral, a place in the antireligion becomes a sharp reversal of the spread of the gospel; false religion, after temporarily retreating, once again claims its own. See *Opera cum quatuor Commentariis*, p. 235 recto, and Cruquius, p. 510

15. See *Craftsman*, no. 225, and *London Magazine* (1732), p. 13. See also Rapin-Thoyras, *History of England, translated into English with Additional Notes, by N. Tindal*, (3rd ed.; London, 1743–47), I, 445 and 505. I have drawn this information from Jay Levine, "Studies in the Neo-Classical Verse Epistle," unpublished dissertation, (The John Hopkins University, 1961).

16. See Butt's note to line 22 of *Dialogue I*, TE, IV, 299.

17. The quoted text is from the Douai translation. In his exegesis of Jer. 1 : 10, Cornelius à Lapide acknowledges and quotes Horace's *murus aheneus*; see *Commentaria*, pt. II, p. 577.

18. P. 235 verso.

19. Cornelius à Lapide, pt. XV, p. 308, and Matthew Poole, IV, col. 1196. Lapide also associates "spirit and truth" with the active and contemplative lives.

20. If any identification of Bug is necessary, I would suggest Lord Hervey who, as Pope's favorite enemy, is otherwise conspicuously absent from this poem, and who, moreover, was similarly characterized in the *Epistle to Arbuthnot* as "this Bug with gilded wings" (309).

21. Dacier, VI 383–84. Pope's use of the word "Reynard," which Butt attributes to the influence of Creech's translation, could just as easily have come from this note of Dacier's.

22. *Ibid.*, 384 : "Belua multorum es capitum] Le peuple n'est pas seulement un Lion, c'est un monstre à plusieurs têtes, qui ne sont jamais animées par le même esprit."

23. See Hugo de Sancto Charo, VII, 403 verso, col. I, and Gagnaeus' annotation in *Biblia Maxima,* ed. John de la Haye (Paris, 1660), XVII, 852. Almost all commentators further agree in identifying the beast's leonine and ursine characteristics with *superbia, avaritia,* and *ambitio* (Cornelius à Lapide, pt. XV, p. 215).

24. IV, 115.

25. See Wasserman, *Bathurst,* pp. 49–51.

26. Dacier, VI, 388.

27. IV, 116–17.

28. Merlin was, according to Arthurian tradition, sired by a demon, and mythographers frequently ascribe Proteus' ability to change his shape and appearance to the same sort of diabolical origin: see Alexander Ross, *Mystagogus Poeticus* (London, 1653), pp. 371–72, and Natale Conti, *Mythologiae,* p. 443, col. 2.

29. Dacier compares the first two lines of this paragraph to an unidentifiable locus in St. Jerome: "Et sapientia prima stultitia caruisse] Le commencement de la sagesse c'est d'être exempt de toute sorte de folie. . . . La science & l'ignorance font la même chose à l'esprit. S. Jerome avoit en vûë ce passage d'Horace quand il écrivoit, *Prima namque sapientia est caruisse stultitia; sed stultitia caruisse non potest, nisi qui intellexerit illam*" (VI, 369). Similar statements, however, may be found in Job 28:28, "And unto man he said, Behold, the fear of the Lord, that is wisdom; and to depart from evil is understanding," and, in Prov. 1:7, "The fear of the Lord is the beginning of knowledge: but fools despise wisdom and instruction." All this demonstrates once again the correspondence of pagan and Christian opinions in the Renaissance view, and indicates the kind of specifically religious coloration of the traditional Horace.

30. See Singleton, *loc. cit.*

31. IV, 101. In former editions it read "Br—'s cause."

32. IV, 100.

33. On climacteric years, see Lynn Thorndyke, *History of Magic and Experimental Science* (New York, 1958), VI, 139–40, and VII, 92, 110, 189. See also Claudius Salmasius, *De Annis Climactericis* (Leyden, 1648), second and fourth pages of the synopsis, and pp. 57–59. Although attempting to explode the theory, Salmasius presents all its tenets in great detail.

34. See for instance Ascensius, p. 67 recto, second pagination, and Dacier, VI, 350.

35. Attributed by Butt to Pope, TE, IV, 279, but it appears to be Warburton's comment (IV, 102).

36. See Dacier, VI, 352, and Landino, pp. 232 verso-233 verso.

37. See also Gen. 41:35–36; Job 22:22; Prov. 10:14; Matt. 6:19–20; II Tim. 4:8; James 5:3.

38. It is interesting, as an indication of how traditional even Pope's rhetorical practices are, to note that Cruquius identifies Horace's lines 11 and 12 as *epilogus proemi* and *protasis narrationis* respectively; this is exactly the manner in which Pope employs their English equivalents. See Cruquius, p. 513, col. 1.

39. See also Prov. 10:22; 11:24; and 14:24. Instances of this sort might be multiplied indefinitely; the basic idea is so common in scripture that the simple statement of the apparent paradox would appear to be sufficient to call to mind its religious implications.

40. 234 verso.

41. IV, 102–3.

42. So at least Pope's friend Atterbury understood the Christian's duty. See "Of Religious Retirement: A Sermon Preach'd before the Queen at St. Jame's Chapel, on Friday, March 23, 1704/5," in Francis Atterbury, *Sermons and Discourses on Several Subjects and Occasions* (London 1740), I, 347–75.

43. All three are noted by Butt, TE, IV, 281.

44. Whitby, II, 402–3.

45. See Wind, *Pagan Mysteries in the Renaissance,* p. 88: "'There is,' as we may remember from Pico, 'this diversity between God and man, that God contains in him all things because he is their source, whereas man contains in him all things because he is their centre.' In the centre the opposites are held in balance, but in the source they coincide. In so far as man therefore approaches his own perfection, he distantly imitates the deity. Balance is but an echo of divine transcendence."

46. See *Essay on Man,* I, 165–72, and II, 53–92, 191–210.

47. Dacier, VI, 395.

48. Cornelius à Lapide, pt. II, p. 573.

49. Saint Augustine, *On Christian Doctrine,* trans. D. W. Robertson, Jr. (New York, 1958), pp. 89–90.

50. See *The Consolation of Philosophy,* book II, for a situation almost exactly parallel to the one presented in lines 180–86 of Pope's poem.

51. I quote from Pope's "Argument of the Fourth Epistle," TE, III, pt. i, p. 127. In section VI of that epistle, Pope specifically rejects the gifts of Fortune as sources of happiness; see lines 167–308.

52. It is important to note in this connection that the exegetes associated the figure of Sapientia as a cloud or vapor with the spirit that brooded over the abyss in Genesis, and consequently linked her, in this form particularly, with God's creative activity. See, for instance, Cornelius à Lapide, pt. V, p. 509.

53. "Discourses on the Heroic Poem," in Gilbert, *Literary Criticism: Plato to Dryden,* pp. 500–501.

Epilogue

Speculations

THE PRECEDING CHAPTERS raise—for me at least—certain questions that seem well worth asking. If Pope is not an exception to the Augustan world, save in his genius, then the broader aspects of his art and thought should be typical or representative in some degree of the whole character of his age; and the qualities we discern in him may well help to define the phenomenon or phenomena we label neoclassicism. His conception and use of imitation, in particular, touch on an issue central to this problem, that of the nature of the *classicism* of neoclassicism.

The fundamental difficulty in our approach to neoclassicism derives essentially from the same source as our difficulty in approaching the *Imitations of Horace*. Just as critics have always seen Pope's Horace as their Horace, so too we have tended to interpret neoclassicism largely in the light of our own sense of Greece and Rome. Moreover, we have too often compartmentalized the literature of the Restoration and eighteenth century, and sealed it hermetically from its Renaissance predecessors. The classicism of Dryden and Pope must inescapably be the sense of the pre-Christian past that the Renaissance formed and nourished; correlatively, our understanding of the very name "Augustan" must depend not on the simple fact of Augustus Caesar, but on the intricate, ambiguous, and often contradictory complex of ideas that he represented to the late Renaissance. What did the imposition of the Pax Romana mean to literate men of the late seventeenth century? What was its significance as an analogue to the restoration of the Stuarts? Even more fundamentally, what did the collapse of the

Roman republic and the establishment of the Julian monarchy denote to English politicians and poets? What are we to make of such ambiguous figures as Cato and Seneca? And ultimately, beyond all other questions, why was it important to the Augustans that there be a classical precedent, an antique model, for their major actions and thoughts and modes of expression? What does the whole doctrine of imitation mean in its broadest cultural context?

There are as yet no answers to many of these questions. Some are perhaps completely unanswerable. But they do point to an area of investigation that seems quite likely to reward careful reappraisal: the function of classical models in the poetry of the Restoration and eighteenth century. The contours of the classical poem underlying any given English one are almost always discernible: the content, however, remains more often than not an enigma. How much, one wonders, might we learn of Cowley's Pindarics by a judicious study of the Renaissance editions of Pindar? Dryden's accomplishment in translating Virgil was guided and shaped by the commentators: how much light would a careful investigation of this cast not only on the contemporary understanding of Virgil but on the total conception of epic form and content? The same, of course, applies to Pope's translation of Homer, which could probably reveal more about the whole problem of the epic than all the Renaissance arts of poetry put together. The interest in pastorals, the spate of verse epistles, English elegiacs—illumination of all these would seem to depend on our recapturing, in so far as it is possible, the contemporary understanding of their classical precedents and models. And this does not begin to approach the larger problems raised by the mock heroic, by the presence of classical fragments in otherwise original verse, by the nature of allusion itself, and—most complex of all—by the manner in which individual talents utilize the materials of common tradition.

The antithesis of all this is equally important. If Pope's practice is not typical, if the ancients and their poetry should appear to mean something different to other poets than they do to him, then a whole new set of questions is raised. The problem then becomes one not of defining neoclassicism, but of distinguishing the varieties of neoclassicisms.

I

The publication of Samuel Johnson's first imitation of Juvenal (*London*) within a few months of Pope's last *Imitation of Horace* provides some interesting and instructive parallels and contrasts. While it is probably true to say that there are ultimately as many neoclassicisms as there are neoclassicists, I would suggest that for the purposes of criticism we may profitably distinguish two main branches: a neoclassicism of form and a neoclassicism of matter. To these, Johnson's and Pope's poems respectively correspond.

What the *Bolingbroke* imitates we have already seen. It is not concerned with the form and tone of the Horatian epistle (indeed, it and the other *Imitations* frequently enough depart from both) but with its content, with the total statement of the poem—not, let it be remembered, with the bare sentences of the Latin text, but with their import as they had been explained and amplified by generations of readers and commentators. What Pope reproduces in his English poem is primarily the Horatian matter as it was understood by the late Renaissance: an ethical doctrine of eternal and unchangeable validity, whose temporal applications may vary infinitely without in the least altering the essential content of the poem. (This indeed may be the only full explanation of Pope's plea to "Let me *be* Horace.") The *Bolingbroke* presents to the reader the ethical stance and the moral teaching of Horace's first epistle almost precisely as they were understood by the late Renaissance.

Johnson's imitation, although apparently dealing with the same sort of material in a similar manner, is substantially different. It echoes a tone, a style, a format—the famous Juvenalian *saeva indignatio* and an equally famous diatribe against city life: what it does not reproduce is the essential matter of Juvenal's poem in anything like the manner in which Pope presents Horace's. Johnson imitates primarily the surface statement, not the underlying core of the poem: thus *London* contains what one rarely finds in Pope's *Imitations*, a major passage (194–209) that is entirely inapplicable as a criticism of eighteenth-century England. Even the bare bones of the rhetorical structure that served to support Pope's poems are missing from Johnson's: all that is reproduced is a tone of voice and a bare format, the linear and topical progression of Juvenal's poem. *London* lacks the Renaissance pedigree of Pope's *Imitations*, and this seems to me to constitute an *essential* difference between the two. *London* and poems like it—much of the poetry of the later eighteenth century—form the real poetry of statement, and to lump them all together with Pope's poems or Dryden's seems a needless critical confusion.

Johnson's criticism of Pope's *Imitations* applies much more accurately to his own, and indicates exactly how great the gulf is between the two generations. The real disjunctions in the history of literature take place at points like this, when one idea, one world view, has lost its validity, and another rises to replace it. The distinction between Renaissance and neoclassical is, in the sense in which it is normally used, meaningless: the convenient century marks and political events that literary historians have tended to rely upon can tell us nothing of importance about the ways of poetry. The important difference is between a "neoclassicism" that encompasses both form and matter—literally a new classicism in its own right—and a "neoclassicism" that consists primarily in formal imitation of the ancients and observance of supposedly classical proprieties. Thus Johnson in his criticism assumes that his and Pope's ideas of poetry are identical because of their formal similarities, while his failure to grasp the true nature of Pope's *Imitations* reveals the substantial difference between them.

[198]

Johnson's criticism of Milton's *Lycidas* reveals nothing so much as this fact: his inability to see the value and function of myth, his objection to the propriety of linking shepherds and pastors indicate his loss of the framework of thought in which these things made not only sense, but poetry. His derision of the Lodona story in Pope's *Windsor Forest* is entirely consistent with this critical viewpoint. What Johnson seems to possess are the rules, the standards, the critical terminology of the earlier neoclassicism without the substance that had previously accompanied them. The simple fact of his birth in 1709 seems to have denied his great critical intelligence the right to understand poetry as more than verbally serious: for him and his age, poetry can only be a heightened and condensed form of rhetoric.

His comments of the Metaphysicals seems to me to illuminate this:

> But Wit, abstracted from its effects upon the hearer, may be more rigorously and philosophically considered as a kind of *discordia concors*; a combination of dissimilar images, or discovery of occult resemblances in things apparently unlike. Of wit, thus defined, they [the Metaphysical poets] have more than enough. The most heterogeneous ideas are yoked by violence together; nature and art are ransacked for illustrations, comparisons, and allusions; their learning instructs and their subtilty surprises; but the reader commonly thinks his improvement dearly bought, and, though he sometimes admires, is seldom pleased.

The nature of wit clearly remains purely verbal: it is an ingenious rhetorical device by which essentially disparate ideas are forcefully linked for the purpose of surprising or impressing the reader. The conception of *concordia discors* itself seems equally one-dimensional: it quite obviously does not—cannot—exist for him as a fundamental law of the universe, or even as a meaningful analogy, but only as an intellectual conceit, a brilliant but basically meaningless play of the mind upon farfetched similarities. The distance between this and Pope's understanding of it shows graphically the revolution or devolution that had taken place in thought in the intervening years. Between Pope's and Johnson's formulation of the idea there is only a formal or verbal similarity, while Cowley's definition of wit—temporally equidistant from Pope—appears almost identical to what we can judge of the latter's conception:

> What is it then, which like the *Power Divine*
> We only can by Negatives define?
> In a true piece of *Wit* all things must be,
>> Yet all things then *agree*.
> As in the *Ark,* joyn'd without force or strife,
> All *Creatures* dwelt; all *Creatures* that had *Life*.
>> Or as the *Primitive Forms* of all
>> (If we compare great things with small)
> Which without *Discord* or *Confusion* lie,
> In that strange *Mirror* of the *Deitie*.

For Cowley and for Pope, *concordia discors* constitutes the underlying rationale of wit and poetry; it forms the essential pattern of the universe, linking God and nature, man and art, in a series of mutually explicative analogies. For Pope, it provides a valid and coherent mode of understanding the universe, an intellectual foundation on which poetry and philosophy are built. Johnson is, by historical accident, unable to hold this view. He does not—obviously cannot—share its presuppositions: yet he inherits a poetic mode based upon them and conceptions like them: and that is precisely the distinction between his neoclassicism—the neoclassicism of the later eighteenth century—and that of Pope.

II

All of this may also suggest reasons for the importance of satire in Augustan literature. The triumphs of *concordia discors,* as Pope chronicles them, are more often personal ones, executed in the sphere of art, than the larger victories of the

political and philosophical worlds. In those areas, since the
last of the Stuarts, there is only satire, cataloguing man's
failings as measured against the yardstick of the harmonic
ideal. This idea and others like it—the great chain of being,
the analogy of kingship and divinity, man as microcosm—
are seemingly still intellectually valid, for this is the way
the world *should* be organized; but the facts all too frequently neither fulfil nor support them. The inevitable result must be satire—cherishing the idea and scorning the
world for failing it—and, after that, the passing of the idea.
Donne's line was prophetic, but only partially true: the new
science called all in doubt, but so did the new politic, the
new philosophy, the new psychology, and even the new
society. What once was felt as a complete reality became a
theory, then an unattainable ideal, and ended as a rhetorical
trick. Obviously, this did not happen overnight: there must
have been many in Pope's own lifetime for whom this and
similar conceptions were already meaningless. But we can
see that for the generation of Johnson, most of these ideas
were entirely void: the *Lives of the Poets* bears witness that
within forty years of Pope's death his poems were in fact no
longer understood. The Renaissance poetic mode was finished: what remained was simultaneously a dead legacy and
and as yet unfulfilled promise.

APPENDIXES

Appendix A

Table of Index Guides

THE FOLLOWING TABLES of index guides are based primarily upon Warburton's edition; the line numbers follow the text of the Twickenham Edition.

I

Table of Index Guides for Pope's "Imitation of Satire II.i."

HORACE		POPE	
CATCHWORD	LINE	CATCHWORD	LINE
[1] Sunt quibus	I	[1] There are	I
[2] sine nervis	2	[2] The Lines	5
[3] Trebati!	4	[3] I come	8
[4] Quiescas	5	[4] I'd write	11
[5] verum nequeo	7	[5] And for	12
[6] Ter uncti	7	[6] Or rather	17
[7] Aut, si	10	[7] Or if	21
[8] multa laborum	11	[8] You'll gain	22
deficiunt: [9] neque	13	Sir [9] *Richard*	23
[10] Attamen &	16	[10] Then all	29
[11] Nisi dextro	18	[11] Alas! few	33
[12] Quanto rectius	21	[12] Better be	37
[13] Cum sibi	23	[13] Ev'n those	41
[14] Quid faciam?	24	[14] Each mortal	45
[15] Castor gaudet	26	[15] *F*—loves	49

HORACE		POPE	
CATCHWORD	LINE	CATCHWORD	LINE
[16] me pedibus	28	[16] I love	51
[17] Lucanus an	34	[17] Verse-man or	64
[18] Sed hic	39	[18] Satire's my	69
[19] Tutus ab	42	[19] I only	71
[20] O Pater	42	[20] Save but	73
noceat [21] cupido	44	[21] Peace is	75
[22] Flebit, &	46	[22] Slides into	78
[23] Cervius iratus	47	[23] Slander or	81
[24] Ut, quo	50	[24] Its proper	85
[25] Scaevae vivacem	53	[25] So drink	89
[26] Ne longum	57	[26] Then learned	91
[27] Quisquis erit	60	[27] Like *Lee*	100
[28] O Puer	60	[28] Alas young	101
[29] Quid? cum	61	[29] What? arm'd	105
[30] Detrahere &	64	not [30] strip	115
Scilicet [31] Uni	70	[31] To Virtue	121
[32] Quin ubi	71	[32] There, my	125
[33] Cum magnis	76	[33] *Envy* must	133
[34] Nisi quid	78	[34] What saith	142
[35] Equidem nihil	79	[35] Your plea	143
[36] "Si mala	82	[36] Consult the	147
siquis [37] mala	83	[37] *Libels* and	150
[38] Solventur risu	86	[38] In such	155

II

Table of Index Guides for Pope's "Imitation of Epistle II. ii."

[a] missing		[a] missing	
[b] Si quis	2	[b] A Frenchman	3
[c] Ille ferat	17	[c] If, after	21

HORACE		POPE	
CATCHWORD	LINE	CATCHWORD	LINE
ᵈ Dixi me	20	ᵈ Consider then,	27
ᵉ Luculli miles	26	ᵉ In Anna's	33
ᶠ Romae nutriri	41	ᶠ Bred up	52
ᵍ Singula de	55	ᵍ Years foll'wing	72
ʰ Denique non	58	ʰ But after	80
ⁱ Praeter caetera	65	ⁱ But grant	88
ᵏ I nunc,	76	ᵏ Go, lofty	108
ˡ Ingenium, sibi	81	ˡ The Man,	116
ᵐ Frater erat	87	ᵐ The *Temple*	127
ⁿ Carmina compono	91	ⁿ Thus we	135
ᵒ Ridentur mala	106	ᵒ In vain,	153
ᵖ Obscurata diu	115	ᵖ In downright	164
�q Praetulerim scriptor	126	�q If such	180
ʳ Nimirum sapere	141	ʳ Well, on	198
ˢ Ac non	143	ˢ Soon as	206
ᵗ Si tibi	146	ᵗ If, when	212
ᵛ Si vulnus	149	ᵛ When golden	218
ʷ Si proprium	158	ʷ If there	230
ʸ Emtor Aricini	167	ʸ Heathcote himself	240
ᶻ Sit proprium	172	ᶻ Loose on	249
ᵃ Gemmas, marmor,	180	ᵃ Gold, Silver,	264
ᵇ Cur alter	183	ᵇ Talk what	268

(Index guides c and d are missing from both texts.)

ᵉ Utar, E	190	ᵉ Yes, Sir,	284
ᶠ Pauperies immunda	199	ᶠ What is't	296
ᵍ Non es	205	ᵍ "But why	304
ʰ Vivere si	212	ʰ Learn to	322

III

Table of Index Guides for Pope's "Imitation of Epistle I.i."

HORACE		POPE	
CATCHWORD	LINE	CATCHWORD	LINE
[a] missing		[a] missing	
[b] Spectatum	2	Why [b] will	3
[c] Veianius	4	modest [c] Cibber	6
[d] Herculis	5	[d] retir'd to	7
populum [e] extrema	6	Nor[e] fond	10
[f] Est mihi	7	[f] A Voice	11
Solve [g] senescentem	8	your[g] Muse	13
et [h] versus	10	then [h] Verse	17
Quid [i] verum	11	What [i] right	19
[k] Condo, et	12	this [k] harvest	21
[l] quo me	15	what [l] Doctors	23
[m] Quo me	15	the [m] storm	25
mersor [n] civilibus	16	a [n] Patriot	27
[o] rigidusque	17	[o] and as	30
Aristippi [p] furtim	18	my [p] native	33
[q] Ut nox	20	[q] Long, as	35
tarda[r] fluunt	23	th' [r] unprofitable	39
gnaviter [s] id	24	That [s] task	43
[t] Restat, ut	27	[t] Late as	47
regam [u] solerque	27	some [u] comfort	48
[w] Non possis	28	[w] Weak tho'	49
prodire [x] tenus	32	to [x] go	53
[y] Fervet Avaritia,	33	thy [y] blood	55
et [z] magnam	35	[z] Between the	58
sunt [a] certa	36	which [a] fresh	60
[b] Invidus,	38	Be [b] furious,	61
[c] Amator,	38	[c] Slave to	62

HORACE		POPE	
CATCHWORD	LINE	CATCHWORD	LINE
Nemo [d] adeo	39	Low-dutch [d] Bear	63
[e] Virtus est,	41	[e] 'Tis the	65
quae [f] maxima	42	no [f] bugbear	67
Per [g] mare	46	And [g] ease	76
cures [h] ea	47	[h] Here, Wisdom	77
" [i] Vilius argentum	49	[i] "Seek Virtue	77
" [k] O cives,	50	[k] "Get Mony,	79
haec [l] Janus	51	From [l] low	82
[m] Laevo suspensi	53	whose [m] quills	83
Est [n] animus	54	in [n] spirit	85
[o] Plebs eris	56	a [o] Cit,	89
[p] at pueri	55	ev'ry [p] child	91
Hic [q] murus	57	thy [q] Screen,	95
[r] Roscia, dic	59	[r] And say,	97
Maribus [s] Curiis	61	at [s] Cressy	100
[t] Isne tibi	62	[t] Who counsels	101
Ut [u] proprius	64	a [u] Box	105
An, [w] qui	65	Or [w] he	107
[x] praesens hortatur	66	And, [x] while	109
[y] Quod si	67	If [y] such	110
ut [z] porticibus	68	the [z] Palace	113
quod [a] vulpes	70	answer [a] Reynard	114
[b] Belua multorum	73	The [b] People	121
gestit [c] conducere	74	Their [c] Country's	126
[d] Crustis et	75	Some [d] with	130
[e] Multis occulto	77	[e] hundreds stink	133
[f] Verum	77	each [f] pursues	134
[g] Nullus in	80	Job [g] sail'd	138
[h] lacus et	81	[h] Up starts	140
si [i] vitiosa	82	that [i] Dev'l	143
[k] lectus genialis	84	the [k] Stocking	148
[l] Si non	86	[l] The Fool,	150

HORACE		POPE	
CATCHWORD	LINE	CATCHWORD	LINE
[m] Quo teneam	87	ever [m] Proteus	152
Quid [n] pauper?	88	the [n] Poor—	154
mutat [o] coenacula,	88	their [o] weekly	155
Balnea, [p] tonsores;	89	They [p] hire	159
[q] Si curatus	91	[q] You laugh,	161
[r] mea cum	94	when [r] no	165
[s] Aestuat,	96	One [s] ebb	168
[t] Diruit,	97	I [t] plant,	169
[u] Insanire putas	98	[u] You never	171
Nec [w] Medici	99	Nor [w] once	173
rerum [x] tutela	100	my [x] Guide	177
[y] Dives!	103	Rich [y] ev'n	182
[z] honoratus!	104	[z] honour'd while	182
[a] pulcher!	104	Lov'd [a] without	183
[b] Liber!	104	[b] free, tho'	184
uno [c] minor	103	Just [c] less	186
[d] Rex denique	104	and [d] much	186
[e] Nisi cum	105	[e] except what's	187

Appendix B

Two Structural Experiments: The Poem as Sermon

POPE'S ADAPTATIONS of Horace's poems take many forms and use many methods. Up to this point, the poems discussed have been assimilated to Christianity and to eighteenth-century culture largely through an alteration of their contents, a reorientation of their themes toward specifically Christian ends. The two poems to be discussed below depart from this pattern by extending the process of assimilation to their poetic media. These poems employ the structure of the Christian homily, and constitute, in effect, two sermons on temperance.

I

Various books of advice to young clergymen offered the aspiring preacher diverse plans for the construction of his sermons. Some of these were scholastically complex, splitting the basic form into as many as five major divisions and endless subdivisions;[1] however; the most common and popular form had no more than three essential parts, which tended to be rather elastic in length and content. All theoreticians of the form agree that the sermon's starting point should be a carefully selected text from Scripture, which was to be immediately followed by the first major section, an explanation or clarification of the text and a statement of the doctrine it contains. The second section was to consist of the proof, reasons, or causes of the chosen text. The third and most important section of the sermon consisted simply of the text's application and use, which could be either general or particular.[2]

Pope's Imitation of Ep.I.vi. adopts this latter, more flexible form. It opens by announcing its text, appropriately set off in quotation marks:

"Not to Admire, is all the Art I know,
To make men happy, and to keep them so."

(1–2)

The next two lines parody the usual attribution of text (e.g.,
"the words of Isaiah, the third Chapter, the twelfth verse"):

[Plain Truth, dear Murray, needs no flow'rs of speech,
So take it in the very words of *Creech*.]

(3–4)

This enunciation and identification of text helps to mark Pope's
poem from its outset as a satiric sermon.

Pope's next three paragraphs (5–27) explain the precise
meaning of *nil admirari*; they distinguish between the Christian's
calm reliance upon God and the sinful pursuit of worldly ends, and
locate virtue at the mean point between dread and desire. This
section also prepares for the themes of the main body of the
sermon by associating the sinful extremes with the court and its
low-church Whiggish supporters.

The second section extends from line 28 to line 53. Pope
herein lists several earthly aims, and shows their absolute futility
in the face of death: all worldly attainments are meaningless compared to the spiritual goal for which the Christian is to strive.
This passage also presents a three-fold division that Pope loosely
follows in his application:

But wherefore all this labour, all this strife?
For Fame, for Riches, for a noble Wife?

(38–39)

Pope's application then opens with a brief paragraph describing the way of virtue, which is simultaneously moral and political:

Would ye be blest? despise low Joys, low Gains;
Disdain whatever Cornbury disdains;
Be Virtuous, and be happy for your pains.

(60–62)

This is immediately followed by concrete consideration of the antithetical paths of vice, beginning with those who strive for riches (63–96). This section concludes with a couplet that unites it with the main theme of the epistle and demonstrates the fruitlessness of the pursuit of wealth:

> If Wealth alone then make and keep us blest,
> Still, still be getting, never, never rest.
>
> (95–96)

The second part of the application is concerned with the absurdity and corruption of those who strive for fame (97–109), and is once again presented as simultaneously moral and political. The third possible pursuit that Pope has indicated, that of a "noble Wife," he has actually disposed of in passing in the previous sections (40–43; 77–80), so that the third section of his application is devoted to those whose goal is to gratify lust, gluttony, and the physical appetites generally (110–29). After this, there is nothing left for him but to draw the obvious conclusion, that his original advice, to shun worldly desire, was best:

> Adieu—if this advice appear the worst,
> E'en take the Counsel which I gave you first:
> Or better Precepts if you can impart,
> Why do, I'll follow them with all my heart.
>
> (130–33)

Pope's political argument is reticulated over this framework in an especially effective manner. He has managed to insinuate an analogy between moral and political evil, and to incorporate this into the primary movement of the Imitation. Beyond this, he has employed a traditional sermon device, the *exemplum,* to carry a heavy portion of his political meaning. The *exemplum* is ordinarily a vignette used by the preacher for the purpose of graphic illustration of the consequences of vice and the rewards of virtue. In Pope's hands, it retains this basic character, but is reoriented in the direction of political significance. Cornbury, for instance, becomes an *exemplum* of political and moral rectitude

(60–62), while Tindal is employed as his exemplary opposite (63–66). The whole section on the pursuit of political power (97–109), adapted from Horace to fit eighteenth-century England, falls neatly into this same pattern. The *exemplum* of co-ordinate lust and political corruption in the Ulysses passage (118-25) is a perfect illustration and proof of Pope's entire argument, and is representative of the way in which he has adapted the resources of the sermon format to his own ends. Corruption in morals is a symbol of corruption in politics. Pope's imitation of Horace's Ep.I.vi. bases itself firmly on that premise, and by this means becomes a sermon simultaneously damning the analogous sins of worldliness and Whiggery.

Of these basic materials, Pope has wrought his Imitation. It is not a complex poem; entrance to the core of its meaning is provided by the simple realization of the essential differences between a Stoic ethical treatise and a Christian homily. In a very real sense, the poem, as Pope works it out, centers around the ambiguity of the key Latin word *beatus,* whose two meanings, "happy" and "blessed," express in concentrated form the tensions that animate the epistle. For Horace, the concept of *beatus* represents man living the life of reason, insulated by a Stoic apathy from the perturbations of the world and, therefore, within the rather strict limits of human nature, "happy." Pope knows this concept, but possesses in addition the specifically Christian idea of beatitude as the life of grace and divine blessing. Because of this duality, he can render *beatus* once as "happy" (2) and once as "blest" (95); at one time he can equate Horace's "vis recte vivere?" (29) with "Would ye be blest?" (60), while at another, he translates "Si bene qui caenat, bene vivit" (56) as "If to live well means nothing but to eat" (111). Even in this latter instance, however, the concept of the good life has been "contaminated" by its occurrence in the company of peculiarly Christian ideas on that subject, and Pope's moral stance is as a result markedly different from that of Horace's poem.

II

The Second Satire of the Second Book Paraphrased is an earlier and structurally more elaborate attempt to utilize the sermon form. Pope is careful to identify the genre he is employing by referring to the body of his poem as "Bethel's Sermon" (9). The text of this sermon has already been announced:

> What, and how great, the Virtue and the Art
> To live on little with a chearful heart,
> (A Doctrine sage, but truly none of mine)
> Let's talk, my friends, but talk before we dine.
>
> (1–4)

The sermon proper begins with Bethel's speech; his lines 11–24 constitute a brief explanation of the doctrine of the text, and the remainder of his speech (25–128) contains the reasons and proofs of that doctrine. The final section of the poem (129–80), in which Pope offers a semi-biographical narrative, amounts to an extended *exemplum,* which is in itself the sermon's application.

Although Pope has labeled this poem a paraphrase rather than an imitation and would seem to imply thereby a greater degree of fidelity to his Horatian original, he has nevertheless taken a great deal of freedom with Horace's satire. This is most apparent in his reapportioning of emphasis and in his co-ordinate deletions of passages from the Latin poem. Pope's point is to shift the orientation of the poem from a Stoic fortitude in the face of both the favors and mischances of the world—roughly the same doctrine as the *nil admirari* of Ep.I.vi., but here discussed more specifically in terms of personal indulgence—to unequivocally Christian temperance and all that it implies. To this end, Pope has eliminated approximately twenty of Horace's lines from his Latin text,[3] almost all of them dealing with foolish wonder at cost, size, or appearance, and has firmly fixed the center of his poem's attention on the capital sin of gluttony. Having specifically to do with appetite, gluttony can easily become metaphor for all sin, which is generally the abuse or improper fulfilment of desire. By virtue of its essential corporeality, it becomes for Pope a unique symbol of the bonds that tie man to earth and prevent his rising to heaven. It exemplifies man's inordinate attachment to the things of this world and his neglect of his spiritual goal; it is a concrete sign of man's fallen state and self-chosen depravity.

In the poem, Bethel's explanation of the doctrine of temperance makes these facts clear by succinctly locating the pleasure of, and consequently the responsibility for, intemperance "in *you,* and not the meat" (16). Thus affection for merely physical pleasures amounts to a submission to the chance rule of Fortune and a concomitant forgetting of spiritual certitudes. Bethel makes this attitude explicit in his final, summary lines:

> Who thinks that Fortune cannot change her mind,
> Prepares a dreadful Jest for all mankind!
> And who stands safest, tell me? is it he
> That spreads and swells in puff'd Prosperity,
> Or blest with little, whose preventing care
> In Peace provides fit arms against a War?
>
> (123–28)

This submission to Fortune rather than to God and the correlative preference of the temporal to the spiritual intrinsically involve a disruption of the harmony of the divine scheme. This has been skilfully foreshadowed in the carefully counterpointed discord of Bethel's description of the glutton's contrariness (21-24). This same discord is the essential characteristic of Pope's sketch of the glutton at table, just as it has been of all his perverse evil-doers in other poems:

> By what *Criterion* do ye eat, d'ye think,
> If this is priz'd for *sweetness,* that for *stink?*
> When the tir'd Glutton labours thro' a Treat,
> He finds no relish in the sweetest Meat;
> He calls for something bitter, something sour,
> And the rich feast concludes extremely poor:
> Cheap eggs, and herbs, and olives still we see,
> Thus much is left of old Simplicity!
>
> (29–36)

The array of unharmonious opposites—"sweetness," "stink," "bitter," "sour"—and the final inversion of "old Simplicity" act once again, as their ideological counterparts so often do in Pope's verse, as the external signs of the interior discord inherent in all sinners.

This discord is most fully expressed later in Bethel's homily, in two successive verse paragraphs that serve as a culmination of this line of argument and are, in a sense, the ethical centers of the poem. The first one treats specifically of the glutton's discord:

> Now hear what blessings Temperance can bring:
> (Thus said our Friend, and what he said I sing.)
> First Health: The stomach (cram'd from ev'ry dish,
> A Tomb of Boil'd, and roast, and flesh, and fish,
> Where Bile, and wind, and phlegm, and acid jar,
> And all the Man is one intestine war)
> Remembers oft the School-boy's simple fare,
> The temp'rate sleeps, and spirits light as air!
>
> (67–74)

This passage springs from Horace's graphic *tumultum* (57) to a fullblown "intestine war" whose components invoke and invert the macrocosmic relations of the reconciled opposites of God's universe and the "little world of man." Just as the great world is composed and held together by the balanced contention of the four elements, so the microcosm of man is sustained by the harmonious conflict of those same elements, or of their counterparts, the four humors. The conflict Pope is here describing is, however, anything but harmonious: the glutton's spiritual state is mirrored in his physical disorder, in the fact that what should give life has become a "Tomb," and he longs hopelessly for the innocence of his past when his spirits—in a meaningful tautology—were properly "light as air." The succeeding paragraph (75–80) knits up all the threads of the argument in one final image of monstrous perversion and sacrilege with the vision of the purely corporeal body engulfing the gross and corrupted soul.[4]

Opposed to all this is the mean of temperance, which Bethel urges:

> He knows to live, who keeps the middle state,
> And neither leans on this side, nor on that:
> Nor stops, for one bad Cork, his Butler's pay,
> Swears, like Albutius, a good Cook away;
> Nor lets, like Naevius, ev'ry error pass,
> The musty wine, foul cloth, or greasy glass.
>
> (61–66)

This mean has the great virtue of being in itself the natural reconciler of the "intestine war" that intemperance raises:

> 'Tis yet in vain, I own, to keep a pother
> About one Vice, and fall into the other:
> Between Excess and Famine lies a mean,
> Plain, but not sordid, tho' not splendid, clean.
>
> (45–48)

The final couplet exemplifies the idea of reconciliation exactly by linking the opposites of excess and famine, sordid and splendid, within the confines of the medians, plain and clean, and by harmonizing them within the end-stopped "mean-clean" rhyme. Even the emphatic initial and final positions of the words "plain" and "clean" in line 48 indicate the balancing and reconciling of the thus enclosed extremes.

Pope's first lines in the poem (129–32) present him as an exemplification of what Bethel teaches, that is, as the living application of the doctrine of Bethel's sermon. This explains his emphasis on copying and imitating Bethel's lesson: such imitation formally identifies the autobiographical narrative that follows as the sermon's application. His subsequent remarks serve as an immediate *exemplum* of the meaning of Bethel's final comments on independence of Fortune (123–28): Pope is as happy now as when, "In *South-sea* days," he thought himself "The Lord of thousands" (134); even though double-taxed, he remains indifferent to wealth (151–52). His lightly done but repeated political allusions serve not only to satirize the Walpole administration, but also to exemplify graphically to contemporary Englishmen the ways of Fortune in their time. The South Sea Bubble (133), the threatened Excise Bill (134), changes of administration (139), religious penalties (152), and the standing army (154)—all such evils stand ready to swallow one's substance; and it is only a truly temperate man, like Pope, who can be free from anxiety on their account.

The doctrine of temperance that Pope elaborates in reply to Swift is both the final proof and the fullest statement of this poem's total meaning.

"Pray heav'n it last (cries Swift) as you go on;
"I wish to God this house had been your own:
"Pity! to build, without a son or wife:
Why, you'll enjoy it only all your life."—
Well, if the Use be mine, can it concern one
Whether the Name belong to Pope or Vernon?
What's *Property?* dear Swift! you see it alter
From you to me, from me to Peter Walter.

(161–68)

Pope has abandoned all reference to eating or to any other physical pleasures; his attention is now resolutely focused on possession of material things in themselves. The argument is based on traditional themes. Pope describes himself as a tenant rather than an owner, or a user of property rather than a possessor. This is in part drawn from the famous dictum of Lucretius:

For life is not confin'd to him or thee;
'Tis giv'n to all for use; to none for Property.[5]

It is also in part drawn from the Roman legal distinction between *usufructus,* the right to use property and enjoy its produce, and *dominium,* the right of ownership. This distinction was perpetuated in Christianity by the casuists' definitions of *dominium* and *possessio,* and by such philosophic distinctions as Aquinas' separation of God's sovereign dominion from man's right to use creatures. But the heart of Pope's argument lies in traditional Christian thought about the relationship of man to the temporal objects that surround him, and about their roles in his life: they are never to be desired in themselves, but only in so far as they are necessary to life and do not interfere with the pursuit of spiritual goods of more lasting worth.

It can readily be seen that it is this sort of doctrine that Pope's lines reproduce, and it is precisely this area of thought that the poem as a whole has been concerned with. The satiric attacks on gluttons, on the prodigal and avaricious, have been moral condemnations of those who view the things of this world with "the attachment of a lover" rather than "the moderation of a

[219]

user." To do so is to submit oneself to the irrational rule of Fortune, which is bound to time, forever fleeting and impossible to be possessed:

> What's *Property?* dear Swift! you see it alter
> From you to me, from me to Peter Walter,
> Or, in a mortgage, prove a Lawyer's share,
> Or, in a jointure, vanish from the Heir,
> Or in pure Equity (the Case not clear)
> The Chanc'ry takes your rents for twenty year:
> At best, it falls to some ungracious Son
> Who cries, my father's damn'd, and all's my own.
> Shades, that to Bacon could retreat afford,
> Become the portion of a booby Lord;
> And Hemsley once proud Buckingham's delight,
> Slides to a Scriv'ner or a City Knight.
>
> (167–78)

The actual nature of such subservience to Fortune is exemplified in the heir of 173–74, who, ambiguously "ungracious," thinks that he actually owns what can never be held, and ironically considers his father damned. Opposed to this is the doctrine of the poem: the whole purpose of learning "the Virtue and the Art/To live on little with a cheerful heart" (1–2) has been to free the soul from the senseless domination of Fortune and worldly attractions, to leave it stable and reasonable and cognizant of the true order of the world. Temperance can teach this, and it is temperance that the final lines of the poem (importantly altered from Horace's, as Warburton notes)[6] pointedly advise:

> Let Lands and Houses have what Lords they will,
> Let Us be fix'd, and our own Masters still.
>
> (179–80)

1. See W. Fraser Mitchell, *English Pulpit Oratory from Andrewes to Tillotson* (London, 1932), p. 95.

2. See, for example, James Arderne, *Directions concerning the Matter and Stile of Sermons* (1671), ed. John Mackay (Oxford: Luttrell Society,

1952), p. 9: "But if you demand, which is the most useful and teaching method? I think, where the matter will bear it, it is that of Proposition, Confirmation, and Inference. This last is the same with which the best Rhetoritians advised to make up the Peroration: all this is in plain terms, no more than Doctrine, Reason, and Use. You may have known many Preachers at present, who are very shie in naming those words, because they are so frequent amongst the dissenting Ministrie; but they may remember withall that this very method is both praescribed and practised by the excellentest Church-Orators of the *Roman*-Communion." Joseph Glanvill makes basically the same points in *An Essay concerning Preaching: Written for the Direction of a Young Divine* (London, 1703), pp. 39–53.

3. For example, between lines 8 and 9 of Pope's Latin text, five lines of the original have been eliminated, and between his lines 13 and 19, almost ten lines have been dropped.

4. See discussion of this passage above, pp. 28–29.

5. *De Rerum Natura*, III.971: Dryden's translation (Kingsley), I, 409, lines 173–74.

6. Warburton, IV, 97: *"Let Lands and houses, etc.,*] The turn of his imitation, in the concluding part, obliged him to diversify the sentiment. They are equally noble: but Horace's is expressed with the greater force."

INDEX

Index